BATHROOMS

DESIGN ■ REMODEL ■ BUILD

CREATIVE HOMEOWNER®, Upper Saddle River, New Jersey

Author: Jerry Germer
Editorial Director: David Schiff
Editor: Laura Tringali
Contributing Editor: Mort Schultz
Assistant Editor: Patrick Quinn
Copy Editor: Candace B. Levy, Ph.D.

Art Director: Annie Jeon
Graphic Designers: Michelle D. Halko, Fernando Colon Jr.
Illustrators: Paul M. Schumm, Ed Lipinski, Jim Randolph

Cover Design: Annie Jeon
Photo Researcher: Alexander Samuelson

Manufactured in the United States of America

Current Printing (last digit)
10 9 8 7 6 5

Bathrooms
Library of Congress Catalog Card Number: 94-69651
ISBN: 1-880029-31-6

CREATIVE HOMEOWNER®
A Division of Federal Marketing Corp.
24 Park Way, Upper Saddle River, NJ 07458
Web Site: **www.creativehomeowner.com**

Photo Credits

Front Cover: Susan Rosenthal, ISID & Clarie Nightengale, ASID
        Melabee M Miller Photography, Hillside, NJ

p.1-Phillip H. Ennis Photography, Freeport, NY
p.6-Melabee M. Miller Photography, Hillside, NJ
p.7-Lawrence Korinda Architects/Melabee M Miller
p.8 (top)- Andersen Flexiframe Windows, Andersen Windows, Inc.
p.8 (bot.)- Countertop:Avonite/Melabee M Miller
p.9 (top)- Phillip H. Ennis Photography, Freeport, NY
p.9 (bot.)- Bevel Mirror Cabinet, Robern, Bensalem, PA
p.10 (bot. l)- Phillip H. Ennis Photography, Freeport, NY
p.10 (bot. r)- Lynn Campbell/Melabee M Miller
p.11- Susan Rosenthal, ISID & Clarie Nightengale, ASID/Melabee M Miller
p.14- Elizabeth Gillin Interiors/Melabee M Miller Photography
p.15 (l)- Kohler Company, Kohler, WI
p.15 (r)- "The Owl & the Pussycat", Absolute, Piscataway, NJ
p.16 (top & bot. l)- Kohler Company, Kohler, WI
p.16 (top r)- Dal-Tile Corp., Dallas, TX
p.16 (bot. r)- Robert J. Bennett Photography, Bridgeville, DE
p.17 (top)- NKBA, Hackettstown, NJ
p.17 (bot.)- Phillip H. Ennis Photography, Freeport, NY
p.18 (l)- Images In Design/Melabee M Miller
p.18 (r)- Kohler Company, Kohler, WI
p.19 (l)- Barbara White Arch. Photography, Laguna Beach, CA
p.19 (r)- Bob Braun, Orlando, FL
p.20- Margie Little, CKD/Dianne Hynes, Pleasant Hill, CA
        photo by David Livingston, courtesy of NKBA
p.21- Florida Tile Industries, Lakeland, FL
p.22- Kohler Company, Kohler, WI
p.23 (top)- Dal-Tile Corp., Dallas, TX
p.23 (bot.)- Kohler Company, Kohler, WI
p.24- Barbara White Arch. Photography, Laguna Beach, CA
p.26- Barbara White Arch. Photography, Laguna Beach, CA
p.27- Phillip H. Ennis Photography, Freeport, NY
p.28 (top l)- Framed Door Cabinets, Robern, Bensalem, PA
p.28 (bot. l)- Kohler Company, Kohler, WI
p.28 (r)- Clairson International, Oscala, FL
p.29 (l)- Joe Canderosi/Melabee M Miller
p.29 (r)- SawHorse Design/Melabee M Miller
p.30 (top l)- Clairson International, Oscala, FL
p.30 (top r)- Kohler Company, Kohler, WI
p.30 (bot.)- Eric Roth Photography, Boston, MA
p.31 (top)- Frameless Pivot Door, Alumax Corporation, Dallas, TX

p.31 (bot.)- Kohler Company, Kohler, WI
p.32 (top l)- Barbara White Arch. Photography, Laguna Beach, CA
p.32 (top r)- Phillip H. Ennis Photography, Freeport, NY
p.32 (bot.)- Eric Roth Photography, Boston, MA
p.33 (all), 34, 35- Phillip H. Ennis Photography, Freeport, NY
p.36 (l)- Rosemarie Cicio, IFDA/Melabee M Miller
p.36 (r)- Barbara White Arch. Photography, Laguna Beach, CA
p.38- Velux-America Inc., Greenwood, SC
p.40 (l)- Kie Birchfield Design/Richard Gross Photo, Grants Pass, OR
p.40 (r)- Eric Roth Photography, Boston, MA
p.41- Fabrette TM Fabric Blinds, Hunter Douglas Corp.
p.42- Phillip H. Ennis Photography, Freeport, NY
p.46- Kohler Company, Kohler, WI
p.49 (top)- Margie Little CKD/Dianne Hynes, Pleasant Hill, CA
        photo by David Livingston, courtesy of NKBA
p.49 (bot.)- Barbara White Arch. Photography, Laguna Beach, CA
p.50- BathEase, Inc., Palm Harbor, FL
p.51- Kohler Company, Kohler, WI
p.52, 54, 56 (top/bot. l)- Phillip H. Ennis Photography, Freeport, NY
p.56 (r)- Classic Restorations, Cambridge, MA/Eric Roth Photography
p.57- Armstrong World Industries, Lancaster, PA
p.58- Satinglo, American Olean, Lansdale, PA
p.59 (top)- Bill Rothschild Photography, Wesley Hills, NY
p.59 (bot.)- Barbara White Arch. Photography, Laguna Beach, CA
p.60- Kohler Company, Kohler, WI
p.61 (top)- Brite & Matte, American Olean, Lansdale, PA
p.61 (bot.)- Phillip H. Ennis Photography, Freeport, NY
p.62 (top)- Eric Roth Photography, Boston, MA
p.62 (bot.)- Hammonds Construction/Richard Gross Photo
p.63- Beth Mellina/Melabee M Miller
p.64 (top)- Phillip H. Ennis Photography, Freeport, NY
p.64 (bot.), 65 (top)- Dal-Tile Corp., Dallas, TX
p.65 (bot.)- Kohler Company, Kohler, WI
p.66- Phillip H. Ennis Photography, Freeport, NY
p.78- Barbara White Arch. Photography, Laguna Beach, CA
p.92- Bill Rothschild Photography, Wesley Hills, NY
p.110, 142, 160, 174- Phillip H. Ennis Photography, Freeport, NY

Back Cover
(top)- Florida Tile Industries, Lakeland, FL
(middle l)- Sojourn Corner Whirlpool, Kohler Company, Kohler, WI
(middle r)- Robern, Bensalem, PA
(bot. l)- "The Owl & the Pussycat", Absolute, Piscataway, NJ
(bot. r)- Kohler Company, Kohler, WI

SAFETY FIRST

Though all the designs and methods in this book have been reviewed for safety, it is not possible to overstate the importance of using the safest construction methods possible. What follows are reminders; some do's and don'ts of basic carpentry. They are not substitutes for your own common sense.

- *Always* use caution, care, and good judgment when following the procedures described in this book.

- *Always* be sure that the electrical setup is safe; be sure that no circuit is overloaded and that all power tools and electrical outlets are properly grounded. Do not use power tools in wet locations.

- *Always* read container labels on paints, solvents, and other products; provide ventilation, and observe all other warnings.

- *Always* read the manufacturer's instructions for using a tool, especially the warnings.

- *Always* use hold-downs and push sticks whenever possible when working on a table saw. Avoid working short pieces if you can.

- *Always* remove the key from any drill chuck (portable or press) before starting the drill.

- *Always* pay deliberate attention to how a tool works so that you can avoid being injured.

- *Always* know the limitations of your tools. Do not try to force them to do what they were not designed to do.

- *Always* make sure that any adjustment is locked before proceeding. For example, always check the rip fence on a table saw or the bevel adjustment on a portable saw before starting to work.

- *Always* clamp small pieces firmly to a bench or other work surface when using a power tool on them.

- *Always* wear the appropriate rubber or work gloves when handling chemicals, moving or stacking lumber, or doing heavy construction.

- *Always* wear a disposable face mask when you create dust by sawing or sanding. Use a special filtering respirator when working with toxic substances and solvents.

- *Always* wear eye protection, especially when using power tools or striking metal on metal or concrete; a chip can fly off, for example, when chiseling concrete.

- *Always* be aware that there is seldom enough time for your body's reflexes to save you from injury from a power tool in a dangerous situation; everything happens too fast. Be *alert!*

- *Always* keep your hands away from the business ends of blades, cutters, and bits.

- *Always* hold a circular saw firmly, usually with both hands so that you know where they are.

- *Always* use a drill with an auxiliary handle to control the torque when large-size bits are used.

- *Always* check your local building codes when planning new construction. The codes are intended to protect public safety and should be observed to the letter.

- *Never* work with power tools when you are tired or under the influence of alcohol or drugs.

- *Never* cut tiny pieces of wood or pipe using a power saw. Cut small pieces off larger pieces.

- *Never* change a saw blade or a drill or router bit unless the power cord is unplugged. Do not depend on the switch being off; you might accidentally hit it.

- *Never* work in insufficient lighting.

- *Never* work while wearing loose clothing, hanging hair, open cuffs, or jewelry.

- *Never* work with dull tools. Have them sharpened, or learn how to sharpen them yourself.

- *Never* use a power tool on a workpiece—large or small—that is not firmly supported.

- *Never* saw a workpiece that spans a large distance between horses without close support on each side of the cut; the piece can bend, closing on and jamming the blade, causing saw kickback.

- *Never* support a workpiece from underneath with your leg or other part of your body when sawing.

- *Never* carry sharp or pointed tools, such as utility knives, awls, or chisels, in your pocket. If you want to carry such tools, use a special-purpose tool belt with leather pockets and holders.

Contents

1

Designing Your Bathroom

The bathroom is the most frequently remodeled room in the house, according to the National Kitchen and Bath Association. Why? Because homeowners want not only more bathrooms, but more amenities as well.

The changing lifestyles of today's families also call for new approaches to bathroom design. With many women now working outside the home, bathrooms must often accommodate two adults during the morning rush hour. Typically, children's bathrooms also need to serve two or more. New demands mean new design approaches: double sinks, separate tubs and showers, and separate dressing rooms, to name a few.

To cope with the increasing stresses of modern life, today's homeowners are relying more and more on spas, whirlpools, steam compartments, and exercise equipment. These items challenge the conventional notion of the bathroom as a small room with three fixtures. What services do you want your bathroom to provide? You may not want or need all of the amenities mentioned, but the many choices available will allow you to customize your bathroom to suit your lifestyle and personality.

What Do You Want from Your Bathroom?

Your first step might be to set some goals that can lead to a plan of action. A good way to start is to write down your bathroom's shortcomings.

List the Present Problems

You probably know your bathroom's problems very well. Others in the household probably have their own gripes. A detailed list of each person's complaints can be valuable in guiding your planning. Here are some questions to help spark discussion:

♦ Are the present bathrooms located conveniently?

♦ What's wrong with the mirror above the sink? (too small? poorly placed?)

▲ Modern life demands bathrooms with more space and more amenities. Often, one bathroom must serve two adults at the same time during morning rush.

▲ The bathroom of today often breaks out of its traditional role to include an exercise area, and perhaps a place to relax and read.

♦ Are electrical outlets near wet areas ground-fault protected (GFCI)?

♦ Does anyone regularly wash or dye their hair in the bathroom sink? If so, is the faucet suited to this use?

♦ Do you have enough storage space in the present medicine cabinet(s)?

♦ Can drugs and other substances be stored so that small children can't get to them?

♦ Do members of your household prefer to wash in a tub, shower, or both? Do the present fixtures accommodate these preferences?

♦ Do any fixtures leak?

♦ Are the effects of accumulated moisture apparent, such as mildew on tiles, curled floor tiles, or loose paint or wallcovering?

♦ Do you have adequate ventilation to remove odors and moisture?

♦ What is right and wrong with your bathroom lighting?

Make a Scrapbook

Use your list of problems to begin a scrapbook or file of improvement ideas. You might include the following:

♦ Ideas for improving efficiency, such as whether it might be better to improve the present bathroom for use by two persons or to add another bathroom.

♦ Pictures of fixtures from magazines and promotional literature.

♦ Pictures clipped from magazines showing attractive bathroom features.

♦ Ideas for storage of towels, washcloths, and personal hygiene items.

♦ Ideas for floor and wall finishes.

♦ Empty pages for jotting down or sketching ideas for improving the layout of your bathroom.

♦ Business cards, newspaper ads, and names and addresses of designers, suppliers, and builders.

Do It Yourself or Hire a Specialist?

As you move from the scrapbook stage to planning, you will have to decide whether to do the work yourself, hire a contractor, or some of both. Doing your own work can save you money and give you the satisfaction that comes from creating something of value. But not everyone can or should undertake every task. To help you decide, see if you can answer yes to these five questions:

1. Do I really want to do this task myself? If you don't, you shouldn't consider the other four questions. You probably have good reasons for wanting to avoid certain tasks, even if you can do them. You probably won't give your best efforts to a chore you are doing just to save money, and it can cost you even more if your work has to be corrected by someone else.

▲ Every bathroom has a mirror for personal grooming. The wall of mirrors in this bathroom also makes the room seem larger and increases the amount of light gathered through the window.

2. Do I have the time to complete this task?

The answer to this question depends on knowing how long the job will take and if it has to be completed in one install- ment. If you have done similar projects in the past, you have a basis for estimating. If you haven't, ask a knowledgeable friend. Also ask if the task must be completed in one session. You don't want to have the water system to the whole house shut down any longer than necessary.

3. Do I have the neces- sary skills to complete the task successfully?

As with Question 2, you'll know you can do it if you have done it before. If not, don't give up without first finding out just what's required. Maybe simple plumbing is something you would like to learn and, having

▲ This majestic master bath, with its large whirlpool tub and magnificent view, is the perfect retreat from the stresses of life.

▲ Little kids can't reach sinks set at standard height. Stools left in the bath- room are an invitation for groggy adults to stub their toes. This bathroom neatly solves the problem with bottom drawers that are really built-in steps.

mastered, would find satisfying. Perhaps you could do the task working alongside an experienced friend.

4. Am I physically capable? If you haven't done the task before, find out what physical demands it requires. To replace a faucet, you need good finger dexterity in both hands. More extensive remodeling of the plumbing, such as replacing a tub, shower, or toilet, requires strength and a good back.

5. Can I save enough money to justify doing it myself? If you take time off from your job to remodel your bathroom, you have to decide whether the amount you will save doing your own remodeling is greater than the income you lose.

Finally, don't forget safety. While your municipality may permit you to do your own plumbing or electrical work, you must be able to do it safely and must meet local building codes. If you don't think you can attain these standards, you're better off hiring a licensed professional.

Don't Pour Money Down the Drain

It's hard to resist the urge to remodel when you see those maga- zine articles that show how to transform a bathroom with three white fixtures into a room that's a pleasure to be in. But even though the typical bathroom is smaller than the other rooms in the house, it is packed with expensive systems. So before you pick up a paintbrush or hammer, decide why you want to remodel and what changes you need. Do you want to add value to your home, satisfy personal desires, or both?

Increasing the Resale Value of Your Home

Getting your money back may not be your first priority when you ponder bathroom improvements. Should it be? People move more frequently today than ever before. If it seems likely you'll sell your home in the next few years, you should weigh any remodeling investment more carefully than if you think you will stay long enough to recoup your money in the form of greater benefit. But that is only a vague guideline.

Taking the hard view toward remodeling dollars, you should aim to spend no more on total remodeling costs for your entire home than you can get back at sale time. One rule of thumb advises not adding more than 20 percent of the value of your home in total improvements. At most, don't spend more on improvements than the difference between the price you paid for your home and the average sale price of other homes in the area.

▲ If resale is a primary concern, choose colors and simple styling that will have mass appeal.

But this advice doesn't tell you how much to spend on bathroom remodeling. To answer this question, it will help to find out what kind of bathroom facilities home buyers expect in your area. You may get a rough idea by asking the opinion of a local real estate agent. Ask how many bathrooms buyers expect and what kinds of amenities they look for in a house with the number of bedrooms your house has.

Improving an Existing Bathroom

Whatever buyers want, bringing an existing bathroom up to modern standards is usually money well spent. You can expect to recoup almost all of the costs of the improvements if you do the work yourself, but expect a return of only 40 percent or so if you hire someone to do the work for you. Perhaps more important than the dollars returned is the likelihood that your improvements will help your home sell more quickly, thus you must consider your plans carefully. Bringing a master bathroom up to par makes more sense than splurging on a new guest bathroom. If you are updating

▲ Resale, aside, the most important people to please are the members of your family. If you love to read in the bathroom, why not make it double as a library?

▲ Adding a shower stall to an existing bathtub can be a cost effective way to update a bathroom.

▲ This handsome old-fashioned claw-foot bathtub is comfortable, appropriate to a Victorian home, and makes great use of a small space.

the only bathroom in the house, consider revamping it to serve two people: provide two sinks and a separate shower and tub.

Here are some other tips to keep in mind that will ensure that your bathroom improvements appeal to future buyers:

♦ Style your remodeling for mass appeal. Play it safe with colors, textures, and fixtures. Consider regional factors. An outdoor deck adjacent to the bathroom might be great in sunny San Diego, but a waste in Buffalo.

♦ Provide quality. Whether you do it yourself or hire specialists, use quality materials that look good and wear well. For work you plan to do yourself, make sure you are capable of professional-looking workmanship.

♦ Plan improvements to fit the house. Remodeling that does not blend with the basic style and character of your house will detract from its appeal. A modern-style bath in an Early American home looks out of place. With care, you can have up-to-date amenities and still retain the traditional mood of your home.

Adding a New Bathroom

Deciding whether to add another bathroom is a tough call. If your house has fewer bathrooms than other houses in the neighborhood, adding one can be a good investment. But if you have three bathrooms in a two-bathroom neighborhood, you probably won't recoup your expenses by adding a fourth.

Where you locate the new bathroom also plays a part. Adding a new bath in an unused or underused room next to an existing bathroom or laundry area is relatively cost efficient. It takes much more money to put a bathroom in a part of the house that is remote from existing plumbing or to add onto the house.

Remodeling for Your Own Comfort and Convenience

After puzzling over the economic aspects of remodeling, you may decide you need to go ahead and make improvements even though you may not recover the costs when you sell your house. Maybe you've been putting up with purple tile in a cramped shower long enough. It's high time to get the bathroom you have always wanted, you think, even if the improvements don't add to the resale value of the house.

No argument here. After all, your home is your personal space, and any change that doesn't make your bathroom better for you and your family misses the real mark. If you can meet your own goals and add real value to your home, so much the better. If you have to compromise, it's probably better to hedge on the side of satisfying your present needs rather than trying to out-guess the tastes and desires of unknown future buyers.

How Much Can You Afford?

Whatever your investment strategy, before getting tied down to a plan of action, it's a good idea to determine just how much you can spend. You can set limits on what you ought to spend from the guidelines discussed earlier. What you can afford will be set by one or more of the following factors:

♦ Your available cash

♦ The amount of financing you can obtain

♦ The amount of your monthly loan payments

♦ Your overall financial goals

An idea of the actual costs of improvements can help you set a budget. The total cost of your project depends on the extent of the remodeling and how much of the work you plan to do yourself. Obviously, the more work you do yourself, the more you stand to save on the total costs of your improvements. If you do all of the work yourself and pay only for materials, you may do the job for about half the cost of hiring someone to do it for you.

Finding the Right Pro for the Job

Knowing which jobs you will do yourself and those you will entrust to outsiders is only the first step. Next comes tracking down contractors who have a good track record and will be easy to work with.

Hiring a builder, plumber, electrician, or other contractor who is licensed guarantees that the provider has satisfied the state's requirements to perform a certain service. It makes no guarantee for the quality of the service. How do you find the best person for your job? Start with the recommendations of your friends and business associates. If you can't find leads there, look in the yellow pages. When you phone prospective providers, ask if they have worked on projects such as yours and whether they would be interested in looking over the plans.

Ah yes, the plans. You will need, at least, a floor plan and a written specification sheet describing your fixture selection, cabinetry choices, electrical items, and finishes. For all but ordinary designs, drawings of each wall (elevations) and cross sections are helpful.

Most building contractors will draw up plans and specifications for you. If you have decided to hire a general contractor—one who will oversee the other subcontractors such as plumbers and electricians—and you have a good idea of what you want to do with the bathroom, this can be a good approach. Usually, the contractor will draw up plans as well as a specification sheet at no charge, in hopes of getting the work. Sometimes, they will charge for the plans and specifications only if you choose to use another general contractor.

Armed with the plans and specifications, you can ask for bids from other general contractors. It's important to use the same plans and specifications for all bids— otherwise the lowest bidder may be saving money by using cheaper fixtures and other materials.

If you don't have a clear picture of how you want your bathroom to be, consider hiring a designer who can produce scale drawings and specifications for you. Invite the designer to come to your house to look over the situation and to discuss your proposed changes and what you would like in the way of planning or design assistance.

When you have your plans and specifications, mail a copy to selected general contractors or subcontractors. Invite them to look over your home, so they can come up with a construction bid for the work or their part of the work. At the meeting, discuss details about fees and method of payment, how soon work could begin, how long the job would take, and anything else you want to know. And, most important, ask for the names and phone numbers of at least three recent clients for references—you will need to get some sense of the quality of work provided by each contractor as well as whether the contractor is financially capable of completing your project. If you have the slightest doubt, ask the contractor for a bank reference.

Do You Need a Permit?

Permits and inspections are a way of enforcing the building codes. A permit is essentially a license that gives you permission to do the work, while an inspection ensures that you did the work in accordance to the codes. For minor repair or remodeling work you don't usually need a permit, but you may need one if you add or resupport walls, extend the water supply and drain, waste and vent system, or add an electrical circuit. You will nearly always need one if your new bathroom is in a new addition to your house. Most states allow a homeowner to work on his or her own house, including wiring and plumbing, if a permit is obtained first.

Depending on the scope of the work, your permit application should include the following items:

♦ A legal description of the property. You can get this from city or county records, or directly from your deed.

♦ A drawing of the proposed changes. This needn't be drawn by an architect, but it should clearly show the structural changes you plan to make and identify the type and dimension of all materials. Most building departments will accept plans drawn by a homeowner, as long as the details are clearly labeled. Always note the size, span, and dimension of existing materials as well as the new materials.

♦ A site plan drawing. This shows the position of the house on the lot, and the approximate location of adjacent houses. It should also show the location of the well and septic system, if any.

Inspections. Whenever a permit is required, you'll probably have to schedule time for a city or county building inspector to come out and examine the work. He or she will check to see that the work meets or exceeds the building codes. When you obtain your permit, ask about the inspection schedule. On small projects an inspector might come out only for a final inspection; on a larger project you might have several intermediate inspections before a final inspection. In any case, it is your job to call for the inspection, not the inspector's job to figure out when you might be ready for a visit.

Zoning Ordinances

If you are planning to add a bathroom, zoning ordinances might require you to enlarge your septic system. If the bathroom is an addition that increases the "footprint" of your house you must make sure it complies with zoning restrictions. For example, most zoning ordinances require that any addition to your house be "set back" a certain minimum distance from your neighbors' properties and from the road. Though most bathroom projects won't run afoul of zoning ordinances, it's always a good idea to check with local officials before you start.

How This Book Can Help You

This book will take you through the process of bathroom remodeling, from helping you figure out what you want (in terms of improvements) to planning, constructing, and finishing the space. The first six chapters will help you make decisions. The last seven chapters tell you how to implement the decisions you made. Each of the "how-to" sections begins by rating the level of difficulty of the particular task. The level of difficulty is indicated by one, two, or three hammers:

Easy, even for beginners

Moderately difficult but can be done by beginners who have the patience and willingness to learn

Difficult. Can be done by the do-it-yourselfer, but requires a serious investment in time, patience, and specialty tools. Consider hiring a specialist.

Where to Find Help When You Need It

Whether you need the services of several specialists or only one, it will help to know what's available.

Planning and Design Assistance

Architects. Architects can help you translate your ideas into plans that you or a contractor can build from. Architects charge a percentage of the construction cost (usually 5 to 15 percent), an hourly rate, or a lump sum. For a bathroom project, you might ask the architect to quote you an hourly rate or fixed fee for a few hours to assist you with planning and design only. If you want to do the planning and design yourself, the architect can review your drawings and make helpful suggestions.

Bath designers. A bath designer can work independently (or as a specialized interior designer) or for a kitchen and bath supplier. Theses specialists can help you organize the interior layout and pick color schemes, fixtures, furnishings and wall and floor finishes. Independent consultants charge a flat fee, an hourly rate, or a percentage of the cost of items they specify, such as cabinets, fixtures, and tile.

If you buy your equipment through a single supplier who specializes in kitchens and baths, you may get design assistance included in the cost of the equipment.

Design and drafting services. These services also provide interior layout work, for which they charge a flat fee or hourly rate. Drafting services may or may not do design. Call on them if you know exactly what you want and need only someone to draw it to scale.

Construction Help

You can hire a general contractor to manage part or all of your project. If you want to deal with only one party, entrust a contractor to be responsible for the entire project. The contractor will hire, oversee, and pay subcontractors such as plumbers and electricians. If you don't hire a general contractor, you have to hire, schedule, and pay each subcontractor separately. Find the names of general contractors who do only residential work under "Contractors-General," "Home Builders," or "Builders" in the yellow pages.

Specialty Subcontractors

Here's a list of the most likely trade contractors who can do parts of your remodeling that you can't do or don't choose to do.

Carpenters. Rough carpenters, or framers, specialize in putting up floors, walls, and roofs of wood-framed structures. Call on finish carpenters for trim, cabinetry, and detail work.

Drywall contractors. These specialists hang and finish drywall and cement backer board.

Electricians. Electricians install wiring and lighting, configure circuits, and locate outlets. If you need one or more additional circuits for your bathroom remodeling project, hire an electrician unless you are competent to do it yourself. Even so, it's a good idea to ask an electrician to review your approach before beginning. One way you can save money if you are not confident in your wiring skills is to do all the wall opening and other rough work so the electrician just has to install and hook up boxes.
 Lots of electricians shy away from working on old houses because the work it is often not straightforward and they can't estimate the job cost accurately. But if you are willing to take on the responsibility of creating the pathways, electricians often are more responsive.

Masons. Ceramic tile, glass block, and cut stone in walls and floors are installed by masons.

Painters. It is helpful to know that painters not only paint but also install wallcoverings.

Plumbing and heating contractors. Do-it-yourself plumbing is more accessible today than ever, thanks to plastic and copper alternatives to steel and cast-iron piping. But plumbing is unforgiving—the smallest leak spells failure. You may also need a plumbing and heating contractor to extend heating ducts or piping to your new bathroom.

A list of tools and materials required for the work is also provided. Certain tools are basic to most of the remodeling tasks described, so when you read "basic carpentry tools," you will know that you should have the following items at hand:

Basic Carpentry Tools

☐ Carpenter's level	☐ Carpenter's square
☐ Hammer	☐ Handsaw
☐ Measuring tape	☐ Pencil
☐ Phillips screwdriver	☐ Pliers
☐ Plumb bob	☐ Pry bar
☐ Standard screwdriver	☐ Utility knife

To rework plumbing and electrical systems, you will need other basic tools. A list of basic plumbing and electrical tools is given at the beginning of the chapter dealing with fixture installation and wiring. Following the tool list for each project, step-by-step instructions show you how to complete the work successfully.

2
Selecting Fixtures

One of the first things you'll notice when you start poring through bathroom catalogs and product literature is the vast number of choices of fixtures and accessories available today. Gone are the days of the purely utilitarian room furnished with three white fixtures jammed in side by side. Now you can breathe new life into your bathroom with a rainbow of colors, a multitude of styles, and a host of amenities stretching from whirlpools and bidets to saunas and steam baths. In this chapter, we'll scan the menu to help guide you through the choices. We'll see how to install fixtures in later chapters.

Sinks

Sinks (or washbasins) are called "lavatories" by the fixture industry. With standard fittings, they accommodate shaving, washing, and tooth brushing. You can adapt them for shampooing by equipping them with special features.

Shapes and Sizes

Sinks come as ovals, rectangles, circles, hexagons, and other special shapes. Manufacturers have gone to great lengths to give sinks appeal by sculpting their forms, but the simpler shapes are both more practical to use and easier to keep clean. Sizes vary from a 12x18-inch rectangle to a 19x33-inch oval.

Materials and Colors

Sinks used to be made of glazed vitreous china or enameled (porcelainized) cast iron or steel. Fused to the base material by firing in a kiln, these finishes proved impervious to water, mold,

▲ This six-sided brass sink is one example of the wide array of sink shapes and materials available today.

▲ A classic Edward Lear nursery rhyme adds a touch of whimsey to this child's bathroom sink.

▲ This stainless steel sink is mounted below a solid marble countertop. This type of mounting requires a strong, water-impervious counter surface.

and mildew; they dulled only after years of abrasion. Today, you can also purchase sinks constructed of plastic compounds, custom-glazed china, wood, or metals such as steel, copper, or even brass. Augmenting the tried-and-true white of the past is a pallet of colors to match any decor.

Plastic sinks open endless possibilities for shapes, colors, and patterns, but are much more susceptible to scratches than china and enameled cast iron. The durability of wood basins over the long term has yet to be proven.

Freestanding Sinks

A good place to begin your sink selection is to decide whether you want a freestanding single fixture or one built into a countertop. The norm until the 1950s, freestanding sinks are now making a comeback. You can choose from models designed to be mounted directly on the wall, including sinks designed to go in corners. Or you can choose a pedestal sink. Freestanding sinks are available in colors, shapes, and sizes to suit any taste. Freestanding sinks come with flat tops or have raised backsplashes where they meet the wall. If you choose a freestanding sink over one mounted into a countertop, make sure you allow enough space. Wall-mounted units will look and feel cramped if they

▲ Freestanding sinks add a classic elegance to any bathroom, especially if you allow plenty of room at both sides of the sink.

abut a wall or other fixture with no, or little, clearance at the sides. While you can stuff a pedestal sink into a space as narrow as 22 inches, it will look better with a generous open space on each side.

Vanity-Mounted Sinks

Vanity-mounted sinks became popular when bathrooms shrunk to the 60x84-inch size that marked much of the housing built after World War II. For extra storage, the space under the fixture was enclosed in a cabinet; any extra space above could be used to hold accessories such as drinking glasses, toothpaste, or soap. Combination vanities and sinks start as narrow as the sink itself and can be as wide as the room. If you are stuck retaining three fixtures in an existing bathroom measuring 60x84inches or less, a vanity-mounted sink may be the only way to get enough storage.

Sinks for vanity cabinets can be molded as part of the countertop or installed separately into holes cut in the countertop. In the latter case, the sink can be self-rimming or can be installed with a metal trim piece to join it to the countertop. Sinks can also be

▲ Separate sink basins can be installed in a vanity (above) or the basin can be molded as part of the countertop, making it easier to keep clean (below).

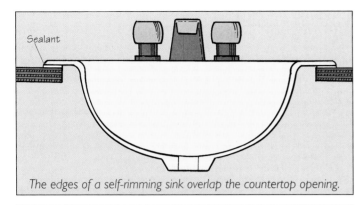

The edges of a self-rimming sink overlap the countertop opening.

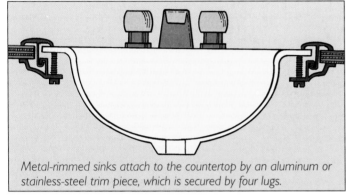

Metal-rimmed sinks attach to the countertop by an aluminum or stainless-steel trim piece, which is secured by four lugs.

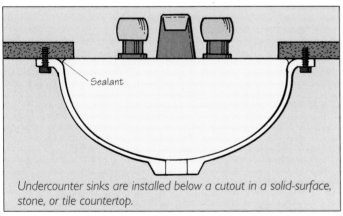

Undercounter sinks are installed below a cutout in a solid-surface, stone, or tile countertop.

installed from below, with the countertop overlapping the rim of the sink; however, the edges of the countertop must be able to withstand constant water. Molded solid-surface countertops, solid marble and ceramic tile work well for this application, but plastic laminate, which has a seam at the edge, will not hold up.

The way the sink is mounted in the countertop has both aesthetic and practical consequences. The exposed edge of a self-rimming sink sits atop the vanity surface. Though attractive, the edge prevents water splashed onto the counter from draining into the basin. Metal rims overcome this drawback by aligning the edge of the basin with the countertop, but the metal trim creates a less elegant look than the self-rimming model has. Sinks mounted below solid-surface, ceramic tile, or stone countertops allow water to drain and provide a pleasing separation between countertop and sink.

One-piece sink/countertops molded from monolithic plastic material offer seamless construction that can be contoured to drain into the washbasin. Many of these units contain built-in soap dishes.

Toilets

Toilets (or "water closets" as they are formally called) now come in a great variety of styles, shapes, and colors, though colors other than white usually cost more. Vitreous china still prevails as the most common material.

You can choose between toilets that contain the tank and base in a single molded unit and toilets that have a separate tank. The most common type puts the tank directly behind the base. Another version, which raises the tank high on the wall, is available for people who want a Victorian motif.

When selecting a toilet for a small room, it will help to know basic toilet sizes. Tank widths vary from 20 to 24 inches. Toilets with the tank mounted high on the wall are around 15 inches wide. Toilets project out from the wall (the depth) 26 to 30 inches, requiring a minimum room depth of 44 and 48 inches, respectively.

Regardless of its color or style, you want a toilet that will function

▲ If you would rather not look at the toilet, you can tuck it under an extension of the vanity counter (above). Another approach is to select a toilet that blends into the decor. In this case (below), the rounded edges of the toilet and tank complement the rounded vanity countertop.

▲ The old-fashioned look of a raised tank lends authenticity to a Victorian-style bathroom.

dependably and quietly. Another factor to consider is water conservation. Until recently, toilets required 5 to 7 gallons for each flush, making them the largest single user of household water. But with water getting scarce in many parts of the United States, conservation has become a top concern. California responded to a prolonged drought by mandating that all new residential construction must install toilets that use 1.6 or less gallons per flush. Other states followed with similar laws, prompting the federal government to enact a national standard that limits the water use by residential toilets made in the United States after January 1, 1994, to 1.6 gallons per flush (gpf). Manufacturers are meeting the challenge with improved versions of standard gravity toilets and new designs that use air pressure.

Water-conserving toilets presently cost a bit more than the older 5-gallon units, but the money you save in water use will eventually make up for the difference. You will see other advantages if you depend on a well for your water and a septic system to handle waste. Less water per flush means less demand on your electric well pump and a smaller load on the septic system.

Gravity Toilets

The traditional gravity toilet has been improved to reduce the water required for flushing. Taller and narrower tanks, steeper bowls, and smaller water spots (the water surface in the bowl) account for most of the improved design. While users report general satisfaction with 1.6-gpf models, 1-gpf models sometimes require more than a single flush to clear the bowl.

Pressurized Tank Toilets

Some toilets use the water pressure in the line to compress air. The compressed air then works with a small amount of water to empty the bowl. One model draws as little as 0.5 gallon per flush, but it costs two to three times more than the standard gravity-operated toilet.

Pumped Toilets

A new toilet design uses a small pump to push water through the toilet. You can set the amount of flush water at either 1 or 1.6 gpf with the press of a button. New in 1994, this unit's list price made it the most expensive of all low-flush toilets.

Bidets

A bidet is used for personal hygiene. It looks like a toilet without the tank or lid. Sitting astride the bidet, the user can cleanse the pelvic area more conveniently than by using other methods. Water of the desired temperature is supplied by a spray mounted on the back wall or bottom of the bowl.

Used by European women for years, bidets have only recently made much of an appearance in American bathrooms. Now they are made by all major fixture manufacturers in the same range of colors and styles as other fixtures. They require a hot and cold water supply and a drain. You should allow at least 30 inches of clear width and plan for the fixture to project out from the wall 25 to 27 inches.

▲ The bidet next to the toilet is becoming increasingly common in North America.

▲ A separate shower is more comfortable than a shower combined with a bathtub. This one features a seat and a moveable spray nozzle.

Showers

Showers are a must-have fixture in most households. Showers are the most economical way to cleanse the whole body and save both time and water. You probably rely on a shower for your regular hygiene even if you like an occasional soak in a tub. If space is tight, you can add a shower to your bathtub.

Begin by deciding what kind of shower you want. Will it be small and utilitarian or ample and luxurious? Your choice depends not only on space, but also on your budget and how much effort you want to expend (or pay a contractor for) to get a custom installation. Consider installing a separate shower if you have enough room or if you have a second bathroom that has a tub.

Tub Showers

Showers combined with tubs save money and space, but not without tradeoffs. Because bathtub bottoms are narrower and curved, tub showers are less safe and convenient than separate showers. Another drawback is the way the shower spray is kept from spilling out. Shower curtains have to be long enough to

▲ Most bathrooms don't have room for a separate shower. In this case, combining the tub and shower works quite well.

overlap the inside rim of the tub to work, which unfortunately puts them where they crowd an already tight standing space. Sliding doors, better at keeping water off the bathroom floor, always seem to be in the way when you want to use the tub for bathing.

Separate Showers

If you are like most people these days, you shower more often than you bathe, so you should consider ways to include a separate shower in your remodeling plans. A separate shower offers more space and is safer to use than a tub shower. It can keep water inside with curtains, sliding or hinged doors, or even no doors if space allows (as we'll see in Chapter 5). You can choose a unit completely prefabricated or custom build one into one end or the corner of the room.

Prefab showers and shower/bath combinations are available as single units molded of fiberglass or cast acrylic and as PVC wall and floor components that you assemble in place (referred to as "knock-down," or KD). Single-unit showers come in widths of 32, 36, and 48 inches, with a standard depth of 36 inches and height of 73 inches. Don't choose a one-piece model without first making sure you can get it through your house and into its destination. Measure the widths of doorways and hallways and any points where you will have to turn corners or negotiate stairs. If clearances are insufficient, consider a knock-down type.

Both types of prefab showers come with glass or plastic doors and various built-in accessories such as soap holders, grab bars, and brush and washcloth hooks.

Custom building your own shower demands more time and expertise, but allows you choices not available with prefab units.

For starters, you can build the shower into the space available. You can also choose your floor and wall materials, as well as the type of door and accessories. Even with this freedom, you should start with a space at least 30 inches wide and 36 inches deep so you can move around without knocking your knees and elbows into the walls.

Floors of a custom shower can be site-installed tile over a plastic or copper shower pan or a prefab base of fiberglass. Choosing a prefabricated base eliminates the hassles of constructing a watertight floor but limits your shower to the size and shape of the base. Prefab bases come in squares, typically 32, 34, or 36 inches; rectangles of various sizes up to 60 inches long, and as corner units, with the two wall sides 36 or 38 inches long.

▲ This luxurious bathroom takes advantage of plenty of space with a separate shower that is generous enough to require no door.

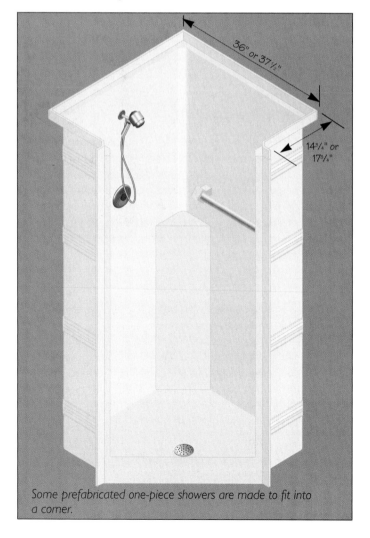

Some prefabricated one-piece showers are made to fit into a corner.

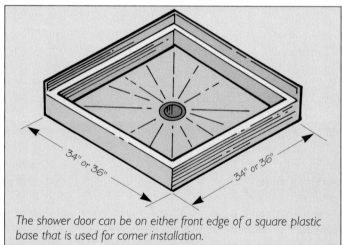

The shower door can be on either front edge of a square plastic base that is used for corner installation.

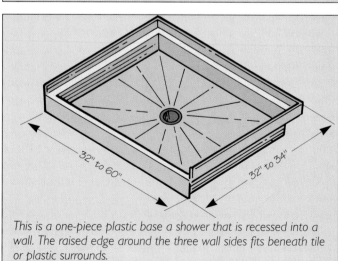

This is a one-piece plastic base a shower that is recessed into a wall. The raised edge around the three wall sides fits beneath tile or plastic surrounds.

▲ There's nothing quite like a long soak in deep old-fashioned claw-foot bath tub.

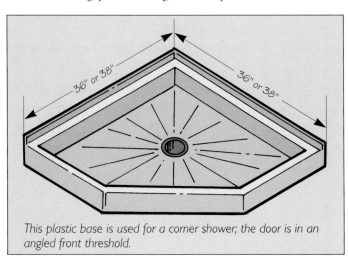

This plastic base is used for a corner shower; the door is in an angled front threshold.

Bathtubs

Every household should have at least one bathtub. Even if you prefer to take showers, you may have to accommodate small children or elderly persons who can't use a shower. Also consider the value of a tub on the resale of your house. Whether you long for a Victorian claw-footed tub or want a more conventional type, there's probably a model that's just right for your bathroom. Enameled cast iron is the material of most tubs today, followed in popularity by cast acrylic and fiberglass. As with sinks, the heat-fused finishes of metal-based tubs stand up to much more abuse than the newer plastic alternatives, but plastic is lighter and enables manufactures to offer a wider variety of forms and surface features. Whatever the material, you can choose between a wide range of pastel tints and bold, solid colors from

▲ Pre-fab showers and shower/bath combinations such as this one are inexpensive, relatively easy to install, and quite durable and easy to clean.

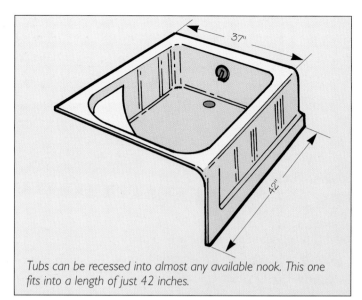

Tubs can be recessed into almost any available nook. This one fits into a length of just 42 inches.

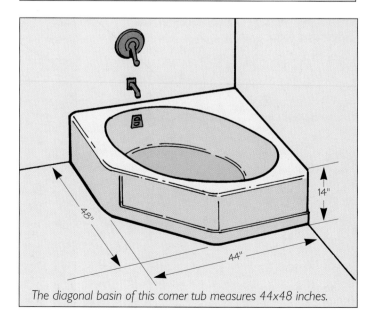

Standard-size tubs are 60 inches long. A 66-inch-long tub affords better leg room.

beet red to ink black in addition to traditional white. The most common size for tubs that back up to a wall is 32x60 inches. Widths from 24 to 42 inches are available. Corner units come in at around 48 inches on the wall sides. Size your tub according to the floor space available, your length, and the level of luxury you desire. For example, if the tub is to serve two people together, the width inside should be at least 42 inches. Claw-footed and other free-standing tubs need adequate clearance on all sides to look their best. Unlike prefab showers, tubs don't come in knock-down models, so check the tub's dimensions against your doorways, hallways, and stairways to ensure that you will be able to maneuver it into the bathroom.

Tubs can be placed at floor level, raised on a platform, or sunk into the floor. If raised, provide steps up with treads at least 11 inches and risers not exceeding 7 inches. Provide grab bars for both raised and sunken tubs to help you climb into and out of the tub.

Whirlpools and Spas

Whirlpools and spas offer the ultimate in relaxation: the chance to soak your cares away in deep, hot water. It's easy to understand their appeal, considering the stresses of modern life.

Whirlpools drain after each use. Spas retain their water. Spas evolved from outdoor hot tubs made of redwood or cedar. Their high, round shape makes them deeper than whirlpools.

The diagonal basin of this corner tub measures 44x48 inches.

Heated by gas or electric heaters, spas can be used indoors or out. Because they cannot double as bathtubs, spas are better adapted for outside installation.

Whirlpools (often mistakenly called Jacuzzis, a trade name) are made of the same materials and in the same colors as tubs. Rectangular sizes start as small as a standard bathtub and range up to 48x84 inches. Like tubs, they can be installed at floor level, recessed into the floor, or raised on platforms.

A whirlpool contains a pump to circulate the water through jets positioned around the sides of the unit. If the unit doesn't come with an in-line heater, it will draw hot water from your home's water heater. The pump is located under or adjacent to the unit and should remain accessible through an access panel at the side, front, or rear. If you have the space and the budget for a whirlpool, you can choose among many optional accessories, such as a telephone or controls for room lights and other appliances.

▲ Whether a long oval stretching under a bank of windows (above) or designed to be tucked into a corner (below), you'll find a whirlpool configuration to fit into any bathroom scheme.

▲ Whirlpools can be installed on raised platforms, or recessed into the floor as shown here.

Home Health Clubs

If a whirlpool doesn't deliver enough luxury for your taste, you may want to consider the next step up: a fixture containing an entire health club in a single enclosure. Some units combine whirlpools topped by an enclosure with glass doors on the front. Inside, you not only have the option of soaking in the turbulent hot water of a whirlpool, but can call up any environment you desire. By pushing a button, you can be baked by the dry heat of a sauna, steamed by a Turkish Bath, irradiated by sun lamps, buffeted by a warm breeze, or soaked by a spring rain.

Some units are freestanding, others mount into the wall. Sizes vary, as do installation requirements. In addition to hot and cold water supply and waste lines, units may require one or two GFCI-protected electrical circuits. If you want to consider a luxury unit, visit a bath specialty store to see what's available—be prepared for the cost, which generally runs into the thousands of dollars. When you make your selection, study the product data for installation requirements.

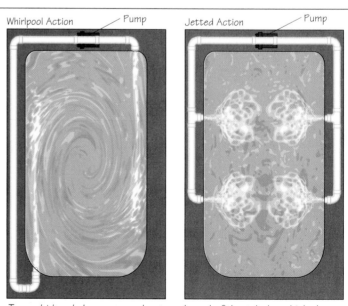

True whirlpools have a nozzle at each end of the tub, by which the water can be moved into a spiral, or whirlpool. Some whirlpools create turbulence by expelling water through jets in the sides of the tub.

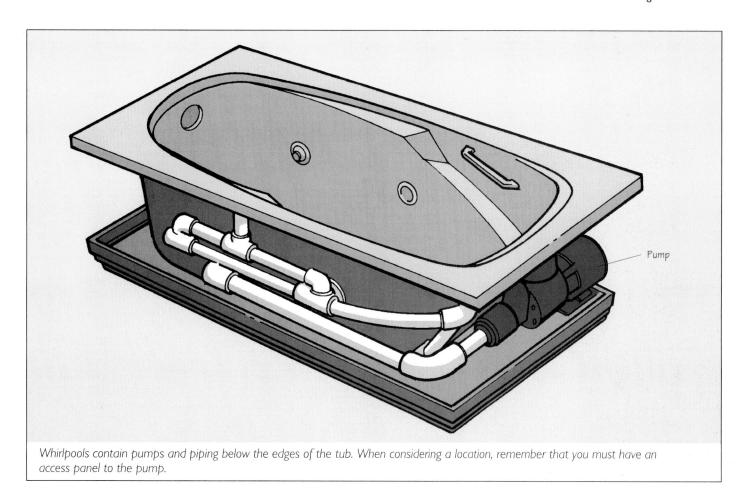

Pump

Whirlpools contain pumps and piping below the edges of the tub. When considering a location, remember that you must have an access panel to the pump.

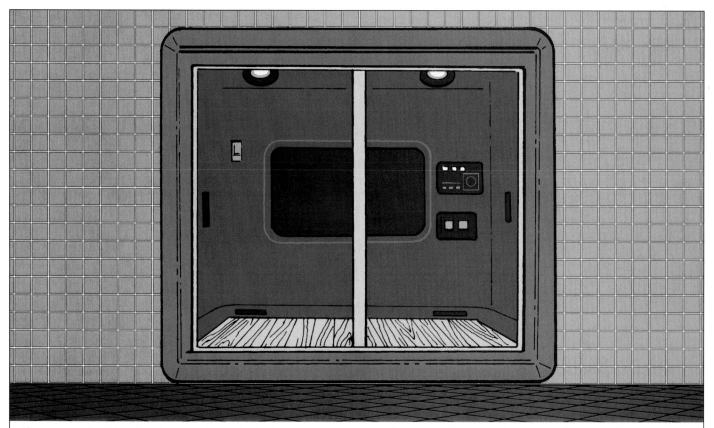

If you want a health club at home and have the budget and space, you can choose a multipurpose fixture that offers not only a shower and bath, but also a whirlpool, steam room, sauna, and sunlamps.

3
Storage and Amenities

A bathroom, like a freeway, doesn't get constant, even use. When it gets jammed during morning rush hours, you want people to spend as little time there as possible. When minutes count, time can't be wasted trying to find toothbrushes, shavers, and hair dryers. Creating top bathroom efficiency for all users requires careful planning of fixtures and prioritizing storage space. The most frequently used items should always be easiest to get at quickly.

Creating a Storage System

Have you ever wondered how so much stuff ends up in such a small room? Let's scan the list of things that commonly live in the bathroom and question how each should be stored.

Medicines

All medicines should be quick and easy to find when needed. Labels should be easily readable without picking up the item. Medicines should be stored where adults can get at them, but where young children cannot. If you can't effectively store medicines in a bathroom cabinet where

▲ Lots of drawers and cabinets help keep this bathroom neat and orderly.

▲ With plenty of storage elsewhere, this pedestal sink is elegantly flanked by narrow, uncluttered shelves.

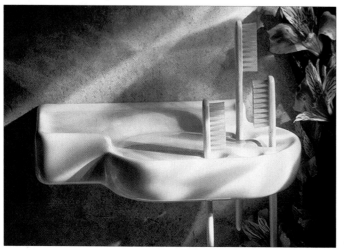

▲ Even a mundane item such as a toothbrush holder can become a bit of sculpture.

they will be out of the reach of small children, consider another location, such as in a high kitchen cabinet. To be really safe, consider fitting a lock on the medicine cabinet (but be sure you can open it in emergencies).

Tooth Care Accessories

Locate toothbrushes and toothpaste within easy reach of the sink. A narrow shelf above a freestanding sink works well, as does a

▲ Wire baskets and racks on rolling slides come in many shapes and sizes to allow you to make maximum use of the space under your bathroom cabinets.

position at the rear or side of a vanity top. Keeping your tooth care accessories visible makes sense, even if you have to watch the toothpaste tube getting steadily uglier with each squeeze. Electric toothbrushes, becoming increasingly popular, need a resting place near an electrical outlet; pay attention to where the cord will end up.

Shaving Gear

Keep shaving gear near the sink but out of sight (and out of the reach of children). The lower shelves of a medicine cabinet with doors fills this bill nicely, as does a bin or tub under a vanity or in a vanity drawer.

If you use an electric razor, you need a way to locate it near a GFCI-protected outlet and a mirror. For maximum convenience, you might keep the razor plugged into the outlet, hung on a nearby hook or narrow shelf. But because cords tend to get in the way of other activities in a cramped space and outlets usually have to be shared with other appliances, a shallow drawer below the vanity might be better.

First Aid

Every home should be equipped with basic first-aid items, and the bathroom is a logical site to store them, since administering first aid usually requires ample clean water. When your child is screaming with a cut hand, the last thing you want is to have to grope around for that box of bandages. The answer is to locate everything in one, easy-to-get-to place. Designate one drawer for first-aid items, and make sure nothing else ends up in that drawer.

most convenient in soap dishes or pump bottles at the side or rear of the washbasin. Built-in shelves and soap dishes and hanging bags and racks can make items used in the shower or bathtub easy to get to.

Towels and Washcloths

Towels and washcloths should be within easy reach of every washbasin, bidet, shower, and tub. Plan towel racks to allow a separate towel bar for each member of the household (for better harmony) and a few additional bars for guests. Fresh towels and washcloths stored on open shelves or in bins in the bathroom can become part of the room decor, or you may want to store them in an adjacent linen cabinet in or near the bathroom.

Most bathrooms don't contain provisions for dirty washcloths and towels. Left wadded up on a fixture or lying on the floor, dirty linen detracts from the room's beauty and gets in the way of other users. A bathroom hamper is one solution; a hamper bin built into the vanity is another.

▲ The bathroom is a logical place for a hamper. This one is built-in to fit with the bathroom's decor.

▲ Cabinets with open shelves keep towels neatly stored and easily accessible.

Besides the convenience of having all your gear in one place, you will be able to pull the whole drawer out and move it to the site of the patient, if necessary.

Personal Grooming Accessories

You can relieve bathroom gridlock by providing space outside the bathroom for grooming routines not requiring water, such as makeup application and hair drying. In addition, a dressing table with several shallow drawers in an adjacent area or bedroom can do much to unclutter the bathroom. Those items that need to be used near a water source can be handily squirreled away in shallow drawers in a vanity near the sink.

Hair Dryers

If you choose to use a hair dryer in the bathroom, store it near a GFI-protected outlet and mirror. A deep drawer in a vanity cabinet is a good place.

Soap and Shampoo

Wet-grooming items need two kinds of storage. Items in current use need to be within easy reach and plain view. Reserve items can be almost anywhere. Soaps for cleansing hands and face are

▲ The storage solution here consists of a combination of drawers and roll-out wire bins.

▲ There's often a bit of wall space left over next to the shower. This is an excellent place to stow towels.

▲ This vanity uses a system of drawers and swing-out bins for easy access to items stored within.

Cleaning and Maintenance Supplies

The odd-shaped space below the sink in a vanity cabinet is ideal for storing cleaning supplies (an advantage that freestanding sinks don't offer). Fit one side of the cabinet with adjustable shelves for small items; keep the other side open for tall items such as cleaning brushes and plungers.

The Means of Storage

Whether you buy your bath storage in the form of prefabricated cabinetry or custom build your own, the most practical storage facilities are suited to the items stored and make use of space not needed for other functions. Each type of storage device has pros and cons.

Drawers

Drawers offer two advantages: Items stored are out of sight when not in use and all items are equally accessible, that is, if you don't pack things on top of each other. To avoid this pitfall, select shallow drawers for small things such as cosmetics and reserve deep drawers for larger items such as hair dryers.

Shelves

Shelves, whether open or enclosed, offer easy access and make good use of shallow spaces on or in walls. Open shelves can display decorative items, such as bottles, colored soaps, and towels. On the downside, open shelves invite dust and clutter.

If mounted on adjustable clips, the height of shelves may be repeatedly changed. Shelves can be shallow or deep, but a greater number of shallow shelves are apt to be more useful than a lesser number of deep shelves (things parked at the rear of deep shelves tend to die there). Open shelving for brightly colored towels and decorative bottles and soaps can add to your decor as well as

▲ Just outside the shower door is the perfect place for towel hooks.

provide storage. If you like the openness of shelves, accentuate this feeling by installing glass ones. Shelving for cleaning materials is better located out of sight behind hinged doors.

Trays

Trays can slide out on guides, like drawers, or pivot off of a pole. Either way, they can provide a lot of shallow storage space for small objects.

Tubs

Plastic tubs can be mounted on guides in the odd-shaped leftover space below the washbasin. Use these tubs to house cleaning materials. Spills or leaks will be easy to clean up and will not soil your cabinetry.

Bins

Bins hinged near the floor or mounted on drawer guides in vanity cabinets make excellent bathroom hampers.

Pegs, Hooks, and Bars

Washcloths and towels in current use need a place to dry out when they're not in service. Locate pegs, hooks, or bars made of wood, ceramic,

plastic, or metal on walls near their point of use. One or two hooks inside the tub/shower area can hold bathing accessories, but locate them where they won't be bumped into.

Amenities

The right kind of storage facilities for the many accessories used in your bathroom can make for a functional, efficient space. But a submarine is also functional and efficient. Something else is needed to make the space special. You can add that extra touch by opening the room to sunlight, incorporating decorative objects, and finishing the space with colors and textures that complement each other and enhance the area. Here are some possibilities:

Plants

Plants thrive in humid bathroom air as long as there is a source of outside light. The challenge, particularly in small rooms, is to locate the plants where they won't get in the way. A wide window ledge is an ideal site, as is an unused corner of the vanity. If space permits, plant shelves can be built adjacent to tubs and showers. You might even hang a single Boston fern from a ceiling hook in a corner of the room not used for foot traffic.

If you live in an area with a mild climate, consider adding an enclosed garden court outside your master bath. One or two French or sliding glass doors could open onto a wood deck surrounded by plants. The courtyard need be no larger than the area required for a chaise lounge and can be kept private by a high wood fence. Even when it's chilly outside, sunlight streaming into the bath through the outdoor plants will help cheer the space within.

▲ Hanging plants add intimacy to this bathing area.

▲ Here are two examples of how pictures and plants can help make the bathroom as beautiful as any other part of the house.

▲ Decorative glass bottles and vases can add elegance to a bathroom as long as they are placed where they won't be knocked over.

Pictures

Like plants, pictures can add interest and warmth to the room. Unfortunately, bathroom wall space is usually in short supply, even in large bathrooms. Mirrors often take up any spare wall space in small bathrooms. But mirrors are more useful in some places than others, as we'll see later in this chapter. The wall space above a toilet or bidet, if not needed for shelves, can make an excellent site for pictures.

Bottles and Vases

While decorative bottles and vases add a touch of luxury to the bath, they must be positioned where they won't be accidentally knocked over. Ledges and window sills may work, if they are out of the line of traffic; a special high shelf is another possibility. Take care where you locate glass items if children use the room. A glass bottle toppled onto a tiled floor will shatter into dangerous shards.

Soaps

Prettily scented soaps please the senses whether heaped in bowls or baskets or displayed on ledges surrounding the tub and washbasin area. They can even be hung in baskets from the ceiling.

▲ Every bathroom needs a mirror over the sink. The bathroom at left adds mirrors to the side so users can see the sides of their heads as well. At right, opposing mirrored walls make the room seem much larger.

Mirror, Mirror on Which Wall?

Mirrors can appear to expand a space as well as serve personal grooming needs, but to do either well, they must be properly located.

Mirrors for Personal Grooming

You'll naturally want a mirror on the wall over the sink, to enable you to see your face. If you also want to see the sides and back of your head, add side mirrors that hinge toward a central mirror. Any medicine cabinet that is to be located directly behind the washbasin should have a sliding or hinged mirror. If you want your medicine cabinet to be off to the side, install a unit that comes with a mirror that hinges toward the central mirror. For people in wheelchairs, consider a fixed or adjustable mirror that tilts toward the floor.

Try to reserve a space on one wall or door for a full-length mirror.

Using Mirrors to Widen the Room

The apparent width of a narrow bathroom can be doubled by cladding one of the long walls with mirrors. Adding mirrors to the opposite side, as well, can make the space seem even wider, though you risk overkill with the confusing series of multiple reflections.

Mirrors behind plants and decorative objects can magnify their effect. If you are lucky enough to have a garden court outside your bathroom, place mirrors on the abutting end walls to draw the garden into the room.

You don't need to mirror an entire wall to get a room-enlarging effect, but if you do, you will save money by using mirror tiles instead of a single large mirror. Mirror tiles come in 12x12-inch squares and can easily be attached to the wall with self-adhesive tabs.

4
Openings for Light and View

Electric lighting and mechanical ventilation can make a bathroom without windows serve basic needs quite well. But opening the wall or ceiling to the outside can make the space come alive. Properly located windows or skylights can cheer the room with sunlight, give views to the outside, and provide natural ventilation, all without sacrificing privacy.

Of course, windows may encourage longer stays, something you may want to deter during the morning rush hour. But wouldn't it be nice if at least one bathroom were a place where you could relax while you showered, soaked, or shaved? This is the room where you should strive to make the most of an outside opening.

You can create an outside opening in an interior bath that sits under a roof by adding a skylight. A bathroom located under other floors with no outside wall cannot, obviously, get access to a window or skylight. In this case, make the room as functional and cheerful as you can by carefully selecting and locating light fixtures, as will be discussed in later chapters.

A well-designed window opening should live up to as many of the following goals as possible:

♦ Let in ample sunlight
♦ Open for natural ventilation
♦ Permit views to outside
♦ Inhibit views to the inside
♦ Be comfortable in cold weather
♦ Be safe to operate

If you are considering a skylight or roof window, your installed unit should:

♦ Let in as much natural light as possible

▲ If privacy isn't an issue, you can use large casement windows combined with skylights to bring the outdoors in.

♦ Distribute the light evenly inside the room, without creating glare
♦ Open for ventilation
♦ Inhibit heat loss in winter and heat gain in summer

How well your window choice meets these objectives depends on how the unit is made, the way it opens, and where it is located in the wall or ceiling. A good place to begin is matching the window frame and glazing materials to your needs.

▲ This elegant archtop window over a shaded awning window achieves privacy while still admitting light and a bit of view.

Window Materials

Today's residential window frames are made of wood, metal, or plastic. Wood frames may be solid—usually ponderosa pine or may be made of pressed wood particles. The most common residential metal windows are made of extruded aluminum, but steel units are also available. Plastic frames come as extruded vinyl (PVC) or fiberglass.

When choosing among finishes, consider first whether you want to repaint the frames from time to time or prefer a finish that requires no maintenance. Wood windows can be clad in aluminum or vinyl, which need no upkeep, or may come primed for painting or staining. Aluminum windows are surfaced with

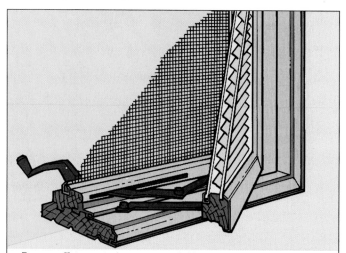

Energy-efficient windows are available in aluminum, wood, and extruded vinyl. The aluminum-clad casement window shown here contains an adjustable shade between the inner and outer pane. With no shade exposed on the inside to pick up water drops, this windows is well-suited for locations above baths and showers.

permanent finishes of baked enamel or electrolitically coated metal. Steel windows come primed for painting. The finish of plastic windows is usually the same material that is used in the frame and never needs to be painted.

During cold periods, even the best windows waste more heat to the outside than the adjacent solid wall. While you naturally want all your windows to be airtight, comfort counts even more in a bathroom. If you have ever sat in a tub below a poorly insulated window on a January night, you know how unpleasant it can be to have a steady stream of cold air wafting down on you.

Fortunately, today's windows are both better sealed against leakage and better insulated against heat loss through the glass. Select insulated windows (two separated panes) wherever you live. If you are located in a cold climate, you'll get even better comfort and energy efficiency in the cold winters by choosing windows protected with low-emissivity (low-E) coating and argon gas in the space between the two sheets of glass. Currently, the window with the highest efficiency encapsulates one or two layers of polyester film with a low-E coating between the glass panes.

Window Types

Because space may be tight in your bathroom, you next need to consider carefully the way your windows will open and close, as well as the shapes and sizes of the units. Here are the most common types of residential windows and the pros and cons of using them in bathrooms:

▲ A glass block exterior wall can flood the room with light while maintaining privacy.

Fixed Windows

As the name implies, fixed windows do not open. They come as glass sheets to be installed into a finished opening or as ready-to-install units enclosed in wood, metal, or plastic frames. Another way to create a fixed window is with glass block. Because it lets in light but distorts through-vision, glass block is an excellent way to achieve privacy while brightening up the interior.

Since fixed windows don't open, they can't ventilate; they are feasible in the bathroom only in combination with operable windows or if you want to rely entirely on mechanical ventilation. An advantage to fixed windows is that they are readily available in many shapes and sizes.

Double- and Single-Hung Windows

Likely, the most common type of window used in homes is the double-hung window, which has an upper and lower sash that ride up and down in their own channels. Newer types allow each section to be tilted to the inside for easier cleaning. Prolonged contact with high bathroom humidity may cause wood sash and guides to swell, making the window hard to open. If placed above a tub or shower, the extra force needed to open a stuck window could lead to slips and falls.

Another possible downside of these windows is their vertical shape. Long and narrow, they afford views through the lower half at a height that can compromise your privacy.

Single-hung windows are like double-hung, but only the lower sash moves; the upper sash remains fixed. While this may be fine

in some cases, before choosing a single-hung window decide whether you will ever want or need to open the upper half. If you draw curtains in front of the lower half for better privacy, for example, you will not be able to open the upper half for ventilation, as you would with a double-hung window.

Casement Windows

While all double-hung windows are necessarily taller than they are wide, casements range in shape from vertical to slightly horizontal. Casement windows are hinged along one side and open outward by use of a crank mounted on the sill. These windows are generally safer than double-hungs to use in a bathroom—you're less likely to slip on the tub floor if you are turning a crank than if you are trying to force a window sash upward. Because the entire window opens and the opened sash directs breezes into the room, casement windows are also better ventilators than double-hung windows.

But there are some disadvantages. Exposure to rain is greater than with other types of windows, and the out-hanging sash may obstruct people from walking by a ground-level open window.

Sliding Windows

Sliders are like double-hung windows turned sideways. They offer the advantages of other horizontally shaped windows, such as privacy and freeing up wall space below the sill. But like double-hungs, wood sliders may stick and become hard to operate when exposed to a high-moisture environment; thus they can become dangerous to use while standing in a wet area.

Awning Windows

Turn a casement on its side and you have an awning window. These windows also open outward and are controlled by a sill-mounted crank. The bottom of the sash on an awning window extends outward. This makes awning windows the best type to deflect rain. Like casements, the full opening is exposed for ventilation, though the open awning window doesn't catch breezes quite as well as a casement window.

Perhaps the best thing about awnings in bathrooms is their horizontal shape. You can place them high on the wall above a shower, with a solid surface below to deflect the water. High placement also allows you to see out—at least while standing—but limits views from the outside to only the ceiling area.

Skylights and Roof Windows

Openings in the roof are excellent ways to flood the bathroom with natural light without taking up wall space. They may be the only way to get outside openings in landlocked, top-story bathrooms. If you choose a unit that opens, you can also get ventilation.

People often refer to any glazed opening in the roof as a skylight. That was fine in the 1950s when the only device for homes was a plastic bubble. Plastic bubble skylights are still available, but today you can also buy roof windows, which closely resemble traditional

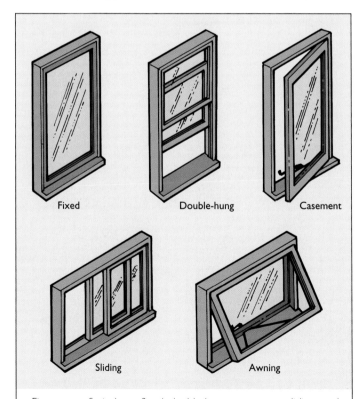

Five types of windows: fixed, double-hung, casement, sliding, and awning. Horizontally shaped windows such as sliding and awning units are better choices for locations above tubs and showers.

▲ If your bathroom is directly under a roof, a skylight is a terrific way to enjoy light and a view of the sky without compromising privacy.

▲ Hot, steam-filled air rises. As a result, operable roof windows are an excellent way to ventilate a bathroom.

wall windows. The difference between skylights and roof windows has become blurred. Whereas skylights do not open, roof windows can open or not. Some even pivot inward to allow cleaning of the outer pane. Here are some things to keep in mind when choosing between the available products:

Appearance. Flat-profile roof windows change your home's outside appearance less than bubble-dome skylights. If the roof is steeply sloped and figures prominently into the design of your home, you won't want to puncture the roofline haphazardly with windows that look like pimples. Bubble-dome skylights make good sense on a flat roof, however, because they shed rain better and are not seen from the ground.

Cost. Fixed skylights are the most economical, followed by operable skylights, with operable roof windows being at the top of cost scale. Built-in blinds cost more still.

Light and Glare. All roof windows and skylights are efficient sources of outside light. Even units as small as 24x30 inches, if placed near the center of the bathroom's ceiling, can flood all corners of the room with natural light. To avoid the potential glare from overhead sunlight striking a wall window or mirror, order a roof window equipped with built-in adjustable horizontal blinds.

Heat Gain and Loss. Unlike side windows, roof windows and skylights can pose more of a heat gain than heat loss problem,

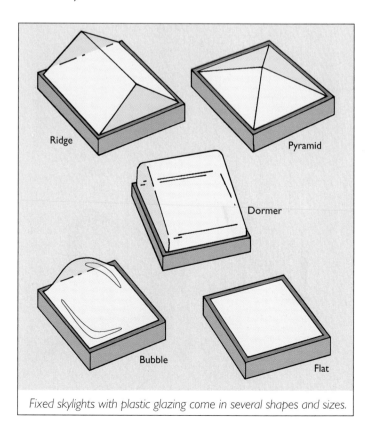

Fixed skylights with plastic glazing come in several shapes and sizes.

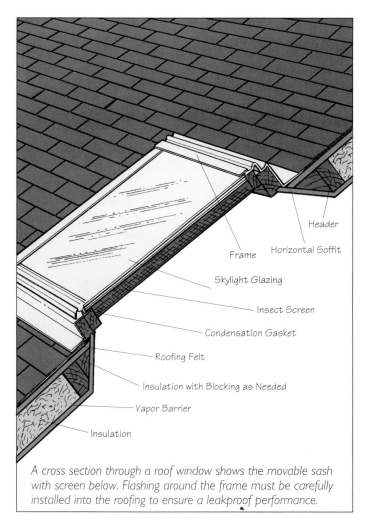

A cross section through a roof window shows the movable sash with screen below. Flashing around the frame must be carefully installed into the roofing to ensure a leakproof performance.

Header
Horizontal Soffit
Frame
Skylight Glazing
Insect Screen
Condensation Gasket
Roofing Felt
Insulation with Blocking as Needed
Vapor Barrier
Insulation

particularly if located on a south- or west-facing slope of a roof. To minimize both heat gain and loss, choose insulated (double-pane) units with low-E coating.

Ventilation. You can get both roof windows or skylights that open, but operating windows that are out of reach requires a remote crank or electrically operated control. If you rely on a portable crank, you'll need a place to store it. Before you buy anything, ask the supplier about the control options.

Light Shafts. The distance between the roof opening and room ceiling below can range from the thickness of the rafters (as with cathedral ceilings) to several feet (when the house has an attic). The shape and construction of the shaft that bridges the gap affects both how much light gets down into the room and how it is distributes once there.

Splaying the shaft walls out from the roof opening to the ceiling creates drama in the room below and distributes daylight to all corners. You can splay just one or two walls—usually the walls at the lowest and highest end of the roof opening—or splay all four shaft walls for the best effect. To promote light distribution, face the shaft walls with drywall and paint them white or off-white.

Straight vertical shaft walls are much easier to build. Since working within the roof space is tough enough under the best of conditions, you may not want to make it any harder than you have to. The end result, however, isn't likely to be as pleasing as splayed walls, particularly if the vertical distance is very great. You run the risk of creating an opening that looks like a vertical tunnel and one that will distribute light unevenly in the room. Chapter 10 tells how to build shafts for roof openings.

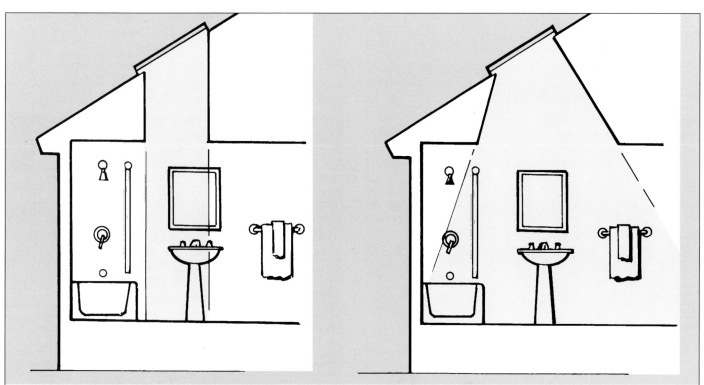

Skylights and roof windows bring sunlight into bathrooms that don't have outside windows. Splayed shafts (right) distribute the light more evenly than straight shafts (left).

Exterior Doors

Opening your bathroom to a garden court will require doors, in place of or in addition to windows. Glazed doors are usually chosen because they allow light and view at all times. Choose between sliding glass doors and French doors.

Sliding Doors

Sliding glass doors come in pairs with overall widths of 60, 72, and 84 inches, and in heights of 84 inches (standard) and 96 inches. You can opt to have a door that has one or two opening panels. When open, sliding doors require no additional space inside or outside to house the open panel. On the downside, sliding doors are hard to seal against drafts, and cold drafts are the last thing you want from a door placed next to a tub or shower.

▲ With frosted glass combined with stained glass, this bathroom provides light and egress to the outside without creating a view into the bathroom.

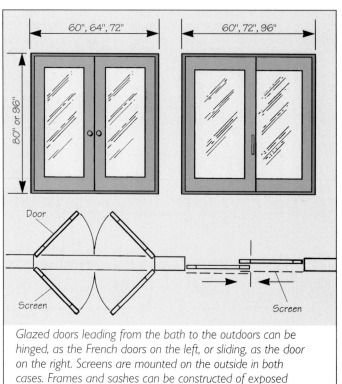

Glazed doors leading from the bath to the outdoors can be hinged, as the French doors on the left, or sliding, as the door on the right. Screens are mounted on the outside in both cases. Frames and sashes can be constructed of exposed wood, vinyl- or aluminum-clad wood, or aluminum.

French Doors

French doors are paired hinged doors with glass panes. You can choose to have one or both doors in the pair open, and they can be hinged either inward or outward. In any case, there must be a clear path for the active door(s) to swing and a place for the door(s) to rest when open. The most common arrangement is to have the doors swing inward, so that screens mounted on the outside can swing outward. The inconvenience of a door that swings compared with one that slides is offset by the advantage of a better seal against drafts.

French doors can be glazed with single-sheet or insulating glass, in one panel or several small panes. In northern climates, choose insulating glass for best comfort and energy efficiency.

Window Accessories

After you choose your windows and decide where they will best work in the walls or ceiling, you may need additional measures to control glare, reduce winter heat loss, block unwanted summer heat, and create privacy—all while preserving the view outside. This tall order calls for flexible controls that respond to the time of day, season, and outside weather.

Window accessories take many forms:

◆ Storm windows of glass or plastic that you add to the inside or outside of the window

◆ Awnings or shutters mounted on the outside

◆ Pleated shades, blinds, and curtains mounted on the inside

Most window treatments can be adjusted, seasonally or daily.

Choose a window control system that will both enhance your comfort while in the bathroom and help create the design expression you are seeking. You can take your first cue from the climate. Window treatments for a hot climate should block direct sunlight. Next consider privacy. If your bath window is vulnerable from the yard or a neighboring house, choose a device that can

▲ Besides adding a decorative flourish, curtains help control the amount of heat and light that flows through a window.

be easily closed to block all views to the interior. Your final selection will have to accommodate the type and size of windows, the appearance you want, and of course, your budget. Here are a few of your choices.

Storm Windows

If you live in a place with cold winters and are beginning with old, leaky windows, you can either replace the windows with newer, more energy-efficient windows or tighten them by caulking and weather stripping and adding a storm window to the inside or outside. Just make sure the storm window can be opened and closed without removing the entire unit, particularly if it is located above the ground story.

Blinds

Adjustable blinds are a good way to control light, glare, and create privacy, though they don't add to the window's energy efficiency. Two types of slatted blinds enable you to direct the sunlight where you want, while maintaining a view to the outdoors. Horizontal miniblinds (Venetian blinds) made of aluminum or vinyl slats are best for south-facing windows, because they can shut out the higher sunlight that comes from the south. They are also the best way to ensure privacy. You can angle them upward, to let light in but prevent view into the bathroom, or close them tight to completely block the light.

For windows on the east and west, vertical blinds work best by blocking out the low-angle sun that adds so much heat on summer afternoons. Available in various tints, fabrics, and widths, vertical blinds can be rotated to direct sunlight where you want it, closed completely, or drawn open to the side of the window.

Shades

Blinds contain slats that block out light when fully closed. Shades let in some light even when closed. The simplest, cheapest models are rolling shades. Cheap describes their appearance, too, since the most economical type that you buy at home centers or discount stores will make your bathroom look tacky. Check out the classier versions that use different fabrics and ride in side tracks. These are available at window accessory stores.

Pleated shades stack, rather than roll up, and ride up and down in tracks. Single-layer pleated shades fold up like an accordion. Another type is made of two layers of fabric and forms honeycomb shapes (viewed from the side) when the shade is pulled shut. The air entrapped within each honeycomb cell helps cut heat loss. Pleated blinds are elegant and allow some light to filter in while ensuring complete privacy.

▲ Horizontal blinds are the best way to control the higher sunlight that comes from a south-facing window.

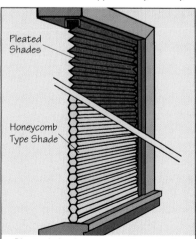
Pleated shades retract upward when open. The air space inside the honeycomb-shaped cells (lower portion) helps stem heat loss.

Labels in illustration: Pleated Shades; Honeycomb Type Shade

Curtains

Curtains can control glare and create privacy. Insulated curtains are available that will provide some control over heat loss and gain. The softness of curtains can humanize a window, while making the interior feel elegant. Horizontal units, such as sliding and awning windows, look best with curtains that close over the entire window. Curtains hung the full length of a vertical window, such as a double-hung or casement, can be awkward at the bottom. The folds are fullest there and likely to hog space in a small room. Consider curtains over only the lower half of the window—this will allow privacy without the excess fabric at the bottom of the window.

Awnings and Shutters

Awnings can block direct sunlight from entering the window. They work best on south-facing windows, though. To keep late afternoon sunlight out of west-facing windows, you'll need awnings that lower to cover almost the full depth of the window or shutters, which are hinged at the sides. Choose awnings or shutters for your bath windows only if you want to fit the other windows on the house similarly; otherwise your bathroom windows will look out of place.

For privacy, you may want to consider interior wood shutters instead of fabric window treatments. You can easily mount them to an entire window unit or the bottom half of a double- or single-hung window.

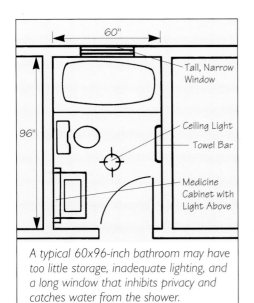

A typical 60x96-inch bathroom may have too little storage, inadequate lighting, and a long window that inhibits privacy and catches water from the shower.

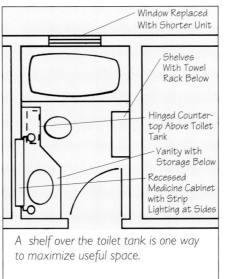

A shelf over the toilet tank is one way to maximize useful space.

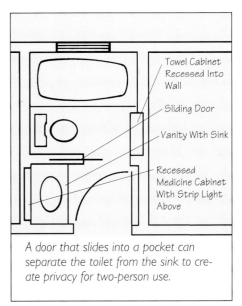

A door that slides into a pocket can separate the toilet from the sink to create privacy for two-person use.

Improving an Existing Layout

Chapter 1 suggested that you start your bathroom planning with a list of shortcomings of the present room. Note your list of gripes on the base plan, to give you a good starting point for changing the layout. Next, see what changes you can make to solve each problem. Use your templates to explore alternatives. The drawings on this page give side ideas for what can be done with a typical 60x96-inch bathroom.

When You Can't Expand

What can you do if you want to add fixtures or amenities, but are stuck with a room of a given size? Be creative and try to find different ways to use the space. Is there unused wall space, for example, that might be used for storage? Can you add a narrow shelf above the toilet tank? If the shelf is low, hinge it to provide access to the toilet tank lid.

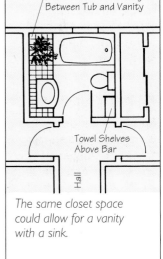

By expanding into the closet of the left bedroom, there is enough room for a corner tub and towel rack, with generous floor space between the fixtures.

The same closet space could allow for a vanity with a sink.

Expanding into an Adjacent Space

If you can't improve the layout without adding space, take a hard look at the rooms adjacent to your bathroom. Most homes have opportunities for adding space without adding to the house. Begin by looking for unused spaces, such as below a stairway. If there are closets nearby, ask yourself if some or all of the space can be used for the bath. Maybe two feet of floor space can be taken from a large abutting room without reducing its usefulness. A small amount of floor space stolen from a closet or adjacent room might be just right for a shower, tub, or vanity.

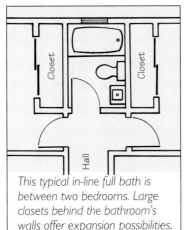

This typical in-line full bath is between two bedrooms. Large closets behind the bathroom's walls offer expansion possibilities.

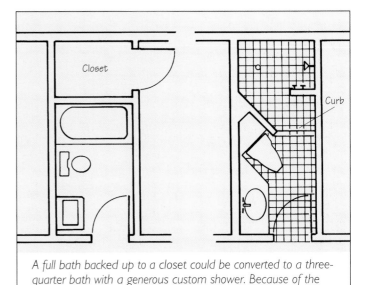

A full bath backed up to a closet could be converted to a three-quarter bath with a generous custom shower. Because of the position of the shower head and shape of the shower, no door or curtain is needed.

Enlarging Outward

A bathroom addition to an outside wall of the house offers the chance to get unencumbered floor space with outside walls for windows or to connect to an enclosed courtyard. The answer to your problems? Maybe, but this kind of space is the costliest to build, since it requires a new outer enclosure.

It may be possible to bump the outer wall out by three feet or so without building a new foundation, by extending the existing floor structure out over the foundation wall. If the present bathroom floor joists run perpendicular into the outer wall, it may be possible to add a "sister" to each joist that will cantilever out and overhang the foundation. If this looks possible, get the help of an architect, engineer, or builder to make sure the structure is sound.

For any addition that enlarges your home's footprint on your property, you will need to make sure that you will not be encroaching into the setback required by the local zoning ordinance.

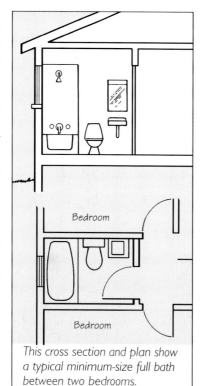

This cross section and plan show a typical minimum-size full bath between two bedrooms.

Making Use of Vertical Space

So far all of our planning has been on the horizontal plane. But you also need to think about how vertical surfaces can be used, for example, for storage or for mounting accessories. Extending a vanity counter-top over an adjacent toilet

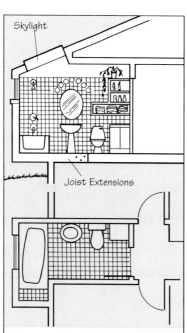

By extending the floor joists out a few feet, you can enlarge your bathroom space without having to construct a foundation. The roof of the house is similarly extended. The original long window is replaced with a smaller, high window and a skylight.

tank provides a useful shelf (be sure that the shelf is hinged or removable, to keep the tank accessible). Another option is to use the cavities between the studs in interior walls for shallow shelving.

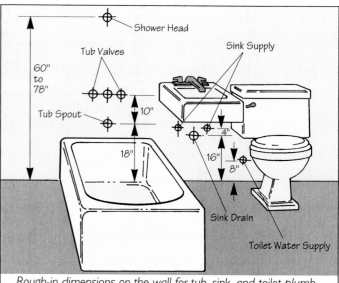

Rough-in dimensions on the wall for tub, sink, and toilet plumbing. Use the manufacturer's product literature for required floor rough-in dimensions.

As you plan the vertical surfaces, include the mounting heights for plumbing fixtures on any drawings you make of the walls. Transfer these later to the walls themselves to locate rough-in holes for piping.

Bathroom Lighting

If parts of your face are in shadow when you stand in front of the bathroom mirror, you need better lighting. Good bathroom lighting puts light just where you need it. A superb lighting scheme also enhances the mood of the room. In Chapter 4, we saw how well-chosen windows and skylights can cheer up a bathroom by bringing sunlight inside. But sunlight is hard to control and not always present, so it pays to get the most from your electrical lighting sources.

Two kinds of lighting are needed: ambient lighting, to illuminate the room in general and to create the desired mood, and task lighting, to throw a focused beam onto a specific spot.

Ambient Lighting

The room's general lighting should illuminate the entire room with enough light to find your way around. In elaborate schemes, general lighting can be expanded to include sources that can be adjusted to create various moods, for example through optional switching and dimmer controls.

The light fixture surrounding a vanity mirror may provide enough light for the entire room if the room is relatively small and open. Larger bathrooms, as well as bathrooms subdivided with toilet or shower compartments, probably need additional room lighting. Whatever you do, don't try to get by with a single lighting fixture mounted dead center in the ceiling. It might keep the room from getting dark, but will cause shadows in the wrong places in any wall mirror.

Ambient light sources can be located on the ceilings or walls, but choose fixtures that don't project into door swings or obstruct the path of foot traffic.

Task Lighting

The main areas needing task lighting are the mirrors intended for grooming. Light from the sides of the mirror is best (place the fixtures at least 30 inches apart so that the light doesn't shine right into the user's eyes). To avoid shadows on the user's face, don't rely on a single light above the mirror. Many medicine cabinet/mirror units are available with lighting fixtures at each side, or you can add strip fixtures to the sides, top, or both, for shadow-free light on your face.

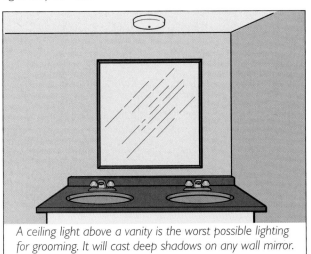

A ceiling light above a vanity is the worst possible lighting for grooming. It will cast deep shadows on any wall mirror.

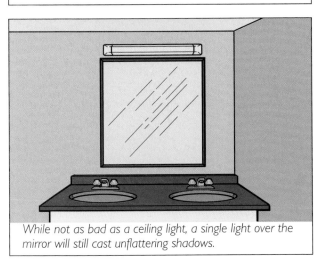

While not as bad as a ceiling light, a single light over the mirror will still cast unflattering shadows.

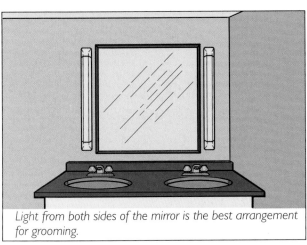

Light from both sides of the mirror is the best arrangement for grooming.

▲ Lighting above the vanity is not ideal, but several less powerful overhead light sources are better than one powerful fixture.

▲ A bank of lights on both sides of the mirror is best for grooming.

6

Planning Bathrooms for People with Special Needs

The standard bathroom found in most homes cannot be comfortably used by people who have disabilities. In fact, people who use wheelchairs may find some bathrooms impossible to use. Unfortunately, making bathroom facilities accessible to a household member who has an impairment can be costly. And some changes may make a facility harder to use for another member of the household. For example, the toilet seat height for wheelchair users is 17 to 19 inches, which is too high for many small children. The trick here is to make compromises so that everyone can safely and easily use the bathroom. And remember, small children will eventually get big enough to use the higher toilet.

To make sure any changes you make meet all your needs, consider these questions:

◆ What difficulties do the standard bathroom facilities create?

◆ Is the family member facing temporary or permanent disability?

◆ If permanent adjustments are necessary, is it more convenient to implement accommodations into only one bathroom or do changes need to be made in all bathrooms?

Individual Needs

The first step in making special accommodations is to assess the specific physical limitations of the person who will be using the bathroom. This will help you tailor the layout and fixtures to meet his or her needs.

Limited Use of Limbs

Some decrease in the ability to reach and bend is experienced by most people as they age, although young people can certainly

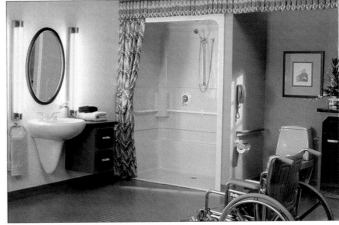

▲ An oversized shower stall with detachable shower nozzle, a low sink and a grab bar by the toilet make this bathroom accessible to a wheelchair user.

have these limitations, too. Adaptations that can make bathrooms easier to use include raised toilet seats, grab bars around the tub/shower and toilet, and tub seats. If your family member has trouble reaching high things, provide storage for personal hygiene and medicines at a level between 36 and 60 inches from the floor. A hand-held shower is useful for people who must sit while showering.

Limited Use of Hands and Fingers

To make life easier for someone who has difficulty turning faucets on and off, consider replacing circular faucet handles with a lever-type faucet. Replace toggle switches with large rocker plates. Instead of small knobs on vanity drawers, use C-shaped handles. Use shallow, open shelves and racks where possible, rather than deep storage behind doors.

▲ This bathroom has no separate shower stall, making it easy to manuever a wheelchair. There are grab bars to facilitate moving to and from the toilet and the shower seat. The space under the sink is unobstructed and the hot water supply is well out of the way.

Reduced Sight

Changes you may make to improve bathroom access for someone with poor eyesight will make the room easier for everyone to use. Start at the floor, and eliminate sudden changes in elevation. Make sure there is an extra long nonslip mat on the tub or shower floor. Mount the room light switch on the outside of the entrance door and use the kind that glows. Provide brighter levels of lighting in the bathroom than you might otherwise install. And make sure there are no unlit corners, such as the tub/shower area.

Wheelchair Accessibility

Accommodating wheelchairs in a bathroom can be difficult. In addition to including specially designed plumbing fixtures, the layout must allow the wheelchair to get in and out of the room and, once inside, to turn around.

Any doors in the pathway to the bathroom should have at least 32 inches clear width (that is, between the stops). Provide at least 60 inches in front of an in-swinging door. Better still, avoid swinging doors altogether, if possible. They always pose an obstacle to wheelchair users. Consider substituting a sliding door. In some cases, such as a private bath off a bedroom, you might even consider skipping the door altogether.

The floor inside the bathroom should have a clear circle measuring 60 inches across to allow the wheelchair to turn around.

Grab bars are essential along the walls of any fixtures that require the wheelchair user to move out of the wheelchair. Horizontal grab bars are mounted 36 inches above the floor. Mirrors should be mounted 40 inches, maximum, from the floor to the bottom edge. They are often angled downward or are adjustable for easier viewing from the wheelchair.

Bathing and showering also require special planning, as described on page 53. Remember that the shower and adjacent room for maneuvering can consume a lot of floor space.

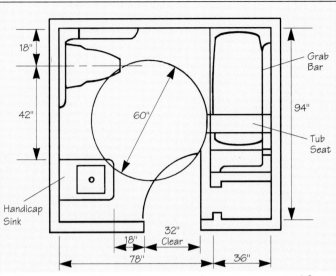

These are the minimum clearances and accessories required for wheelchair access in a tub bathroom. The 60-inch clear circle allows a person in a wheelchair to turn inside the room.

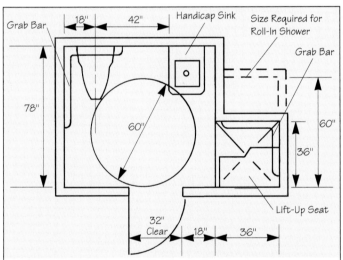

Two types of showers are geared to wheelchair use. People who can leave the wheelchair can move onto the seat of a small square shower. If the person must remain in the wheelchair, a roll-in shower must be installed (indicated by the dashed lines).

Permanent Versus Temporary Changes

It doesn't make sense to construct permanent physical changes to accommodate a family member whose limitations are temporary. After determining what the person can and can't do, look for ways to make temporary adaptations to the bathroom. For example, add grab bars that clamp onto the side of the tub or surround the toilet. Extensions are available to raise the height of a standard toilet seat. Visit a medical products supplier to see what's on the market. You may even be able to rent some of these products.

If a household member is permanently disabled, lasting changes may be warranted. You need to determine whether it is possible to adapt an existing bathroom or whether a new bathroom must

be added. If a larger room is needed for wheelchair use, consider adapting an unused or underused bedroom or bumping the bathroom into an existing closet, as was discussed in Chapter 5. If the family member's limitations make for longer bathroom time, you may want to try to add a second full or three-quarter bath to ease the morning rush and make it possible for all of you to be on time for work or school.

Barrier-Free Fixtures

You can either adapt existing fixtures by adding grab bars and various devices that adjust heights or replace them with fixtures specifically designed for people who use wheelchairs or who have limited mobility. Here are some of the options:

Sinks

Sinks for wheelchair access must allow for knee space below and project out far enough to allow the user to reach the faucets. Exposed hot water pipes beneath the sink should be insulated to prevent users from burning their legs, and fittings should be adapted to the user's needs.

Wheelchair-accessible sinks measure about 20 inches wide and project out from the wall 18 to 27 inches. They should be mounted to allow 34 inches of space from floor to the underside of the front edge. One model mounts on an adjustable wall bracket which allows users to choose the most convenient height. For wheelchair access to a sink, allow 36 inches clear width at the floor level.

Showers

There are two types of showers for people who use wheelchairs. One contains a seat—the person wheels up to the shower and uses grab bars to hoist himself or herself onto the seat. Constructed out of fiberglass or acrylic, these units measure 36, 42 1/2, or 56 inches wide by 37 inches deep by 84 inches high. They come equipped with hand holds, soap ledges, and adjustable hand-held showers. The second type allows the user to wheel into the compartment and shower while remaining in the wheelchair.

Toilets

Toilets for wheelchair users are basically the same as standard toilets, but the seat is 17 to 19 inches above the floor, instead of the more usual height of around 14 inches. Grab bars, preferably at the back and one side, are essential for maneuvering between the wheelchair and toilet. Allow at least 36 inches clear width for the fixture.

You can adapt a standard toilet by placing a portable extension seat over the existing toilet. This approach is useful if the fixture must also be used by small children, who may have trouble reaching a higher seat. Some extension seats come with grab bars attached to the sides. Look for these items in medical products supply stores (check with a doctor or nurse if you have trouble locating this handy device).

7

Selecting Finishes

Before grabbing the hammer and saw, consider one important part of your planning: the finishes. Bathroom floors, walls, and cabinets endure more heat, cold, and moisture than surfaces in other rooms, and you feel the effects more intimately. Since finishes such as ceramic tile are permanent, unlike paint, it's important to select these finishes in colors and styles that you won't tire of. Finally, if you intend to apply these finishes yourself, you will want to know something about the substrate, cost, and skills required of each. We'll review the options in this chapter, winding up with a trick to help you be sure that you've chosen the right colors and finishes.

Making Colors and Textures Work for You

Do you see your bathroom as a sensual place for relaxing or one that serves with machinelike efficiency? The colors you select affect the mood of the room. Red excites; mauve calms. Here are other colors and the moods attributed to them:

Yellow Happiness, warmth

Red Warmth, energy, excitement, anger

Green Refreshment, nature

Blue Coolness, restfulness, peace

You probably won't use primary colors full-strength on walls and ceilings; you'll be more likely to choose blends, tints, and hues, so the mood can be mixed. If your bathroom is small, it can easily be overpowered by strong colors, so you might want to keep walls and ceiling in the off-white or pastel range and reserve strong colors for fixtures and accents.

Textures also trigger associations. Soft, yielding textures broadcast luxury and relaxation (think of the seats in a luxury car). Hard, smooth surfaces suggest no-nonsense efficiency. Because of the importance we place on bathroom surfaces being easy to clean and resistant to water penetration, smooth surface textures on walls and cabinets generally win out.

How Color and Shade Can Affect the Space

How light or dark your walls and ceiling are will affect the apparent size of the room. Light surfaces tend to recede; dark ones foreshorten. You can "square" a long bathroom by selecting dark colors for the end walls and light colors for the side walls. The same trick—painting the ceiling darker than the walls—can visually lower a high ceiling. The shade of walls and ceiling also affects how light diffuses in the room. Light colors reflect light; dark colors absorb it. Light-colored walls will make any daylight that comes through windows more useful for seeing inside the room. To visually enlarge a very narrow space without moving walls, consider full-length mirrors.

Floor Covering Options

All sorts of finish materials cover bathroom floors, but not every material meets every challenge. Take tile, for example. It sheds water like fish scales, but it is slippery to walk on when wet. You won't slip easily on carpet, but carpets are prone to mildew and can pick up odors from entrapped moisture. So what makes an ideal bathroom floor covering? You'll naturally want a surface that's pleasing to the eye. Whether you prefer a hard or soft surface, you'll probably want your floor covering to:

▲ Soft red fabrics give this bathroom a warm look.

▲ By contrast, smooth blue surfaces give this bathroom a cool restful atmosphere.

▲ A throw rug with a non-skid backing makes a hard tile floor easier and warmer on the feet.

A dark-colored end wall draws it closer, while the lighter side wall seems to recede, widening the room.

Reversing the wall colors makes the room seem longer and narrower.

◆ Withstand constant water

◆ Be safe to walk on when wet

◆ Be easy to clean

Let's see how some finishes found on bathroom floors meet these tests.

Resilient Flooring

Thin floor coverings composed of resilient materials such as vinyl, rubber, cork, or linoleum are attractive and durable. While softer than tile, resilient flooring feels hard compared with carpeting. Its surface resists water, but it can be slippery when wet. Offset the hazard with throw rugs placed strategically next to tubs and showers.

Resilient flooring comes in a wide range of colors and patterns in both tile and sheet form. Tiles come in 3/32- and 1/8-inch thicknesses and are usually 12 inches square; sheet flooring comes in rolls 6 or 12 feet wide. Easier, by far, to install than sheet flooring, tiles are never as resistant to water because of the number of joints that can open if the substrate expands. For the best water resistance, set resilient tiles in a troweled-on adhesive. Self-adhesive tiles, while easy to install, can pull up at the corners over time. Resilient tiles are easily cut by scoring them with a scribing tool or utility knife and snapping them in two. Sheet flooring can be cut with a utility knife.

All resilient flooring is easy to maintain, needing only occasional waxing. The shiny surface layer of so-called no-wax floor covering eventually wears down. Eventually, you'll need to wax to restore the original luster.

▲ The long boldly blue countertop and long bold stripes in the resilient sheet floor combine to give this bathroom a striking look.

While resilient floor covering ideally goes over underlayment-grade plywood, you can also apply it over existing resilient flooring, but only if the old floor is tightly adhered and smooth.

Ceramic Tile

Ceramic tiles have long been preferred for bathroom floors because of their ability to withstand water. But glazed tiles are slippery when wet and all tiles can be cold underfoot. To reduce the hazard of slipping, select tiles with a matte rather than a glossy finish. Never use wall tiles on a floor because they will crack. You can cushion the hardness of a tile floor with a throw rug, but make sure the rug is backed by a surface that grips the tiles.

Ceramic floor tiles are available in various pastel and deep colors, in sizes from 2x2 inches up to 12x12 inches. If you like the look of small tiles, the ones that come attached to fabric-mesh-backed sheets are easiest to install. Quarry tiles come in rectangular shapes in sizes from around 4 inches up to 12 inches on a side; they also are available in hexagons, octagons, and other shapes in a range of sizes. Colors run from the earth tones (buff, browns, and reds) to various grays.

For level floors not subject to constant water, the easiest way to install tiles is to "thin-set" them into troweled-on adhesive over a solid subfloor, such as underlayment-grade plywood and cement

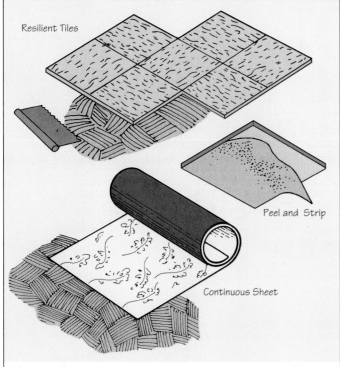

Resilient floor covering comes in tiles or continuous sheet form. Self-adhesive tiles are easier to install, but are riskier in wet areas than tiles set in troweled-on adhesive.

Resilient Tiles

Peel and Strip

Continuous Sheet

▲ Tile patterns emphasize the steps up to this bathtub, making the steps not only more beautiful, but safer too.

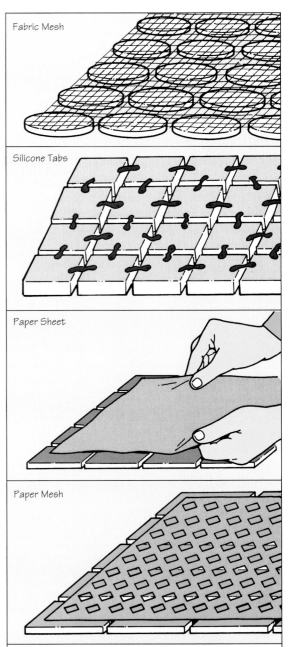

Fabric Mesh

Silicone Tabs

Paper Sheet

Paper Mesh

Small tiles come mounted on a backing of fabric mesh, silicone tabs, paper sheet or paper mesh. Each 12-inch square sheet contains 8 to 64 tiles.

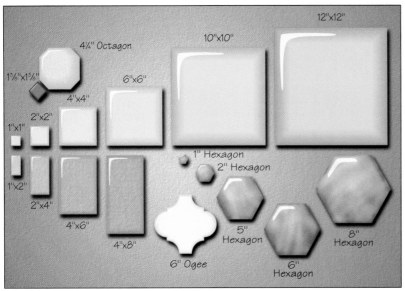

1⅜"x1⅜"

4¼" Octagon

10"x10"

12"x12"

6"x6"

4"x4"

2"x2"

1"x1"

1"x2"

2"x4"

4"x6"

4"x8"

6" Ogee

1" Hexagon

2" Hexagon

5" Hexagon

6" Hexagon

8" Hexagon

▲ Ceramic tiles come in numerous shapes and sizes that you can use to create your own designs.

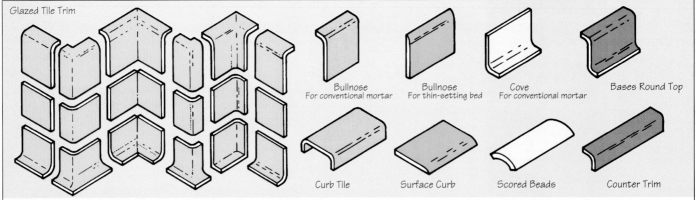

Glazed Tile Trim

Bullnose
For conventional mortar

Bullnose
For thin-setting bed

Cove
For conventional mortar

Bases Round Top

Curb Tile

Surface Curb

Scored Beads

Counter Trim

Trim tiles are available for inside and outside corners, curbs, and edges; but you won't find all of the shapes shown here for every style, color, and type of tile, so know which trim shapes you need before you select your tile.

backer board. Constantly wet or sloping floors, such as in showers and their adjacent drying areas, are better tiled by setting the tiles into a bed of mortar (mud-setting). Whether thin- or mud-set, all joints between the tiles must be filled with cementitious grout.

Stone

Stone adds real class to a bathroom floor. Durability, ease of cleaning, and slipping hazard vary depending on the material and its texture. One thing you can depend on, though, is that this is the most expensive floor you can choose.

The least expensive way to achieve a stone floor is with tiles cut from real stone. Marble, granite, and slate are available in 3/8-inch-thick tiles measuring 12x12 inches or 12x24 inches. They are installed much the same way as ceramic tiles.

Real stone pieces 1-inch or more thick must be set in mortar, and the combined load of stone plus the setting bed may be more than your floor can safely support without structural reinforcement. To cut stones, you'll need a diamond-tipped wet sawblade, skill, and a lot of strength. If you are attracted to a stone floor, you should have your subfloor's structural capacity analyzed by an architect, structural engineer, or builder. Then, if the subfloor and joists are deemed strong enough, you should probably consider hiring a specialist to do the installation.

Carpeting and Rugs

The soft feel of carpeting under bare feet makes it an appealing choice for bathroom floors. Unfortunately, carpeting holds moisture, which can breed organisms that in time smell and may seep into an underlying wood floor, where it can cause rot. For these reasons it is best to avoid carpeting in areas subject to water spillage, such as adjacent to tubs, showers, toilets, bidets, and basins. That doesn't leave much spare floor in most bathrooms. If you like the softness of carpeting underfoot, consider a hard floor covering for the permanent finish and throw rugs with nonslip backing for a cushiony feel.

If your room is large enough to include a portion of carpet in a nonwet area, or you want to carpet an adjacent dressing or vanity area, you have a wide choice of materials, colors, textures, patterns, and underlayments. Prices vary widely, with nylon or polypropylene at the bottom end and wool at the top.

Put a pad under the carpet to increase the softness and to provide the feel of luxury. Carpet can be installed over almost any subfloor by either tackless strips or directly gluing the carpet to the subfloor. Tackless strips are thin strips of plywood embedded with hundreds of bent tacks that poke up to grip the carpet and keep it from sliding around. The strips are nailed around the outer edges of the room. A simpler way to install carpet in a small room is to simply trowel on an adhesive and "glue" the carpet to the subfloor. The downside is that if and when you have to remove the carpet, you're in for a grueling task.

▲ Nothing makes a classier, more durable, or more expensive surface finish than real stone.

▲ Carpet is an unusual choice for a bathroom floor. But if you do use it, choose a short nap such as the carpet shown here.

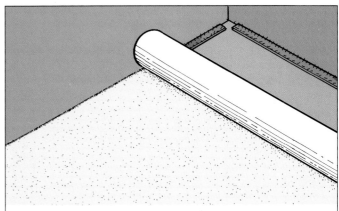
Wall-to-wall carpeting attached to tackless strips can provide a soft feel for dressing areas adjacent to the bathroom.

▲ Wood walls and floors give this bathroom a warm and homey feeling.

Wood Flooring

Wood, though hard, imparts a warm, homey look to any room. Properly sealed, it can be fairly resistant to moisture (witness the growing popularity of wood in kitchens in recent years). Nonetheless, it still isn't a good bet for areas subject to continuous moisture, such as adjacent to tubs, showers, toilets, or bidets.

For portions of the floor away from wet areas, you can choose among unfinished and prefinished flooring. Unfinished wood flooring comes as random-length planks or strips with tongue-and-groove (T&G) edges. Strip flooring measures 2¼ inches wide and 25/32 inches thick, whereas planks come in standard dimensions from 1x4 to 1x10. Oak and maple are available almost everywhere; walnut, fir, and southern yellow pine are less common.

Prefinished wood flooring, an option if your tools, skills, and time are limited, comes in planks that can be glued or nailed to the subfloor and as 12x12-inch parquet tiles that are glued down. Installing parquets is easier than cutting, placing, nailing, and finishing raw wood flooring.

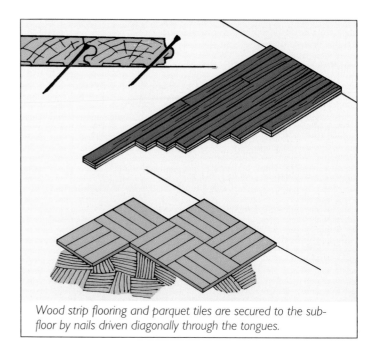

Wood strip flooring and parquet tiles are secured to the subfloor by nails driven diagonally through the tongues.

Wall and Ceiling Finishes

Bathroom walls and ceilings should be easy to clean and resist moisture penetration. Here are the best candidates:

Ceramic Tile

Ceramic tiles are an expensive but unbeatable choice for walls in wet areas. Properly installed, they will last indefinitely. If and when problems occur, they will usually involve cracked grout joints or cracked and loose individual tiles. Fortunately, grout can be restored and cracked tiles can be replaced. Glazed wall tiles are easiest to keep clean.

Wall tiles vary in size from 2x4 inches up to 12 inches square. You can select smaller tiles of a contrasting color to create accents, patterns, or stripes.

Paint

Paint is the most economical and easiest wall finish to apply. Oil-based paints, long preferred for walls and ceilings subject to high moisture levels, are now being phased out in favor of acrylic or latex paints. Because the latter use water as a solvent, they are less harmful to your health and the environment.

When selecting paint, remember that the higher the gloss, the better the finish withstands moisture. The porous surfaces of flat (satin-sheen) paints grow mildew and cannot be cleaned with water and detergents. Choose acrylic gloss enamel (best) and semigloss (next best) for bathroom walls and ceilings. Be warned, though, that glossy finishes show surface imperfections more readily than flat finishes, so getting a smooth, even finish requires extra attention to preparing the surface.

Wall Coverings

Don't call that material you buy in rolls and apply with an adhesive "wallpaper" any longer. Though many wallcoverings are still backed with paper, they are faced with washable vinyl, making them a good material for bathroom walls and ceilings.

For each of the hundreds of colors and patterns available for the wall itself, there are an equal number of patterned borders. You can install roll-stock wallcoverings yourself on almost any smooth, dry, substrate that has been sized (coated with a solution that controls the bond). If your walls already have wallpaper, you'll have to strip it off and apply a solution to remove the adhesive. Walls painted with glossy paint should be dulled by sanding for a good bond.

▲ Tiles can be used to create a variety of patterns. When selecting tiles, be sure to choose colors you'll want to live with for a long time. The neutral white, black and grey used here will work with any other colors the owners choose to use in this bathroom.

▲ Paint is a durable wall surface that is easily changed.

▲ The washable vinyl wall coverings of today are well suited to the bathroom environment.

▲ Wood strips make a bold and beautiful statement around this tub and skylight.

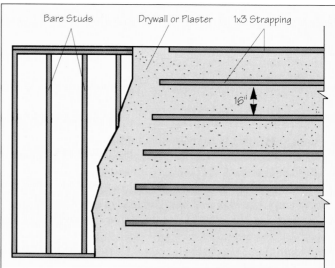

Bare studs can support horizontal wood paneling or boards thicker than 3/8 inch. Attach vertical panels or boards to drywall directly with glue or, better, to 1x3 furring strips spaced at 16 inches.

Many wall coverings now come prepasted, that is, with a self-adhesive coating on the back. Choosing this type will save you the time and effort required to mix a powdered paste and coat each strip separately, but keep in mind that prepasted wallcoverings often don't adhere to the wall as well as the unpasted types.

Wood

Wood can add warmth to bathroom walls but may absorb moisture, depending on the finish. Aim for smooth-textured surfaces with as few joints as possible, and avoid wood altogether in continuously damp areas such as behind toilets. You can get wood veneer paneling in 48x96-inch sheets, prefinished or unfinished. Imitation wood veneer, consisting of a particleboard core printed with a wood pattern, is also available. It's cheaper than real wood, but it doesn't have the classy look of the real thing.

You can create your own wood wall finish by nailing up solid boards of pine, fir, cedar, or redwood in various patterns. Check your lumber supplier to see which sizes and species are regularly stocked. Softwood tongue-and-groove boards are com-

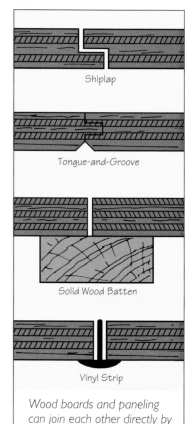

Wood boards and paneling can join each other directly by shiplap or tongue-and-groove joints, or indirectly by solid wood battens or vinyl strips (paneling only).

monly available in nominal 1-inch thickness (actual thickness is 3/4 inch) and nominal widths of 6, 8, and 10 inches (actual widths are 5½, 7½, and 9¼ inches, respectively).

Finishes for Wood in the Bathroom

Prefabricated cabinets such as vanities usually come prefinished with highly durable coatings, so you will be able to judge the final effect before you buy. You will have to finish any wood cabinets you custom build in place and any raw wood used on walls. Two factors are important: The finish should be easy to clean and should resist moisture well.

Paint

Gloss or semigloss paint over two coats of primer can make wood surfaces as cleanable and water resistant as painted plaster or drywall. While paint hides the grain, it allows any joints to show through, so it can even be a good choice on wall paneling or boards.

Natural Finishes

If you aim for the look of wood, start by selecting a species that has the color and grain you like. Oak and fir have strong grain, while the grain in birch and maple is more subtle. If you want a dark wood, choose walnut, cherry, or redwood (bear in mind that too much dark wood in a small room will make the room feel closed in). Semidark woods include cedar and red oak. Pine, maple, fir, spruce, and birch are naturally light woods.

▲ From its solid marble floor and tub surround to its real wood and glass walls, and yes, even a wooden tub, this bathroom is a celebration of the beauty of natural finishes.

The most moisture-resistant finish is provided by a polyurethane or some other varnishlike finish that builds up on the surface. Penetrating oil finishes, which sink into the wood pores, provide a more natural look but offer less protection from water. All finishes darken the wood somewhat. For a different color, you can stain the wood. Alternately, you can use a finish coating that contains a stain, though this approach doesn't look quite as good because the colorant stays on the surface with the finish rather than penetrating into the pores of the wood.

Penetrating oil finishes are simple to apply. You brush or wipe them liberally on the surface, let them sink in for a while, then wipe off with a cloth. These finishes are also easy to repair. Surface finishes are difficult to spot-repair as well as more difficult to apply. The water- and solvent-based varieties are put on differently, so be sure to follow the manufacturer's instructions when applying.

Countertop Choices

Laminated Plastic

Plastic laminate is hard to beat for a bathroom countertop. It's economical, easy to maintain, and resists moisture superbly. Hundreds of colors and patterns are available. Plastic laminate comes in sheets 48x96 inches that are 1/16 inch thick. Installing plastic laminate to a countertop requires cutting the sheets and bonding with contact cement, then trimming with a router.

Ceramic Tile

Ceramic tile makes a countertop that stands up well to moisture and use. A ceramic tile countertop will cost more than one finished in plastic laminate, but costs less than a solid-surface top (see below). But costs range widely—you can bust your budget on custom-designed hand-formed tiles from Mexico or get by with a generic mass-produced domestic tile.

▲ Plastic laminate is inexpensive, durable, easy to keep clean and available in a panoply of colors. No wonder it is the most popular countertop material.

▲ The curved lines of this tiled bathroom is far removed from the rectilinear grid we normally associate with tile.

Your choice of tiles for a countertop range over the whole gamut of floor and wall tiles. In addition to "field" tiles—those used on the countertop surface—you can choose various edge trim tiles in colors and shapes to fit your decor. Your local tile supply store may have some made-up countertops on display and literature that can show you some of the design possibilities.

Setting tiles on a countertop is something you can probably do, if you have the desire, time, and patience to do each step right. After selecting field and trim tiles, you'll need to plan the pattern, cut tiles to fit, and apply them, as described in Chapter 13.

Solid Surface Material

Not too long ago if you wanted the look of marble or granite, you were in for high costs. Now you can add the class of real stone at less cost with a lighter synthetic material that can be cut, drilled, and shaped in much

▲ Like the leaves on a tree, this green tile harmonizes with the natural finish of the wooden vanity.

the same way as wood. This material, sometimes referred to as synthetic marble, consists of stone dust or chips cast into an acrylic or polyester resin. Unlike plastic laminate, solid surface material can be repaired by sanding out any defects and filling them with plastic.

Solid surface material comes in 1/2 and 3/4 inch thickness, widths of 30 and 36 inches, and lengths up to 12 feet. Figure on spending three to five times as much for a solid-surface countertop as you would for plastic laminate. Also, though lighter than stone,

solid surface material is still heavy and difficult to install, so consider having the installation done by a specialist. In addition, you should be aware that some manufacturers of solid surface material will not honor their warranty if you install it yourself.

Making a Finish Sample Board

Coordinating the colors and textures of walls, ceilings, floors, and cabinetry can be made manageable by mounting samples of each material and color on a board. First obtain samples of tile, plastic laminate, and solid surface material from suppliers. Next collect samples of any wallcoverings and paint chips.

Begin by deciding which items you will build the color scheme around. These "anchor" finishes are the ones most likely to stay in place indefinitely, such as plumbing fixtures, ceramic tile, and solid-surface countertops. Glue samples (or color chips that approximate the true color) down to the board first. If you use rubber cement, you can easily make changes. Then add samples of each material that will occur in order. For example, if you started with the toilet color chip, add the chip or sample for the floor material, then the wall, and finally the ceiling.

The completed board will give you a realistic idea of how the various colors look together. If things don't work together, you can quickly pluck out the offending sample and try another until you are satisfied that you will have just the look you want.

▲ Solid surface material costs more than plastic laminate, but it is more durable, versatile and attractive.

8

Remodeling Bathroom Floors

We demand a lot from a bathroom floor. It has to please the eye and blend with the fixtures and other finishes, be easy to clean, and be comfortable to walk on barefoot. Above all, it must shed water like a duck's back. As if these weren't reasons enough to begin your remodeling project with the floor, there may be other demands as well. For example, you may need to reroute piping for plumbing fixtures, reinforce the joists to handle the additional load of a whirlpool, or add insulation above a cold crawl space.

A Bathroom Floor Dissected

Depending on your situation, your floor may require extensive or minimal remodeling. But before you start to tear your floor apart, let's look at the composition of a well-constructed bathroom floor.

The surface that you look at and walk on is called the floor covering. Vinyl and ceramic tile rank as the most popular coverings, but other materials such as wood and stone are also used in bathrooms. Just below the floor covering is some sort of underlayment, which provides a smooth, flat surface to support the floor covering. The underlayment may be made of a variety of materials, depending on the floor covering, but is it never particleboard, which, especially in a bathroom situation, absorbs moisture and swells.

Below the underlayment is the structural part of the floor. For wood floors, this consists of a subfloor—usually plywood or wood planks—supported by joists and beams below. Concrete slab floors are floor structure and subfloor rolled into one, though a plywood subfloor can be installed over a concrete floor that is continually damp, such as in a basement.

Other materials may be needed to insulate the floor from heat loss and to keep water and moisture out of the structure. Thermal insulation can be added between or below the floor joists or above a concrete slab, as we'll see later in this chapter. Plastic vapor barriers go between the thermal insulation and floor covering material.

Removing Flooring and Subflooring

If new flooring figures into your plans, you may be able to apply it directly over the old covering, saving time and money. New resilient floor coverings (sheet vinyl and vinyl tiles) can be installed over existing vinyl or linoleum, if the old flooring is in good condition. But curled or chipped edges, usually found around toilets and near tubs and showers, bespeak of water damage below. Peeling up a few tiles or a part of the sheet should reveal the condition of the subfloor and tell you if it needs replacement.

How to Pull Up Old Sheet Floor Covering

Difficulty Level: 𝕋

Tools and Materials

- [ ] Basic carpentry tools
- [ ] Shims or scrap
- [ ] Clothes iron, hair dryer, or heat gun
- [ ] Putty knife
- [ ] Electric sander

Step 1. *Remove the Base Trim.* Use a pry bar to remove the baseboard and base shoe from where the walls meet the floor. As you pry each portion outward, insert a wood shim behind it to keep the molding away from the wall so that you can insert the

1. *Pry the base shoe from the baseboard with a pry bar. Insert wood shims as you go. When you pry off the baseboard, protect the wall with a wood block.*

2. *Score sheet flooring into strips (left). Heat resilient floor tiles with a clothes iron to loosen the adhesive. A piece of thin fiberboard or plywood distributes the heat (right).*

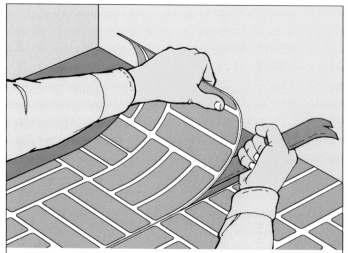

3. *Loosen each tile or strip of sheet flooring with a pry bar. Pull on the freed end as you continue to loosen the back side with a pry bar or putty knife.*

pry bar at the next position. Use a pencil to label where each piece goes, if you intend to reinstall the trim. When prying the baseboard away from the wall, place a block of wood behind the bar to protect the wall from dents.

Step 2. *Score Sheet Flooring or Heat Tiles.* With a utility knife or linoleum cutter, score lines across the surface to divide the flooring into strips that are 6 to 18 inches wide. For resilient tiles, use a clothes iron, blow-dryer, or heat gun to melt the adhesive on the back of resilient tiles. If you use an iron, start with the lowest temperature, increasing the heat as needed.

Step 3. *Pry Off the Strips or Tiles.* Loosen each tile or sheet flooring strip with a pry bar. Grip the freed end of resilient flooring and pull up as you continue to loosen the back with a pry bar or putty knife. Tiles are more brittle so you'll have to pry them off in chunks. Scrape off any adhesive residue left on the floor with the putty knife, or sand it off with a portable electric sander.

If you can't get the floor covering off, remove the subfloor along with the floor covering or install the appropriate underlayment over the top of the existing flooring. Choosing the latter option will result in a raised floor. Also, you may need to undercut the bathroom door and install a transition piece such as a wood or tile threshold where the new floor meets the adjacent room.

Removing Underlayment and Subfloor

Difficulty Level: 🔨 🔨

Tools and Materials

☐ Basic carpentry tools   ☐ Electric drill with 3/4-inch bit
☐ Crowbar   ☐ Wood chisel
☐ Circular saw with carbide-tipped blade

Bathroom floors are constantly subjected to water. Eventually, some of it may find its way through the floor covering and penetrate the subfloor. Your first clue to problems below is a squishy feel when you walk on the floor; the curling edges of resilient flooring also signal moisture seepage. If the problem is localized, you can probably get by with replacing only the damaged portion of the subfloor. But be prepared to replace the entire subfloor, perhaps even some of the floor joists.

Step 1. *Remove the Toilet.* Water damage is most likely near the toilet. In humid weather, water condenses on the toilet; the drops run down the sides and seep into cracks in the floor covering. Before removing the toilet, shut off the cold water to the fixture. After you disconnect it (see "Installing a New Toilet," page 120), store the toilet in a safe place, unless you intend to

Keeping Moisture Out of the Structure

You know that keeping surface water from penetrating the floors and walls is essential to preventing deterioration of wood joists, studs, sheathing, and siding. But do you know that water is not the only menace? Airborne moisture can pose an even worse danger, and bathrooms are notorious moisture producers. The vapor created by showering and bathing raises the indoor humidity to much higher levels than the outdoors. What happens to this moisture?

In the winter, it migrates through walls, floors that are above crawl spaces, and roofs and condenses somewhere inside. In time, it can cause insulation to lose its effectiveness, wood to rot, and paint to peel. When you have your floors or walls stripped to the studs or joists, you have an excellent chance to do something about any moisture problem. Here are some tips:

Install a continuous vapor-retarding barrier over wall studs and floor and ceiling joists on the warm side (in winter) of the insulation. A good bet for a vapor barrier is a continuous sheet of 4- or 6-mil polyethylene (poly) stapled to stud and joist faces; the overlapping seams should be taped. Seal the poly sheet to any electrical or plumbing penetrations with tape and/or caulk.

◆ Install 1 or more inches of foil-faced rigid foam insulation over the studs and joists, if you are rebuilding outside walls and/or ceilings. Tape all joints and seal around electrical outlets and pipe penetrations with caulk.

◆ Provide exhaust fans that exhaust to the outside, not into an attic or crawl space (see "Installing an Exhaust Fan," page 154). Exhaust fans are a must in any high moisture area such as baths and kitchens.

◆ Select double-glazed, low-e windows for the bathroom.

1. *Turn off and disconnect the water to the fixture. Remove the heavy toilet carefully, bending your legs to protect your back.*

2. *Use a circular saw, with the blade set to the thickness of the underlayment, to cut out damaged areas.*

3. *Pull off subfloor along with underlayment if the subfloor is damaged or removing adhesive is a problem.*

replace it. Stuff a rag into the drain hole to prevent sewer gas from seeping into the room.

Step 2. *Remove a Sample of Underlayment.* Set the blade of your circular saw to cut through only the layer you want. Determine this thickness by pulling out a floor grille, if possible, or by drilling a 3/4-inch-diameter hole through the underlayment. Set the depth of the saw blade to the thickness of the underlayment, then cut out a portion of underlayment large enough to tell you whether damage is confined to the underlayment or extends to the subfloor.

Step 3. *Remove All the Underlayment.* If the damage stops at the underlayment, pry it off the subfloor, using a pry bar and hammer. If the underlayment is glued to the subfloor with adhesive, you can try to remove the adhesive with a scraping or sanding tool, but you'll probably find it easier to remove the subfloor along with the underlayment.

4. *Cut out the rotted portion of the subfloor.*

Step 4. *Remove a Portion of the Subfloor.* If the subfloor is damaged, set your circular saw blade to a depth that will cut through the subfloor without cutting into the joists. Cut around the area that needs to be replaced. Be sure to extend the new patch so that both sides bear on one-half of a joist, reserving the other half for the remaining subfloor. Separate the subfloor from the joists with a pry bar and hammer.

Upgrading the Floor Structure

Before you put down a new subfloor, you should remodel the plumbing and electricity as necessary (Chapters 11 and 12). This is also the time to beef up the floor structure and add insulation and vapor barriers.

Reinforcing the Floor Joists

Bathroom floor joists may need reinforcement to support new loads, such as a whirlpool. Any rotted joists should also be reinforced or replaced. You'll be able to assess the extent of the damage after removing some or all of the subfloor or, if possible, by examining the joists from a crawl space or basement. If you don't feel competent to judge the structural condition of the joists, get the opinion of a builder, architect, or structural engineer.

A professional can also tell you whether the floor joists are capable of carrying the additional load of a whirlpool or spa and how to beef up the floor to carry the new load.

Difficulty Level: 🔩 🔩

Tools and Materials

☐ Basic carpentry tools   ☐ Electric drill (optional)
☐ Lumber to match existing joists
☐ 12d galvanized nails or 3-inch galvanized screws (for sister joists)
☐ 1/4-inch dia. x 3½-inch hex-head bolts (for doubling joists)

Step 1. *Install a Sister Joist.* If a joist is damaged, you can reinforce it by adding a "sister" joist to its side. Pick a new joist of the same depth or slightly less, and as long as possible (getting it into place may be difficult). Attach it through the side of the existing joist with 12d galvanized nails or galvanized screws, or use bolts, as described in the following step.

Step 2. *Double the Joists.* Follow the same procedure when doubling the joists to support a new load, such as a whirlpool, with one exception: If you can't extend the new joists to bear over the supporting sill plate, extend them as long as possible and bolt each new joist to an original joist with hex-head bolts, 1/4-inch diameter x 3½ inches long. Space the bolts no more than 12 inches apart and stagger them between the top and bottom of the joist. If necessary, add a cleat at the wall.

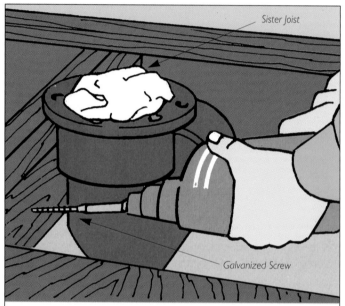

Sister Joist

Galvanized Screw

1. *Reinforce damaged joists by attaching new "sister" joists to their sides.*

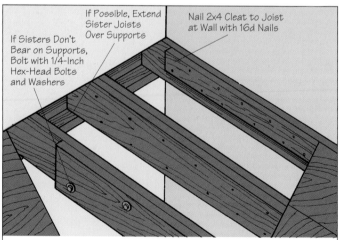

If Sisters Don't Bear on Supports, Bolt with 1/4-Inch Hex-Head Bolts and Washers

If Possible, Extend Sister Joists Over Supports

Nail 2x4 Cleat to Joist at Wall with 16d Nails

2. *When doubling the joists for extra strength, place the ends of the new boards over the supporting plates. If this isn't feasible, cut lengths as long as possible (making sure you can maneuver the new joists into position) and then bolt them to the primary joists. If needed, attach a cleat to the wall with 16d nails.*

Insulating a Wood Floor above a Crawl Space

If your bathroom sits above a crawl space, you can prevent cold feet by making sure there is enough insulation in either the floor or the surrounding foundation. If you insulate the floor itself, you'll need to enclose any water piping on the warm side of the insulation to prevent it from freezing. For this reason, many builders prefer to insulate the foundation wall.

Another must for a crawl space is a continuous plastic vapor barrier placed over the earth, to keep moisture from wicking up through the soil and condensing on the wood structure above. Installing these items is relatively easy to do from above when the subfloor is removed, but more difficult with the floor intact. Working from below in a tight space among spiderwebs and who knows what else is no fun. Equip yourself with a good source of light and protect yourself with a dust mask, goggles, hard hat, full-length trousers and a long-sleeved shirt. Working from above, you probably don't need the hard hat.

Difficulty Level: 🔨 🔨

Tools and Materials

- ☐ Long scissors (or knife)   ☐ Staple gun
- ☐ Staples
    1/4 inch if installing insulation to top of joists
    1/2 inch if installing insulation to the foundation
- ☐ Insulation
    fiberglass insulation
- ☐ Duct tape
- ☐ 4- or 6-mil polyethylene sheet
- ☐ 48-inch-wide housewrap
- ☐ 2x4s or bricks

Step 1. *Place Insulation between the Joists.* Cut lengths of insulation with long scissors or a sharp knife, using a piece of 1x4 as a guide and a piece of wood below as a cutting surface. Fit a piece of insulation between each pair of joists.

If you are working from above the floor, use kraft paper-faced insulation and pull the paper tabs out and over the tops of the floor joists. Staple the tabs at 8-inch intervals. Cut the strips of insulation short enough to manage easily (4 feet or so). Fit each one up in a joist space. Staple sheets of housewrap to the bottom of the joists to keep the insulation from dropping down. If you are working from below, use unfaced fiberglass friction-fitted into place.

Step 2. *Insulate around Pipes and Ducts.* Wrap insulation around each heating duct and water pipe. Use duct tape to make the insulation continuous.

Step 3. *Put a Vapor Barrier over the Ground.* Place strips of 4- or 6-mil poly sheet over the soil, overlapping the joints generously (at least 12 inches). Run the poly sheet up to the top of the wall and staple it to the sill plate.

1. *Install unfaced blanket insulation between the floor joists from below by fitting pieces into the spaces. Staple a sheet of housewrap below the insulation to hold it in place.*

2. *Wrap all heating ducts and water pipes below an insulated floor. Seal the joints with duct tape.*

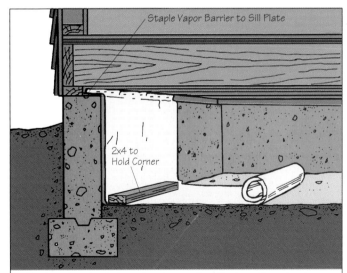

3. *Attach polyethylene sheeting to the sill plate. Completely cover exposed soil, overlapping the poly sheets by at least 12 inches. Weigh down the edges and corners with bricks or 2x4s.*

Insulating the Sides of a Crawl Space

Insulating between the joists, as described on page 71, is often harder than insulating the sides of the foundation and keeping the crawl space heated. The latter approach also does away with the need to wrap pipes and ducts to keep them from freezing. If you choose this method, be sure to close off any foundation vents to the outside. The tools and materials you'll need are the same as for insulating a wood floor, except you'll also need some 2x4s. And be sure to wear appropriate protective wear, as in the previous section.

Step 1. *Hang a Vapor Barrier over the Wall.* Staple strips of 4- or 6-mil poly sheet to the sill plate. Run the strips down the inside of the foundation wall and 12 inches over the soil, overlapping the joints at least 12 inches.

Step 2. *Measure, Cut, and Hang the Strips of Insulation.* Measure the vertical distance between the top of the rim joist and the ground and add 36 inches. Cut strips of insulation to this length. Place one end of each piece of insulation between two floor joists with the facing toward the crawl space and staple the ends to the rim joist. Drape the insulation strips down the inside of the foundation and out over the ground.

Step 3. *Connect the Tabs.* Connect the strips of insulation by stapling the tabs of adjoining pieces together at 8-inch intervals.

Step 4. *Install a Vapor Barrier on the Ground.* Insert strips of 4- or 6-mil poly sheet under the portion of insulation that extends over the soil. The poly should cover all exposed soil. Be sure to overlap the sheets by at least 12 inches.

Step 5. *Use 2x4s to Hold Down the Corners.* Place lengths of 2x4 lumber over the top of the insulation and vapor barrier at the joint between the wall and the ground. This will help hold the bottom edges of insulation in place.

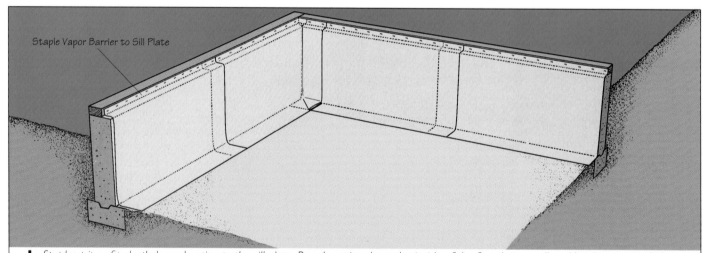

Staple Vapor Barrier to Sill Plate

1. *Staple strips of polyethylene sheeting to the sill plate. Run the strips down the inside of the foundation wall and let them extend about 12 inches over the ground soil. Overlap the sheets by at least 12 inches.*

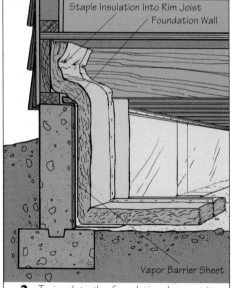

Staple Insulation Into Rim Joist
Foundation Wall

Vapor Barrier Sheet

2. *To insulate the foundation, hang strips of kraft-faced insulation from the rim joist. Run the strips out over the soil 36 inches.*

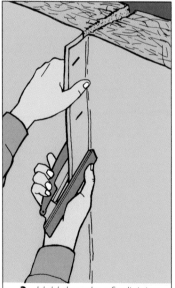

3. *Hold the tabs of adjoining pieces of insulation and staple them together.*

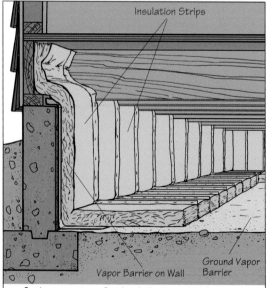

Insulation Strips

Vapor Barrier on Wall

Ground Vapor Barrier

4. *Insert strips of polyethylene under the insulation where it is lying on the soil. The polyethylene should cover the exposed ground, overlapping the joints by at least 12 inches on the sides.*

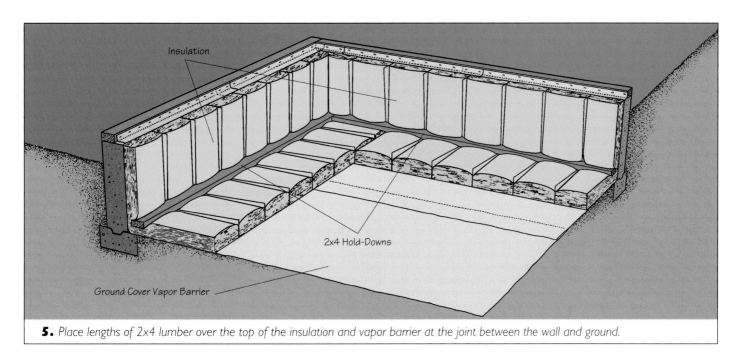

5. *Place lengths of 2x4 lumber over the top of the insulation and vapor barrier at the joint between the wall and ground.*

Installing a New Subfloor

Difficulty Level: 🔨 🔨

Tools and Materials

- ☐ Basic carpentry tools
- ☐ Compass
- ☐ 5/8- or 3/4-inch plywood
- ☐ Construction adhesive
- ☐ Saber saw (or keyhole saw)
- ☐ Electric drill with screwdriver bit
- ☐ L-shaped framing anchors or 12d galvanized nails
- ☐ Circular saw
- ☐ 2x4 lumber
- ☐ Caulking gun
- ☐ 1½-inch galvanized screws

Step 1. *Provide Blocking under the Patched Sections.* If you are patching the subfloor, you'll need to provide blocking between the joists to support the patched pieces. Make these by cutting lengths of 2x4 lumber and attaching them to the joists with L-shaped framing anchors (preferred) or by toenailing (second

best). If you toenail, use galvanized 12d nails (two on one side and one on the other).

Step 2. *Cut Out the Subfloor Sections.* Measure the sections of plywood and cut them out with a circular saw. Plan the layout so that the face grain of the plywood runs across the joists. Stagger the pieces so that the joints fall on alternate joists.

Step 3. *Cut a Hole for the Toilet Drain.* Measure from the center of the existing drain pipe to two adjoining walls. Mark the places on the walls so you can measure from the same spots later; be sure to write down the distances. Lay two pieces of plywood over the existing drain hole so that their edges meet across the diameter of the circle. Now locate the center of the drain hole by using the two distances you measured earlier. Mark the center on the plywood. Using a compass, scribe a circle of the same diameter as the existing drain hole onto the two pieces of plywood. Cut the semicircles out of the plywood with a saber saw.

Step 4. *Apply Construction Adhesive to the Joists.* Working with one piece of subfloor at a time, apply a bead of construction

1. *Nail in pieces of blocking to support your new subfloor. L-shaped framing anchors connect blocking to the main joists.*

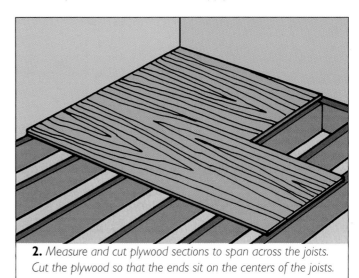

2. *Measure and cut plywood sections to span across the joists. Cut the plywood so that the ends sit on the centers of the joists.*

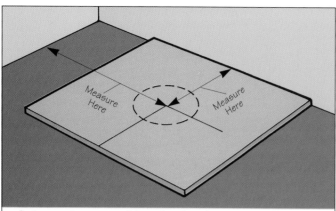

3. *Locate the center of the toilet drain by measuring from two walls. Place two pieces of subfloor over the hole as shown. Mark the center of the drain and scribe the circle with a compass.*

4. *Apply beads of construction adhesive to the tops of the joists before placing new subflooring in place.*

5. *Screw the new subflooring to the joists with 1½-inch galvanized screws. Space the screws 6 inches apart around the perimeter joists and 12 inches apart around the other joists.*

adhesive to the top of each joist that will fall under that particular piece of plywood. Immediately put the plywood in place, because the adhesive starts to film over as soon as it is exposed to air. Attach each piece of subfloor in the same manner.

Step 5. *Permanently Attach the Section of New Subfloor.*
With a screwdriver bit in your electric drill, screw the new section to the supporting structure with 1½-inch galvanized screws spaced 6 inches apart.

Selecting the Right Underlayment

The proper underlayment will ensure that your new floor covering will lie flat, level, and resist water for several years. Selecting the right thickness will help you match the new floor level to that of an adjacent floor, or at least minimize the difference. It's important to match the floor covering to a compatible underlayment. Always avoid particleboard, especially in the bathroom; it swells when wet, causing floor coverings to separate or bubble.

Underlayment Options

Floor Covering	Acceptable Underlayments
Resilient floor coverings	Old floor vinyl or linoleum in sound condition Underlayment-grade plywood Lauan plywood
Wood parquet flooring	Old floor vinyl or linoleum in sound condition Underlayment-grade plywood Lauan plywood Hardboard
Ceramic tile and stone	Old ceramic tiles, if sound Concrete slab Cement board Underlayment-grade plywood

Underlayment-grade plywood made from fir or pine is available in 48x96-inch sheets in thicknesses of 1/4, 3/8, 1/2, 5/8, and 3/4 inch.

Because it can expand, when damp, plywood is not as good a choice for ceramic tiles as cement board.

Lauan plywood, a species of mahogany, is often used under resilient flooring. It is available in 48x96-inch sheets. The usual thickness for underlayment is 1/4 inch.

Cement board is also called tile backer board. It is made of a sand and cement matrix reinforced with fiberglass mesh. It is usually available in 36x60-inch sheets in a thickness of 1/2 inch. This is the preferred tile base for ceramic tile and stone floors

Resilient floor coverings (vinyl, rubber, and linoleum sheet and tiles) and wood parquet can be laid over an existing layer of similar material if the original is in good condition. The existing covering should be tightly adhered and have no cupped edges or evidence of water damage. If the old flooring is not in good condition, remove it and smooth down the old underlayment before installing the new floor covering. If you can't remove the old floor covering, just apply the new underlayment over it.

Ceramic and stone tile can be applied over existing ceramic tile if the original flooring is tightly adhered and in good condition. The tiles can also be applied directly over a concrete slab floor. Except inside showers, tile and stone are usually set onto the underlayment via a troweled-on adhesive. Showers require heavier water resistance and sloped floors, so the best way to meet these demands is by setting the tiles in a mortar base over a plastic or copper pan. When installed on wood bathroom floors, the underlayment of choice for ceramic and stone tile is cement board. Underlayment-grade plywood is the second choice.

Installing Plywood and Hardboard Underlayment

Difficulty Level: 🔨 🔨

Tools and Materials

☐ Basic carpentry tools   ☐ Putty knife
☐ 1-inch ring-shank nails   ☐ Wood filler
☐ Circular saw with plywood blade

The following steps assume a separate underlayment is applied over the subfloor. If the underlayment and subfloor are the same material, such as one layer of plywood, install it as described in "Installing a New Subfloor," page 73.

Step 1. *Measure and Cut.* To prevent nails from popping out, let the underlayment acclimate to the room for a few days before installation. Measure and cut each section of underlayment into lengths that will allow the joints to be staggered. Place the boards over the subfloor so that the joints are offset from the joints in the subfloor (or existing underlayment). Leave a gap of 1/16 inch between sheets and 1/8 inch at the walls. Place full sheets first, then cut pieces to finish up the floor. Cut the underlayment with a circular saw equipped with a plywood blade. Use a saber saw or keyhole saw to cut openings for drain pipes.

Step 2. *Nail the Underlayment to the Subfloor.* Begin at one corner of the room. Nail the underlayment to the subfloor with ring-shank nails. For 1/4-inch-thick material, use 2d nails; for 3/8-inch material, use 3d nails. Space nails in rows no more than 4 inches apart and 1/2 inches in from the edges.

Step 3. *Fill in Holes, Dents, and Cracks.* Fill any holes or imperfections in the boards with a plastic-type wood filler. Sand the filler smooth after it sets.

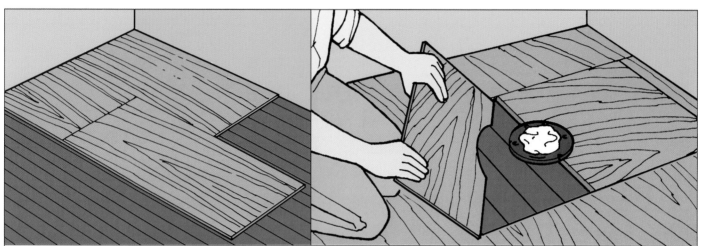

1. *Measure and cut each section of underlayment into lengths that will allow the joints to be staggered. Place the material over the subfloor so that the joints are offset from the subfloor joints. Leave a gap of 1/16 inch between the sheets and 1/8 inch at the walls (left). Cut out the holes for drains with a keyhole or saber saw. Use 2 pieces, as shown (right).*

2. *Use ring-shank nails to secure the underlayment to the sub-floor. Place nails at 4-inch intervals and 1/2 inch from the edges of the boards.*

3. *Use a 3-inch putty knife to force wood filler into imperfections in the underlayment.*

Installing Cement Board Underlayment

Difficulty Level:

Tools and Materials

☐ Basic carpentry tools   ☐ Variable-speed electric drill

☐ Cement board   ☐ Notched trowel

☐ Carbide-tipped bit (1-inch diameter)

☐ Phillips screwdriving bit

☐ Carbide-tipped blades for saber saw or several keyhole saw blades (if circles must be cut)

☐ 48-inch straightedge (or aluminum drywall T-square)

☐ Saber saw (if circular holes must be cut)

☐ 1½-inch coated cement board screws

☐ Fiberglass mesh drywall joint tape

☐ Construction adhesive (trowel-on type as recommended by supplier for cement board)

Step 1. *Mark the Floor.* Because cement board is expensive, heavy to maneuver, and difficult to cut and install, it pays to plan as much of the installation as you can before you buy and cut the material. Begin by marking off the floor surface into sections the same size as the panels.

Step 2. *Cut the Sheets.* Mark the cut line directly onto the cement board. Using a straightedge as a guide, score a 1/16- to 1/8-inch groove along the cut line with a utility knife. Insert a length of lumber (2x4) under the cut line and press down over the panel to snap it in two. Use a utility knife to cut through the reinforcing mesh and separate the pieces. Cut semicircles for toilet drains with a saber saw, using a carbide-tipped blade.

Step 3. *Tape the Joints.* Cover each cement board joint with fiberglass mesh drywall tape. Simply cut and press; the tape is backed with an adhesive.

Step 4. *Set the Cement Board into Adhesive.* With a notched trowel, apply construction adhesive to the substrate where the

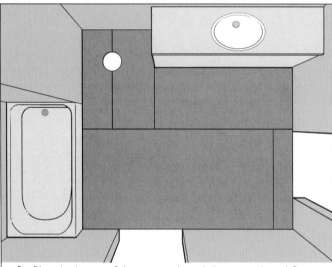

1. *Plan the layout of the cement board sheets on the subfloor before cutting. Use as many full sheets as possible.*

2. *Score the cement board 1/16 to 1/8 inch deep against a straightedge. Then place a piece of 2x4 under the cut line and press down to snap the panel apart.*

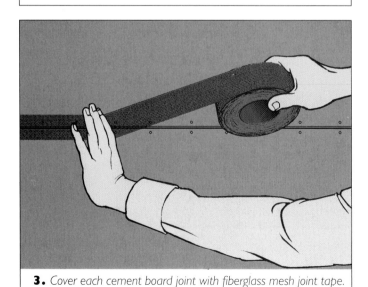

3. *Cover each cement board joint with fiberglass mesh joint tape.*

4. *Set cement board in a bed of construction adhesive. Use a notched trowel to spread the adhesive onto the subfloor.*

first sheet of underlayment will go. Next, set the panel into the adhesive, smooth side down.

Step 5. *Screw Down the Board with Backerboard Screws (bugle-head phillips screws with non-corrosive coating).* Drill pilot holes 4 inches apart at the edges and 8 to 12 inches apart throughout the panel. Drive screws into each hole with your electric drill.

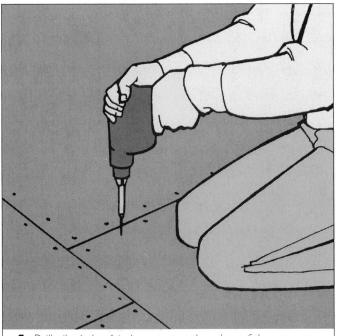

5. *Drill pilot holes 4 inches apart at the edges of the cement board and 8 to 12 inches apart in the board's center. Secure the underlayment with backerboard screws.*

Warming up a Cold Bathroom

Maintaining a comfortable temperature inside the bathroom is extra important because people spend part of their time there unclothed. In winter, any poorly insulated (or uninsulated) ceilings, walls, or floors quickly lose heat to the outdoors, causing higher fuel bills and discomfort. Poorly insulated wall and floor surfaces actually suck heat away from a warmer source such as a naked body.

The key to a toasty warm bathroom in January is adequate insulation. Insulation resists heat flow because of the multitude of tiny air spaces inside the material or reflective foil or both. We measure insulation's resistance to heat flow in R-values—the higher the number, the better the insulating ability. How much is enough depends on your climate. In regions with cold winters, aim for levels of R-38 in the ceiling or roof, R-26 in the outside walls, and R-11 in a floor above a crawl space (or around the outer foundation of the crawl space).

When choosing insulation you have to consider the cost and type, as well as R-value. Here are the R-values per inch and relative cost per unit of some of the most popular materials:

Insulation	R-Value per Inch	Relative Cost per Unit
Blanket and Batt		
Fiberglass	3.3	lowest
Mineral wool batts	3.6	lowest
Rigid Sheets		
Phenolic foam	8.5	highest
Polyurethane/ isocyanurate	7.2	medium
Polystyrene (extruded)	5.0	medium
Polystyrene (beadboard)	4.0	medium
Fiberglass board	4.0	highest
Loose Fill*		
Cellulose (blown in)	3.7	medium
Perlite (pellets)	2.7	medium
Fiberglass (blown in)	2.2	medium
Mineral wool (blown in)	2.9	medium

*If you install any of the loose fills yourself, the relative cost is "lowest."

Blankets and batts are best suited to fit between studs and joists. Rigid boards nailed over the studs or joists are a good way to increase the R-value when these spaces already contain some insulation. Aluminum-foil-faced rigid foam panels can also serve as vapor barriers if the joints are taped. Loose fill insulation is an economical way to insulate a ceiling overhead without having to crawl around inside. Loose fill can also be blown into outside wall cavities, leaving the inside and outside finishes intact. The insulating contractor will drill holes through the siding and fill each stud cavity with insulation. The holes are then, of course, repaired.

9

Rebuilding Walls and Ceilings

The problem with damaged walls and ceilings may look skin deep, but close inspection will often reveal a variety of problems. Even if a wall surface seems in sound condition, it may need to be ripped out to allow access to the mechanical systems or to upgrade the insulation. Whatever work is called for below the surface, do it with care. You will be repaid with a sound foundation for your final wall and ceiling finishes.

Removing the Previous Finish

Wall renovations can vary from nothing more than cleaning the present surface before adding a new one, to gutting the entire wall. The key to keeping the job simple and economical is to not remove any more than you have to. Still, you must be sure to remove enough of a substrate material to ensure good adhesion of the new finish.

Stripping Old Wallcovering

Deciding what to remove and how best to remove it depends on both the condition of the existing wallcovering and the proposed finish material. While old wallcovering may serve as a base for a paint finish, the water in latex paints will cause the wallcovering to bubble away from the substrate unless you first prime the surface with white shellac (oil-based primer will also work, but it's being phased out in most states because of antipollution legislation). If your intended finish is a new wallcovering, your best bet is to strip off the old using a wet stripping method for plaster walls or a dry stripping method for drywall.

If the existing wallcovering is a vinyl or other plastic-surface material, it must be removed before applying the new wallcovering or paint finish. The good news is that you can probably strip off this type of covering by simply making slits and pulling the sections off. Some plastic-faced wallcoverings, called "strippable," are made up of a vinyl facing backed by cloth or paper. When you strip off the surface layer, the backing remains on the wall where it can serve as the base for a new application of vinyl wallcovering.

Wet-Stripping Walls

Non-plastic faced wallcoverings, such as wallpaper, can be removed with water and/or steam. If the substrate is unsized drywall, the water or steam may also remove the facing paper from the drywall as well as the covering. If this happens you face the unfortunate choice of painting over the wallpaper or adding a layer of 1/4-inch drywall. You won't know, unfortunately, until you try removing a section.

Difficulty Level: ⬤

Tools and Materials

☐ Scoring tool	☐ Utility knife
☐ Pail	☐ Sponges
☐ Work gloves	☐ Goggles
☐ Wallcovering remover	☐ Scraper (for plaster walls)
☐ Phosphate-free trisodium	
☐ Steamer (rented from tool rental store or wallcovering supply store)	

1. Score wallcovering by making circular motions with a scoring tool.

2. To make quick work of removing wallcovering, rent a steamer. Wear goggles and gloves to do this job (left). After saturating with steam or hot water, try to peel the wallcovering away (top right). If the wallcovering won't peel away easily, use a scraper, taking care not to gouge the wall (bottom right).

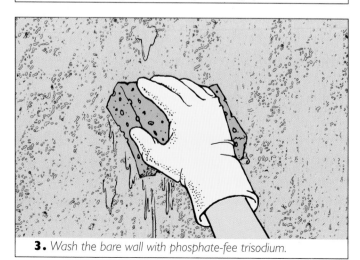

3. Wash the bare wall with phosphate-fee trisodium.

Step 1. *Score the Existing Wallcovering.* Score the wall covering by making circular motions with a scoring tool. (The tool looks like a hamburger and contains two toothed wheels below that perforate the surface of the wallcovering without damaging the substrate.)

Step 2. *Steam and Peel.* A steamer is not the only way to remove wallcovering, but it is the easiest. Hold the perforated plate of the steamer against portions of the wall until the steam permeates the covering and breaks the bond. Then simply peel away the covering (don't pull any harder than necessary). Use a scraper when necessary to coax wallcovering away from the wall, but be careful not to gouge the wall.

Step 3. *Wash the Substrate.* When the walls are bare, mix phosphate-free trisodium in warm water (following the directions on the container) and wash the wall surfaces thoroughly with a wet sponge. Allow them to dry for at least a week.

How to Make a Mock Steamer

If you can't locate a steamer to rent, you can make a wallpaper removal device from a pail or garden sprayer. Here's how:

With a Pail: Fill the pail with a mixture of hot tap water and wallcovering remover (follow the manufacturer's recommended proportions). Protect your hands with gloves, then dip a rag or sponge into the pail and rub the wallcovering with it. Be sure to soak the material well before scraping it off—the wetter, the better.

With a Garden Sprayer: First score the wallcovering. Then fill the sprayer with a mixture of hot tap water and wallcovering remover (follow the manufacturer's instructions). Use the sprayer to saturate the wallcovering with the mixture. Then scrape off the wallcovering.

Gutting a Wall or Ceiling

Think twice before you tear into a wall or ceiling. The work almost always adds up to more than you bargained for at the outset, and the dust and debris somehow finds its way into all corners of the house—even if you take heroic measures to contain it. Still, there are many unavoidable conditions that necessitate pulling off the tile, plaster, or drywall, if not over the entire wall, at least in the area of operation. New fixtures may require new piping. Extensive rewiring may be called for. You may want to insulate the wall and install a vapor barrier. Finally, the old substrate may be showing the effects of years of dampness.

Before you begin, take measures to protect yourself and the house from the stuff that will come loose. Wear gloves, protective eyewear, heavy shoes, and a hard hat. If you buy a hard hat, look for one with built-in eye and ear protectors. Ear protectors can prevent hearing loss caused by exposure to noisy power tools.

Keep the door to the area of operations closed. Line the path to the outdoors with tarps. If the room has an outside window, setting up a chute leading from the window into a dumpster or trash can will save you from carting the debris out through the house.

Difficulty Level: 🔨🔨 to 🔨🔨🔨

Tools and Materials

- ☐ Basic carpentry tools
- ☐ Adjustable wrench
- ☐ Adjustable pliers
- ☐ Masonry chisel (for plaster)

Step 1. *Prepare the Work Site.* Turn off the circuit breaker that controls the room's power. If you will be relocating plumbing fixtures or working on walls containing pipes, make sure the water supply has been shut off before proceeding. Take down any pictures, mirrors, plants, switch plates, outlet cover plates, and heating grilles. Remove any cabinets mounted in or on the wall.

Step 2. *Remove the Trim.* Pull off door and window trim and baseboards with a pry bar. Tap the short end of the bar under the trim with a hammer, then push the bar to lever the trim away from the wall.

Step 3. *Remove Any Wall Tiles.* Pry wall tiles (and the grout) from the substrate one at a time, rather than attacking the wall with a sledge hammer (flying pieces of tile can be dangerous). When removing tiles above a tub that you want to save, protect the tub with old towels, sheets, blankets, or cardboard.

1. *To remove a recessed medicine cabinet, first take out all screws, then pry the cabinet out of the wall with a pry bar.*

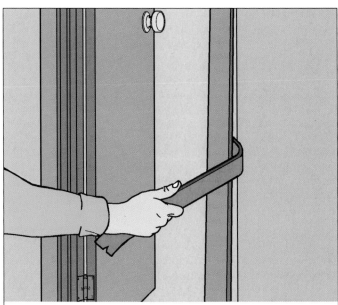

2. *Pry off all wood trim with a pry bar. If you want to salvage the trim, insert wood shims as you move along the length of each piece to keep the trim from breaking in two.*

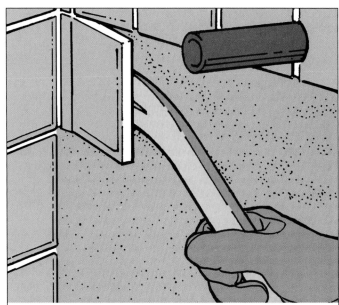

3. *Pry large tiles off one by one. Wear goggles and gloves to protect against flying shards of jagged tile.*

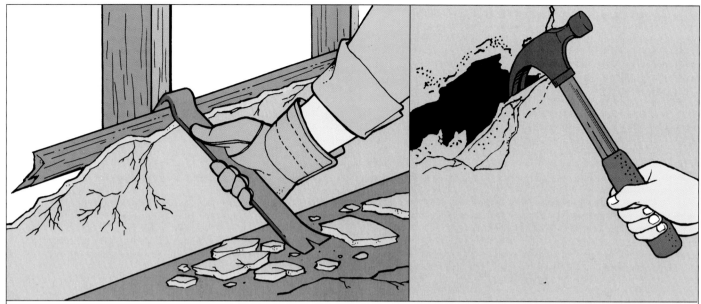

4. *Remove plaster and lath by inserting a hammer or pry bar between the studs and the back of the lath; then pry the section loose (left). Tear out drywall by using the claw end of a hammer; remove all nails as you go (right).*

Step 4. *Remove the Drywall or Plaster.* Bang a starter hole through old drywall with the claw end of a hammer or the pry bar tapped with a hammer. Use the claw of the hammer or pry bar to pull off one large chunk at a time. Remove all nails as you go. Protect your hands with gloves when removing the metal trim edges.

Break plaster walls apart with a hammer. Whack a hole through the plaster, to begin, then pull out a piece of lath near the top. Insert the claw of your hammer or a pry bar between the lath and studs near the top, and pry away lath and plaster pieces in one operation. Finally, remove all nails, leaving the studs exposed and clean.

Caution: *You risk damaging pipes and electrical wiring when you poke into walls and ceilings, so take extra care around areas where you suspect these items might exist. Also cover openings in heating ducts and exposed drains to keep chunks of debris from falling into them.*

Warm, Dry Walls and Ceilings

Chapter 8 stressed the need for vapor barriers and adequate insulation in bathroom floors, walls, and ceilings. This section will describe several ways to add insulation and a vapor barrier to existing walls, with or without gutting the surface finish.

The usual way to install insulation in a stud wall is to fill the cavities between studs. This can be done from the inside, after the wall finish is stripped off, or from the outside, by blowing loose-fill insulation through holes cut through the siding (this method does nothing to improve the wall's resistance to moisture). A third option enables you to add both insulation and a vapor barrier to the inside of the wall without having to first remove the wall finish. This may be your best solution if you can live with a fatter wall. (Plumbing fixtures and other obstructions may make this approach unworkable.)

Insulating Over Head

Bathroom ceilings under attics or roofs should have adequate insulation just above the ceiling itself (with a cold attic space above) or between the rafters (warm attic or cathedral ceiling). The easiest way to add insulation to an attic is by pouring in loose-fill insulation or hiring an insulation contractor to blow in fiberglass.

Before adding insulation, check to make sure there is a vapor barrier. Go into the attic and remove a portion of the insulation (if any) and see if a plastic sheet lies just above the plaster or drywall. If not, consider adding a vapor barrier. You can do this in one of two ways:

♦ Remove the ceiling finish and staple a sheet of 4-mil polyethylene to the joists, then reinstall the drywall (or plaster).

♦ Staple a sheet of 4-mil polyethylene to the room side of the present ceiling finish, then apply a second layer of drywall.

♦ You can add a vapor barrier to exterior walls in the same ways. If the walls need insulation as well, you can add it by one of the following methods:

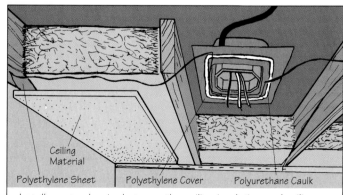

Install a vapor barrier between the ceiling insulation and ceiling material. To prevent moisture leaks around electrical boxes, wrap them with special polyethylene covers caulked to the main sheeting.

1. *Hold blanket insulation down with a board. Using the board as a guide, slice through the insulation with a sharp knife. Cut against a piece of scrap plywood or old carpet.*

Insulating a Wall Stripped to the Studs

Here are the steps to install batt or blanket insulation in a wall cavity. Begin after all alterations to the framing have been completed and plumbing has been roughed in. You can install new wiring after insulating (but before installing the vapor barrier). When working with fiberglass insulation, wear eye goggles, gloves, and a long-sleeved shirt, to protect as much of your skin as possible.

Difficulty Level: 🔨

Tools and Materials

☐ Long scissors (or knife)   ☐ Polyurethane caulk
☐ Housewrap tape or duct tape   ☐ Caulking gun
☐ 4-mil polyethylene sheet   ☐ Gloves
☐ Staple gun with 1/4-inch staples   ☐ Goggles
☐ Kraft-faced or unfaced fiberglass insulation blankets or batts of desired R-value

Step 1. *Cut and Fit the Batts between Studs.* Cut lengths of insulation from rolls or batts using long scissors or a sharp knife. Use a 6-inch wide piece of wood as a guide and a piece of wood below to cut against. Fit each piece of insulation snugly into the stud cavity. If you are using unfaced insulation, the friction between the edges and the studs will keep it in place.

Step 2. *Staple the Facing to the Studs.* For kraft paper-faced insulation, staple the tabs to either the sides of the studs or the stud faces (better).

Step 3. *Insulate around the Pipes.* Tuck insulation around the outside of any water pipes, leaving the room side uninsulated (to keep the pipes from freezing).

Step 4. *Apply a Vapor Barrier.* After any plumbing rough in and electrical wiring have been completed, staple a layer of poly-

2. *Attach kraft-faced insulation to wall by folding the edge tabs over the face of the studs and stapling with 1/4-inch staples.*

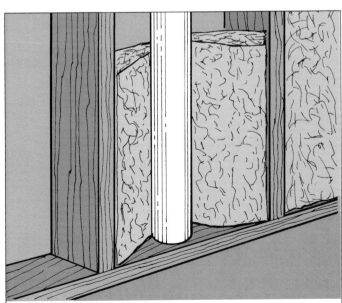

3. *Wrap insulation around the outer face of water and waste piping to prevent freezing. Leave the room side uninsulated.*

4. *After all insulation, wiring, and piping is in place, staple a vapor barrier to the stud faces. Use polyurethane caulk to seal the polyethylene at joints and to abutting surfaces.*

ethylene over the face of the insulation. Set each overlapping edge in a bead of polyurethane caulk before stapling. Wrap polyethylene around all penetrations, such as pipes and electrical boxes, then seal the patch to the face layer with caulk. This tedious and messy step is necessary to prevent moisture leaking into the wall.

Adding Insulation and Vapor Barrier to an Unstripped Wall

If you can afford losing a few inches of floor space to a fatter wall and there are no windows, doors or other obstacles, it may be practical to add insulation and a vapor barrier over the top of the existing wall finish before installing the new wall finish.

Difficulty Level: ⚒ ⚒

Tools and Materials

☐ Basic carpentry tools
☐ Housewrap tape or duct tape
☐ Electric drill with screwdriver bit (if screws used)
☐ Straightedge (or 48-inch drywall T-square)
☐ 2x2 or 2x4 furring strips (strapping)
☐ 1½-inch-thick foil-faced rigid foam insulation
☐ 20d nails or 3-inch screws (Phillips)
☐ Roofing tins (1-inch diameter pieces of tin used to hold roofing felt down)
☐ 10d box nails
☐ Caulk

Step 1. *Install the Furring Strips (Strapping).* Measure lengths of 2x2s or 2x4s (furring strips or strapping) to extend across the face of the wall. Starting at the floor, mark horizontal lines on the wall at 24-inch intervals. Place each strip on the wall so that its bottom edge is on the line, then screw the strips to the studs with 3-inch Phillips screws or nail with 20d nails.

Step 2. *Reposition the Electrical Boxes.* If there are any switch or outlet boxes on the wall, you will have to pull them forward to align with the new wall finish. After shutting off the power to the circuits, detach the box and pull it out of the wall a few inches. Add vertical cleats to support the box, making the cleats of the same stock as the furring strips. Attach the box to the cleats. If there isn't enough wire in the box, you may have to reposition the box slightly to gain some slack. Do not leave the old box in place and make a connection to the new box. Concealing electrical boxes is a fire hazard that violates the National Electrical Code.

Step 3. *Cut the Foam.* Lay a sheet of rigid foam insulation over a cutting surface, such as plywood or carpet. Measure and mark the pieces to fit between the furring strips. Cut through the foam using a straightedge or T-square as a guide. Use a sharp knife and make two or three passes to cut cleanly through the foam and facing material.

Step 4. *Insert the Foam and Tape the Joints.* Fit each piece of rigid foam snugly between the furring strips. Cut smaller pieces, as necessary, to fit around pipe projections and electrical boxes. Then tape each joint with plastic housewrap tape or aluminum-faced duct tape.

1. *Secure furring strips to the wall surface with nails or screws driven through the strips at each stud.*

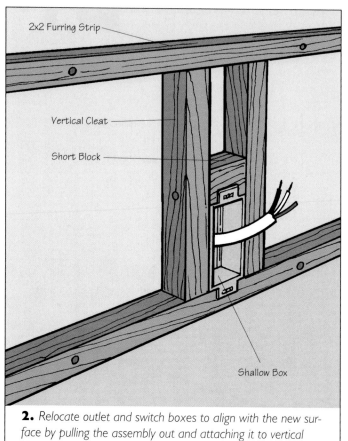

2. *Relocate outlet and switch boxes to align with the new surface by pulling the assembly out and attaching it to vertical cleats between furring strips.*

Step 5. *Caulk Any Projections.* Caulk around all projections in the foam with polyurethane or silicone caulk, taking extra care to seal the backs of electrical boxes. You can now apply drywall over the insulation. Attach it to the furring strips.

3. *Cut through rigid foam insulation with a sharp knife, using a drywall T-square or straightedge as a guide. Place a piece of plywood or old carpet below to protect the floor.*

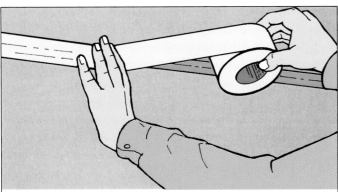

4. *When rigid insulation has been installed between all the furring strips, tape the joints with housewrap tape or duct tape.*

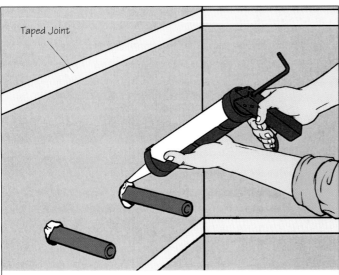

5. *Seal all projecting pipes and around electrical boxes with silicone caulk.*

Installing Drywall

Drywall, also called wallboard, is an amazing material that largely replaced plaster in houses built after World War II. It has a core of gypsum plaster that is sandwiched between two layers of paper. Drywall comes in sheets that are 48 inches wide. Sheets are available in length from 8 to 16 feet in 2-foot increments. Sheets come in thicknesses of 1/4, 3/8, 1/2, and 5/8 inch. For studs spaced 16 inches apart or less, use 1/2-inch drywall. Use 5/8-inch thickness if the studs are spaced 24 inches. In some old houses, studs are spaced still wider or are irregular. In that case, support the drywall from 1x3 or 2x4 furring strips, nailed horizontally across the studs at 16- or 24-inch spacing.

Use standard-grade drywall in dry areas of the room and water-resistant drywall (blue board) or cement board in wet areas to receive tile (cement board is preferred).

Before you begin, make sure the framing is straight and rigid. You can attach wood shims to concave sections of framing to bring them out to the desired line. Studs that can't be corrected with shims should be pulled out and replaced. Mark stud locations on the floor, so you will know where to sink nails or screws.

Difficulty Level: 𝗧 𝗧

Tools and Materials

☐ Basic carpentry tools ☐ Keyhole Saw
☐ 48-inch aluminum drywall T-square (or straightedge)
☐ Electric drill with screwdriver bit (if you use screws)
☐ Drywall nails or galvanized drywall screws long enough to penetrate at least 3/4 inch into the framing

Step 1. *Mark and Cut the Drywall.* Measure the height of the wall and width of the stud bays you want to cover with a single

1. *You can install drywall panels horizontally or vertically. Cut panels so that the edges fall on the centerline of the studs. (top). Score the drywall with a utility knife drawn against a T-square or straightedge (inset).*

sheet. You can install drywall vertically or horizontally. Vertical installation may be easier to install if you are working alone. To prevent cracks avoid making joints directly next to doors and windows. Mark the sheet with a straightedge. Draw the utility knife against the straightedge to score the paper facing (being careful to keep your other hand out of the path of the knife).

Step 2. *Snap the Joint in Two.* Slip a length of lumber under the cut line and gently push down on one side to snap the drywall panel apart, separating the cut through the thickness, but not through the backing paper.

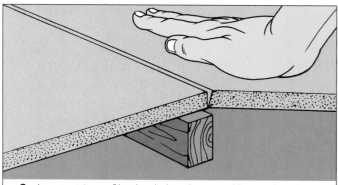

2. *Insert a piece of lumber below the scored line and push down to snap the joint in two.*

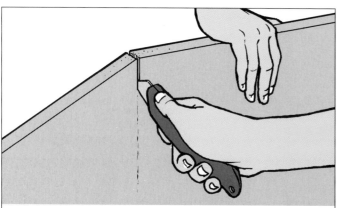

3. *Stand the panel on edge and cut through the paper facing on the back side. This is easier to do if you have a helper.*

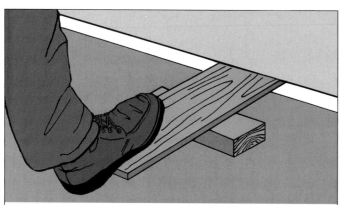

5. *When installing panels vertically, use two pieces of wood, set up as shown, to lever the panels against the ceiling.*

Step 3. *Cut Through the Backing Paper.* Turn the panel up on edge, fold the two cut pieces slightly together, and slice through the paper backing to complete the cut (this step is easier if someone else holds the drywall at the top).

Step 4. *Make Any Necessary Cutouts.* Cut openings for plumbing and electrical protrusions with a keyhole saw. Start by drilling holes in the corners of the shapes or by making repeated passes with the utility knife.

Step 5. *Position the Drywall on the Studs.* Positioning the panels is easier if you have a helper to hold the panel in place while you attach it. If you are installing the panels vertically, cut their lengths about 3/4 inch shorter than the wall height. Place the panel against the wall and use a foot lever, as shown, to push the panel up snug to the ceiling structure. Don't worry about the gap at the floor. It will be covered by base molding.

Step 6. *Attach the Drywall to the Studs.* Have a helper hold the panel against the wall (use your shoulder if you're working alone) as you use your foot to push the drywall snug against the framing and drive a few nails or screws in to hold it in place. Drive nails or screws around the edge, spaced 6 inches or less, and into each stud, spaced at 12 inches apart. Sink the fasteners to dimple—but not break—the facing paper.

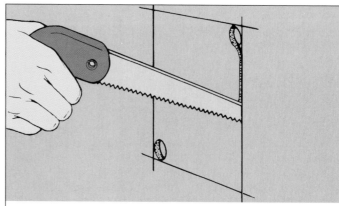

4. *Bore holes at opposite corners of each cutout and cut the piece out with a keyhole saw. You can avoid drilling the corners by making several passes along each edge with a utility knife.*

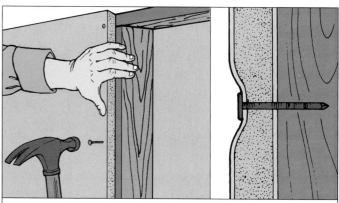

6. *Nail or screw the drywall to the framing at 6-inch intervals around the edges and at 12-inch intervals in the center (left). Drive fasteners just enough to dimple the facing paper (right).*

Finishing Drywall

Drywall intended as a base for wallcovering or paint should be finished with drywall tape and joint compound. The compound should be sanded smooth because even the smallest dents and ridges show through paint, especially paint with a glossy sheen. For a top-notch job, plan on applying joint compound in three stages, sanding the surface after each application. Drywall meant to receive tile simply needs to be taped with one coat of compound.

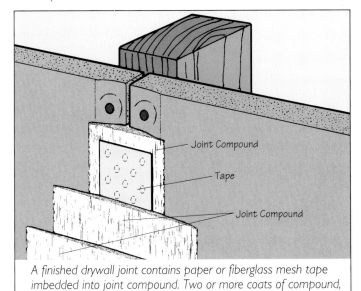

A finished drywall joint contains paper or fiberglass mesh tape imbedded into joint compound. Two or more coats of compound, sanded smooth, ensure a seamless appearance when finished.

Difficulty Level: 🔩🔩 to 🔩🔩🔩

Tools and Materials

☐ Utility knife
☐ 6-inch-wide drywall knife
☐ 12-inch-wide drywall knife
☐ 100-grit sandpaper
☐ Mud pan (or an old loaf pan from the kitchen)
☐ Tin snips (if you need to cut metal corner bead)
☐ Ready-mix joint compound
☐ Perforated paper tape or fiberglass mesh tape
☐ Metal corner bead (only if outside corners present)
☐ Pole sander with swivel head and 100-grit sandpaper inserts (optional)

Nails or Screws?

For small jobs and patches, nails will suffice for drywall. Use 1⅛-inch ring-shank drywall nails for 1/2-inch drywall, and 1⅞-inch nails for 5/8-inch drywall. If you are doing an entire room, though, consider using drywall screws. Use the galvanized screws at least 1 inch longer than the thickness of the drywall. You can drive them with a Phillips-head bit and your variable-speed electric drill, or rent an electric screwdriver from a tool rental store. These devices come with a clutch that prevents the screws from sinking too far into the drywall.

Step 1. *Fill the Mud Pan.* Open the container of joint compound. If liquid has separated from the rest of the material, stir it in. Use your 6-inch-wide knife to put a working gob of compound into your mud pan.

Step 2. *Fill the Drywall Joint.* Begin by applying compound to a joint with the 6-inch knife. Force the compound down into the tapered drywall joints to fill them level with the wall. At butt joints (where the nontapered ends of two panels join) fill the crack and create a slight hump (this will be finished flat later.)

Step 3. *Embed Tape into the Joint Compound.* Cut a length of joint tape and, beginning at the top, place it over the com-

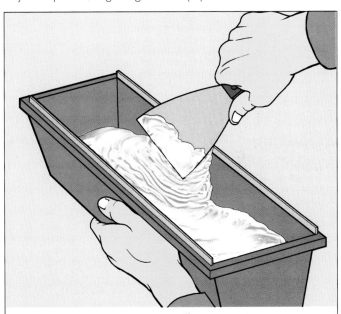

1. *Begin by scooping joint compound out of the bucket and into a mud pan (or into an old loaf pan).*

2. *Fill the joint with compound to a thickness of about 1/8 inch.*

pound-filled joint. Be sure to center the tape over the joint. Spread a thin layer (1/8 inch thick) of joint compound over the tape, holding the knife at a 45-degree angle.

Note: If you use fiberglass mesh tape, apply the tape over the joint before you apply the first coat of compound (it is self-adhering). Fiberglass tape is stronger than paper tape and easier to apply. But because fiberglass won't give, the joints may work apart in time (enough to be noticeable). This is less likely with paper, because it expands and contracts along with the paper facing on the drywall.

Step 4. *Remove the Excess Compound.* Go back over the joint with the drywall knife to scrape away any excess compound. Clean the knife against the edge of your mud pan.

Step 5. *Tape the Inside Corners.* If you are using paper tape, start by filling both sides of the inside corner joints. Fold a length of paper tape along its centerline and place it over the joint. (The tape is precreased for this purpose.) Finally, spread a thin layer of compound over the tape. If you are using mesh tape, apply it first then fill the joint. Remove the excess compound.

3. *Imbed paper tape into the joint with a 6-inch-wide knife, avoiding wrinkles (if using fiberglass tape, stick tape to joint before applying joint compound).*

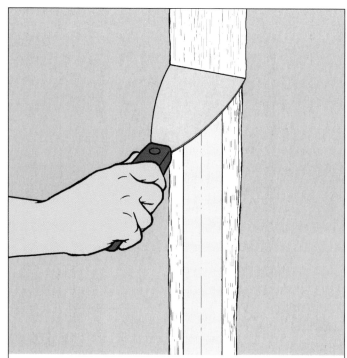

4. *Work from the top down to scrape away excess compound.*

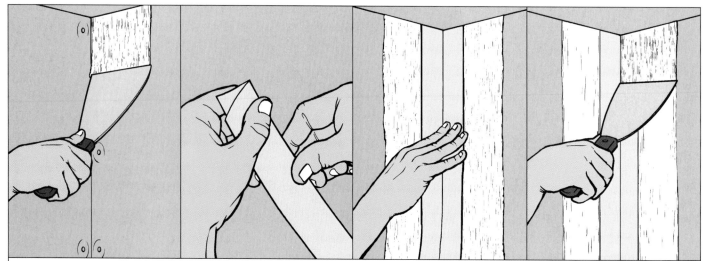

5. *Start finishing inside corners by filling both sides with joint compound, to about 1/8 inch thick (left). Fold paper tape by creasing it along the prescored centerline (second from left). Press the folded tape into joint compound at the corner (if you're using fiberglass tape, put the tape on the joint before applying compound) (second from right). Apply compound to both sides of the tape. Be sure to remove the excess compound (right).*

Step 6. *Fix a Metal Bead to the Outside Corners.* If you have any outside corners, use tin snips to cut a length of metal corner bead to the wall height. Angle the cut ends inward a little to ensure a better fit. Nail the bead to the wall with drywall nails. Fill the edges with joint compound, using the bead to guide your knife.

Step 7. *Fill in the Nail (or Screw) Dimples.* Fill all nail (and/or screw) holes and dimples with joint compound.

Step 8. *Sand the Joint Compound Smooth.* After 24 hours, or when the compound is completely dry, sand all joints and dimples smooth. Fix a sheet of 100-grit sandpaper into your pole sander, if you have one. If you are hand sanding, use a sheet of sandpaper folded into quarters.

Step 9. *Apply the Finish Coats of Compound.* Use a wide (12-inch) drywall knife to apply a second coat of compound to the joints and dimples. Sand again and repeat as necessary until you have a completely smooth surface.

6. *Nail a metal corner bead over any outside corners (left). Fill the corner with joint compound, using the raised bead edge as a guide (right).*

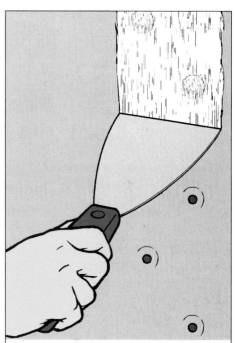

7. *Fill all dimples and dents with joint compound.*

8. *Sand the compound between applications. To make sanding easier, use a pole sander.*

9. *Finish joints and other filled areas with a wide-blade drywall knife.*

Putting Up Cement Board

Cement board makes a better backer for ceramic tile in wet areas than drywall does. Installation is harder, because of the greater weight and difficult cutting. On the positive side, cement board is the same thickness as 1/2-inch-thick drywall, so you won't have to adjust the wall framing where drywall leaves off and cement board begins.

Difficulty Level: ⚒ ⚒

Tools and Materials

☐ Basic carpentry tools   ☐ Variable-speed electric drill

☐ Center punch   ☐ Cement board

☐ Carbide-tipped bit (1-inch diameter)

☐ Phillips screwdriving bit for drill

☐ 48-inch straightedge (or aluminum drywall T-square)

☐ Saber saw (if circular holes must be cut)

☐ 1½-inch coated cement board screws

☐ Fiberglass mesh drywall joint tape

☐ Carbide-tipped blades for saber saw or several keyhole saw blades (if circles must be cut)

Step 1. *Measure and Cut the Cement Board.* Measure each panel carefully so that the edge lands dead center over a stud. Mark the cut line. Using the straightedge as a guide, score a 1/16- to 1/8-inch groove along the cut line with a utility knife.

Step 2. *Snap the Panel in Two.* Insert a length of 2x4 under the groove and press down over the panel to snap it in two.

Step 3. *Cut the Mesh Backing.* Lift up the panel and stand it on end, with the backside facing you. Use a utility knife to cut through the reinforcing mesh, freeing both sides.

Step 4. *Make Any Necessary Cutouts.* Measure the center of any holes for projecting pipes and mark them on the panel. Start the hole by tapping a dent at the center point with an awl or center punch. Then drill through the dent with a carbide-tipped bit. Make the holes slightly bigger than necessary to make installation easier (the edges of the holes will be hidden from view by an escutcheon plate). Start the drill at slow speed and gradually accelerate to prevent the bit from grabbing.

If you don't have a bit of large enough diameter to cut through the hole, make a starter hole with a small diameter (1/2-inch) masonry bit, and use a saber saw to cut out the hole. Use this method also for larger irregular cuts, but be prepared to go through several blades.

Step 5. *Make Sure the Framing Is True.* Unlike drywall, cement board is a rigid material that won't bend to take up minor irregularities in the framing. If you install it over uneven framing, you risk cracks. Use a straightedge vertically on each stud to check for any bows. Then run the straightedge across the studs in several places. Replace any deformed studs, or shim them out with wood shims.

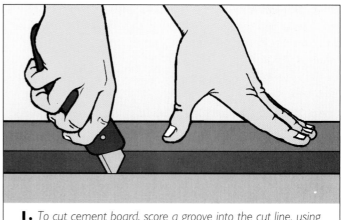

1. *To cut cement board, score a groove into the cut line, using a drywall T-square or straightedge as a guide.*

2. *Place a strip of lumber below the groove, and press down to snap the panel in two.*

3. *Stand the panel up on edge and cut through the mesh at the back to separate the pieces.*

Step 6. *Install the Panels.* Put the pieces of cement board into position and screw them to the studs with cement board screws set 1/2 inches in from the edges. Space the screws 4 inches apart around the edges and 12 inches apart along the studs in the center.

Step 7. *Tape the Joints.* Cover each panel and corner joint with fiberglass mesh tape. Simply cut and press; the tape's adhesive backing holds it to the cement board.

5. *Before putting up cement board, make sure the framing is true. Check the studs vertically with a long, straight board. Replace deformed studs or shim them out at the low spots.*

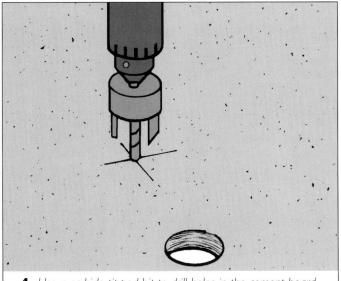

4. *Use a carbide-tipped bit to drill holes in the cement board.*

6. *Screw the cement board to the framing with 1½-inch cement board screws that are spaced 4 inches apart along the edges and 12 inches apart along the studs in the center of the panel.*

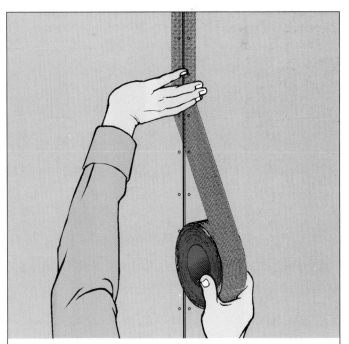

7. *Cover all edge and corner joints with fiberglass drywall tape. You do not need to use drywall joint compound.*

10
Installing Windows, Skylights, and Glass Block

You probably know what's wrong with your present bathroom windows, but when you get around to figuring out what to do about that leaky double-hung window above the bathtub, other questions will undoubtedly arise. Should you trash the old window and replace it with a better window of the same type and size? Should you replace it with a different type of window? Would a new window in another location better?

Let's assume you would like to improve the sash (the movable portion containing the glass). You may be able to install a replacement sash in the old frame if the frame is in sound condition. To tell, look for signs of rot or other deterioration. Poke the frame in several places with an awl or nail. If the frame seems solid all around, you can probably salvage it and replace the sash only. But if any part of the frame seems spongy, offering little resistance to a sharp object, you're better off replacing the entire window (that is both sash and frame).

Installing a New Sash in an Old Frame

Visit your home center, window supplier, or building products store to check out the various types of replacement sash available. Some, such as the one described at right, require a precise fit into the old frame. Others, such as all-vinyl (PVC) units, come with their own frames, which can be adjusted to fit into misaligned existing frames.

Here's how to replace an existing double-hung sash with new wood replacement sash units that ride in vinyl guides (called jamb liners), instead of being suspended from ropes or chains

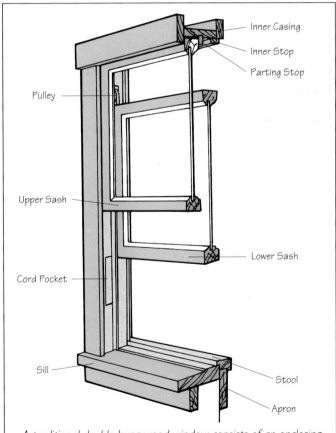

A traditional double-hung wood window consists of an enclosing frame and casings, into which are set two movable sashes. Cords attached to the sashes ride on pulleys in the side of the frame. Inside the frame's sides, cylindrical iron weights keep the open sash from falling down. Replacement windows use springs, rather than weights, to control window operation.

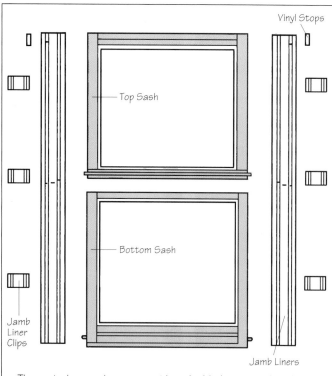

The typical parts that come with a double-hung wood replacement window kit include jamb liner clips (to attach the jamb liners to the frame); vinyl jamb liners; and a preglazed top and bottom sash.

concealed in the frame. Unlike the old window, this type of window not only slides up and down, but each sash tilts inward on a pivot for easier cleaning. You can adapt this method for installing other types of replacement sash.

Difficulty Level: 🔨

Tools and Materials

☐ Basic carpentry tools   ☐ Sash replacement kit
☐ Chisel   ☐ 8d finishing nails
☐ Loose-fill insulation (vermiculite)

Step 1. *Measure the Sash's Opening Width.* With a measuring tape, measure the inside opening dimensions, starting with the width. Be sure to record the actual width across the frame rather than the distance between stops. Take one measurement across the top and one across the bottom. If the two dimensions are different by more than 1/8 inch, you will need the type of replacement sash that can accommodate variations in frame width.

Step 2. *Measure the Sash's Opening Height.* Next measure the opening height, from where the sash abuts the top frame to where it abuts the topmost part of the sill. Use the width and height dimensions to order your replacement sash unit. Measure the opening height for all sash you will replace—even if they look to be the same size they may vary a bit, especially in older homes where windows were built on site.

Step 3. *Pry Off the Old Inner Stops.* If you're lucky, the stops will be secured with screws and not stuck in place by layers of paint. In this case all you have to do is remove the screws. But

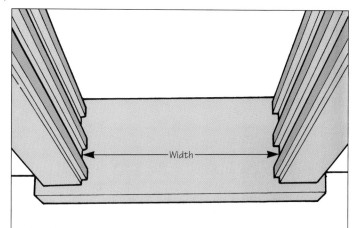

1. Measure the width of the frame, taking one measurement across the top and one across the bottom.

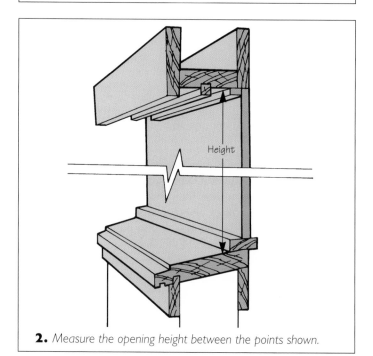

2. Measure the opening height between the points shown.

3. Run a utility knife down the length of the sash stops to break the paint seal, then pry the inner stops off with a pry bar or chisel.

4. *Take out the bottom sash, then pry off the parting stop.*

6. *Cut new jamb liners to the required length with a hacksaw, then secure them to the sides of the opening.*

more often, you'll find that the stops are painted and attached with small nails. In this case separate the paint between the sash stops and adjacent trim by scoring the joint with a utility knife. Pry off the stops from the sides and top of the sash.

Step 4. *Remove the Sash.* Remove the bottom sash from the frame and disconnect the cords for the weights from the sash. Be sure to lower the weights before letting go of the cords. Then pry off the parting stop (the vertical guide piece between the upper and lower sash). Finally take out the top sash, disconnecting the cords in the same manner.

Step 5. *Insulate the Frame.* Open the sash weight cover in the lower part of one of the jambs. Pull out and discard the old ropes and weights, and then replace the cover. Next remove the pulleys and fill the voids with loose-fill insulation. Enlarge the openings with a drill or keyhole saw to enable you to pour the insulation inside more easily. This step is important—it makes no sense to install an energy-efficient window in an uninsulated frame.

Step 6. *Install the New Jamb Liners.* Measure and cut the jamb liners (guides) to the proper height with a hacksaw, then position them in place and attach to the frame; this is usually done with two preset nails at the top and bottom.

Step 7. *Install the New Top Sash.* Insert the top sash into the jamb liners, holding the sash at an angle. Make sure the clutch

7. *Place the top sash into the jamb liners at an angle. Engage the clutch pivot above the clutch in the outermost track on both liners.*

5. *Remove the sash weights, cords, and pulleys. Enlarge the pulley opening with a drill and pour loose-fill insulation inside the cavities at each side of the window.*

8. *Level the top sash and tilt it up to vertical, pressing in the liners while pushing the sash to the outside track, one side at time. Slide the sash down to engage the clutches, then slide it back up.*

9. *Insert the bottom sash the same way as the top sash, but use the inside tracks of the jamb liners.*

10. *Replace the original stops. If they were damaged during removal, install new ones.*

pivot (the projecting hardware at the side of the sash) is above the clutch in the outside track on both sides.

Step 8. *Level the Sash.* Turn the top sash to a horizontal position and tilt it up to vertical, pressing in the liners while pushing the sash to the outside track, one side at time. Slide the sash down to engage the clutches, then slide it back up.

Step 9. *Install the New Bottom Sash.* Install the bottom sash using the same methods as explained in Steps 7 and 8, only use the inside tracks of the jamb liners.

Step 10. *Replace the Stops.* Replace the original stops or install new ones, if the original ones cannot be salvaged.

Replacing an Old Window Unit Entirely

Installing a complete unit, including the sash and frame, begins with removing the old unit—trim, sash, and frame. You may then need to alter the framing of the rough opening to accommodate the new unit's size or shape. Here's how to install a new window in a wood-frame wall, which is clad with siding. Many of the same steps also apply to brick-veneer walls, but to avoid having to change the brick, choose a replacement window of the same size as the old one. Begin the job by removing the old sash as described in Step 3 on page 94 and Step 4 on page 95.

Difficulty Level: **T T**

Tools and Materials

- ☐ Basic carpentry tools
- ☐ 1/2-inch plywood for header
- ☐ 1¼-inch roofing nails
- ☐ 8d, 10d, 12d, and 16d common nails
- ☐ Drywall finishing tools
- ☐ 6 mil polyethylene sheet
- ☐ Joint compound (if needed)
- ☐ 2x4 lumber for studs and sill
- ☐ Lumber as needed for header
- ☐ Staple gun with 1/4-inch staples
- ☐ Roofing nails (if window has flange)
- ☐ Finishing nails (if window has brickmold)
- ☐ Exterior-grade caulk (polyurethane, acrylic latex)
- ☐ Reciprocating saw (if needed to cut through studs)
- ☐ Plywood (if necessary to close part of opening)
- ☐ Drywall (if necessary to close part of opening)
- ☐ 2 adjustable jack posts (if needed for a bearing wall—rent from a tool rental store)
- ☐ L-shaped framing clips (if necessary to attach sill to jack studs)

- ☐ Circular saw
- ☐ Paint
- ☐ Metal drip cap
- ☐ Wood chisel
- ☐ Nails
- ☐ Caulking gun
- ☐ Housewrap
- ☐ Wood shims
- ☐ Trim
- ☐ Paint brush

Removing the Old Window Unit

Step 1. *Remove the Stops and Casings.* Remove the old window unit entirely. First pry off the inside and outside trim and the stool using a pry bar and hammer. If you want to salvage the inside trim, pry each piece off bit by bit, inserting shims as you go. Insert blocks between the prying tool and the wall to prevent damage to the plaster or drywall.

Step 2. *Remove the Old Frame.* After removing the trim and any nails holding the window frame to the house framing, pull out the frame.

Enlarging the Rough Opening in a Bearing Wall

If you have to enlarge the opening to fit the new window unit, make sure you don't cut through the studs until you know you will not be damaging a bearing wall or have a plan for replacing the necessary supports. Get the opinion of a builder or architect as to whether the wall is a bearing wall and if so, how to reframe the header beam to maintain the wall's integrity. In general, you can probably widen an exterior window opening to as much as 96 inches without temporary shoring in the following cases:

♦ The window is below a floor, rather than a roof (the rim joist can likely carry the load of the floor joists).

♦ The window is under a roof, but in the gable end.

If the window sits below the eaves end of a roof, it carries the weight of the roof and ceiling. You should support these loads with temporary shoring while you replace the header above the window opening with a longer one.

1. *Pry off the exterior and the interior trim with a pry bar and hammer.*

Window Frame

2. *Remove the window unit, including the frame and any protruding nails.*

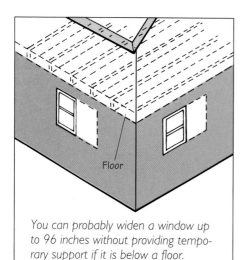

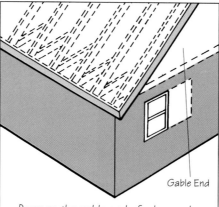

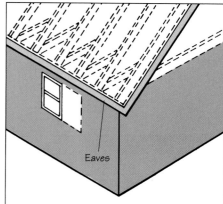

You can probably widen a window up to 96 inches without providing temporary support if it is below a floor.

Because the gable end of a house does not usually carry the weight of the roof, you won't need to provide temporary shoring while you enlarge a window below it to 96 inches or less.

Before widening a window below the eaves side of a roof, take precautions to support the structure temporarily and properly size a new beam above the window.

Step 1. *Cut an Opening in the Outside Wall Facing.* After determining the required rough opening size from the instructions or catalog description of your new window, mark the rough opening dimensions on the outside of the house. Use a circular saw to cut through the siding and sheathing, and then remove them. This will allow you to see what will have to be done to rework the framing for the new window.

Step 2. *Remove the Inside Wall Facing.* Remove the wall cover from the studs above and below the existing window and at the side where it will be widened (see page 81, "Gutting a Wall or Ceiling").

Step 3. *Provide Temporary Support.* Place a 2x10 plank on the floor, about 24 inches from the wall. The plank should be at

least 24 inches longer than the new window opening. Place one adjustable jack post at each end of the plank, to align with the sides of the window opening. Adjust the jack posts to the approximate height needed by setting the pins in the correct holes, then place a second 2x10 plank above the jacks, under the ceiling. Screw the threaded rod at the top of each jack upward until the 2x10 is tight to the ceiling, but do not tighten beyond this point.

Step 4. *Plan the Reframing and Cut Out the Old Members.* Using the rough opening dimensions specified with your replacement window, first determine the size of the new header. Use the size recommended by your builder or architect or use the following rule of thumb to size the header:

1. *Mark the rough opening dimensions on the outside. Cut through siding and sheathing with a circular saw. Tack a guide board to the siding to provide a smooth surface for the saw.*

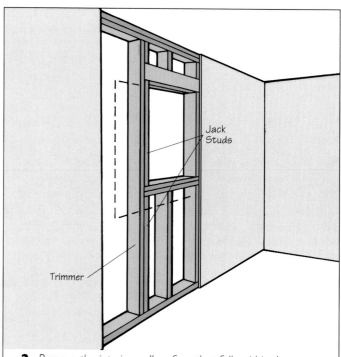

2. *Remove the interior wall surface that falls within the area of the rough opening.*

Installing the Unit

Step 1. *Frame the Roof Opening.* Reinforce the rafters at the sides of the openings and install double headers, in the same way you framed the ceiling opening (see Step 4, "Frame Out the Ceiling Opening" on page 102).

Step 2. *Install the Skylight or Roof Window.* Follow the manufacturer's instructions for installing the window. Secure it in only one place until you have made sure that the window is properly aligned. If it is not straight, you'll likely notice it when you trim out the inside.

Step 3. *Flash the Curb and Repair the Roofing.* Replace the shingles, installing aluminum step flashing as you go. Aluminum

step flashing comes in packages of precut pieces. Interweave one flashing piece to overlap and underlap each successive shingle, as shown. Apply roofing compound under flashing and shingles.

Step 4. *Complete the Shaft.* Frame the sides of the shaft with 2x4s. Measure the angles with an adjustable bevel gauge. Cut the angles accurately (a circular saw makes this easier). Insulate the sides with fiberglass; carefully cut to fit between the framing. After insulating, staple a sheet of 6-mil polyethylene over the inside face of the studs for a vapor barrier. Use polyurethane caulk to seal the sheet to the existing ceiling barrier (or backside of the ceiling drywall if there is no barrier). Finally, apply drywall as described in "Installing Drywall," page 85. Apply wood trim, if necessary, at the joint between the roof window and drywall.

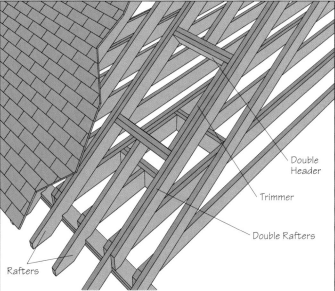

1. *Frame the roof opening in the same way you framed the ceiling opening. Use double headers to span the uncut rafters and trimmers to adjust the width.*

2. *Mount the skylight or roof window according to the manufacturer's instructions.*

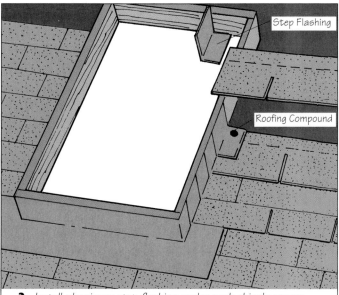

3. *Install aluminum step flashing under each shingle as you go, applying a bed of roofing compound over each layer.*

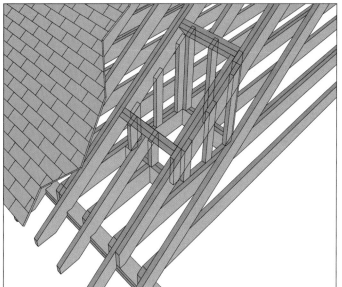

4. *Frame the shaft sides with 2x4s, measuring angles with an adjustable bevel gauge. Insulate the sides with fiberglass, then staple a 6-mil poly sheet over inside face of studs.*

Making a Glass Block Wall

Glass blocks let light pass through but obscure vision. A wall made from glass blocks can divide one part of the bathroom from another without making a small room seem even smaller. Glass blocks come in modular sizes, 6x6, 8x8, 12x12 inches—all nominally 4 inches thick. You can lay them into straight walls or, by setting each block at a slightly different angle, create curved walls. Imagine how you might use walls of glass to define toilet stalls, showers, and baths. Best of all, the installation is simple enough for most do-it-yourselfers.

The downside is high cost, even if you do the work yourself. Also, you must reinforce the subfloor to take the weight of an 8-foot-high masonry wall. As to the cost, first estimate how many blocks you will need to complete the job, then ask a local masory products supplier how much materials will cost. Reinforcing a wood floor will mean doubling or tripling the joists in the vicinity of the new block wall. To be on the safe side, get the opinion of a builder, architect, or structural engineer (concrete slab floors that rest on the ground can safely support an 8-foot glass block wall). When you install glass block next to a wood-framed wall, you'll need to place the new construction near an existing stud or add a new stud inside the existing wall.

Difficulty Level: 𝗧 𝗧

Tools and Materials

☐ Basic carpentry tools
☐ Lumber for sill curb forms
☐ Plastic jointing tool
☐ Glass block mortar mix
☐ Foam plastic expansion strip
☐ Lumber (as needed for blocking)
☐ Lumber (for sister joists if needed)
☐ Pressure-treated 2x4s (if needed)
☐ L-shaped framing clips (if needed)
☐ Plastic joint spacers (1/4 inch)
☐ Metal wall anchors (available from block supplier)
☐ Caulking gun and silicone caulk
☐ Wire joint reinforcement (of size to match type of block units selected)
☐ Concrete dry mix (if you build a curb, one bag per each cubic foot of curb needed)

☐ Mason's trowel
☐ Stapler and staples
☐ Plastic mortar tub
☐ 10d common nails
☐ Glass blocks
☐ Rubber gloves
☐ Wood shims

Preparing the Project

Step 1. *Reinforce the Wood-Framed Floor.* If your glass block wall will run across the floor joists, add solid blocking between the joists that lie underneath the wall. Toenail the blocking into the joists or hang from metal joist hangers. If the glass block wall will align with an existing floor joist, reinforce that joist with a sister joist nailed into the original with 10d common nails spaced 8 inches apart at the top and bottom. If the glass block wall will run parallel to and between two joists, double up both joists and add solid blocking between them at 16-inch intervals.

Step 2. *Provide Bracing at the Side Wall.* Place your glass block wall against a wall stud, if possible. If the glass wall falls between studs, remove the intervening wall cover, install a bracing stud inside the cavity, and then patch the wall (see "Rebuilding Walls and Ceilings," page 79). To avoid tearing into the wall, add two pressure-treated 2x4s at the wall joint, and connect them to the floor and ceiling framing with L-shaped framing clips. Cover the 2x4s with tile or wood trim.

Step 3. *Build a Top Plate (Optional).* You may run the glass block right up to the ceiling or end it below the ceiling, to allow for a strip of ceramic tile, wood, or wallboard trim. If you want to install trim, you'll need to build a top plate for the wall. Determine how far down from the ceiling you want the top plate to extend, then nail the appropriate number of 2x4s to the ceiling to achieve this thickness. If the top plate runs parallel to but between the ceiling framing members, you may have to get up

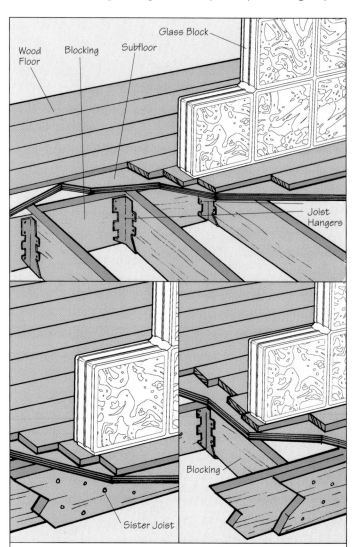

1. *If your block wall will run across the joists, reinforce the floor with solid blocking toenailed into the joists or hung from metal joist hangers (top). To reinforce a floor under a glass block wall that runs along the top of a joist, nail a sister joist to the supporting one (bottom left). For a glass block wall that runs parallel to and between two joists, reinforce the floor with two sister joists. Add blocking between them (bottom right).*

into the attic and install two or three crosspieces (so you will have something to attach the top plate to).

Step 4. *Build a Raised Curb (Optional).* You will want to start the glass block at or above the raised edge of a prefabricated shower stall. But if you are enclosing a toilet stall, you can start the blocks right at the floor level. After the shower base has been installed, build a form around the sides to the desired height, using 2x4s or 2x6s. The form should be 3⅝ inches wide (the thickness of the glass blocks). Mix a batch of concrete

according to the manufacturer's directions, and fill the form, tamping down the concrete to consolidate it into the corners. With a trowel, remove the excess mortar from the top of the form. Cover with plastic, and let the concrete set overnight.

Setting the Blocks

Step 1. *Mix the Mortar.* Use white-colored mortar mix specifically made for glass block. Mix one package at a time, following

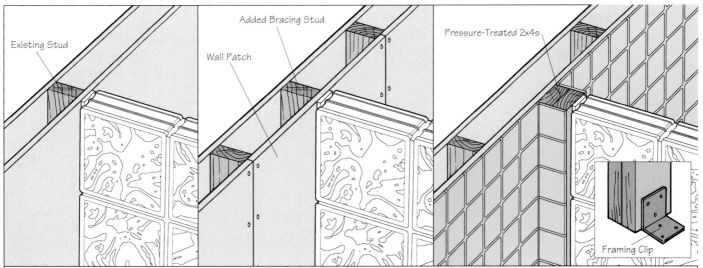

2. *You can avoid the need to add extra wall bracing by locating your glass block wall against a wall stud (left). If your glass block wall will fall between studs, remove the wall cover and install a bracing stud inside the cavity, then patch the wall (center). Another option is to add two pressure-treated 2x4s between the proposed glass block wall and existing bathroom wall. Connect the lumber to the floor and ceiling with L-shaped framing clips. Cover the 2x4s with tile or wood trim (right).*

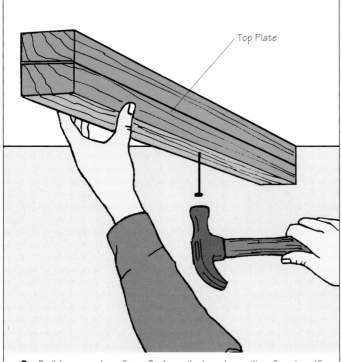

3. *Build a top plate from 2x4s nailed to the ceiling framing. If there is no framing above the plate, go into the attic and nail blocking across the nearest ceiling joists.*

4. *Build a form for a base curb using 2x4s or 2x6s. The form should be 3⅝ inches wide.*

the directions on the package and using as little water as possible to make a stiff mix. You can tell when you have it right if you can make a "baseball" out of the mortar. Mix the mortar in a plastic tub.

Step 2. *Install Wire Joint Anchors, Expansion Strips and Mortar Base.* Joint anchors and expansion strips are used where the block meets the walls and ceilings. If you are using 6-inch block you'll need an anchor every third block. For 8-inch block use an anchor every other block. The anchors come 24 inches long. Cut each piece into two 12-inch-long anchors and bend them so there is a 4-inch leg. Nail the 4-inch leg of the anchors along the walls and ceiling, positioned as needed for the block you are using. Cut the foam plastic expansion strip to a width that will fit between the ridges on the glass block. Staple the strip along the walls and the ceiling. When you come to a joint anchor, cut the strip to cover

the 4-inch leg, then continue the strip along the wall or ceiling. Next, spread a bed of mortar 1/2-inch thick on the curb or floor.

Step 3. *Install the First Block.* Glass blocks are installed with spacers between them. As shown in the drawing, the spacers are used as supplied where four blocks come together, but are cut into an "L" shape for use in corners and a "T" shape for use where blocks meet walls, floors or ceilings. For the first course, you'll need to cut two "L"s for the corners and "T"s for between each block. Press the first block firmly in place with it's "L" spacer against the expansion strip. Insert the "T" spacers below and above as shown in the drawing.

Step 4. *Complete the first course.* Put a 1/2-inch-thick layer of mortar on one vertical edge of the second block. Put it in place against the first block. Install spacers and complete the first

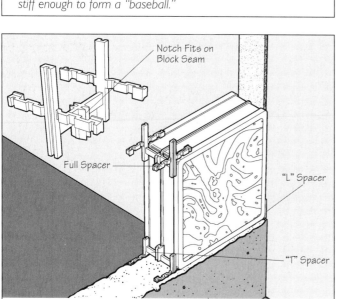

1. *Mix prepared glass block mortar mix in a plastic tub or wheelbarrow, using as little water as possible. Make a mixture stiff enough to form a "baseball."*

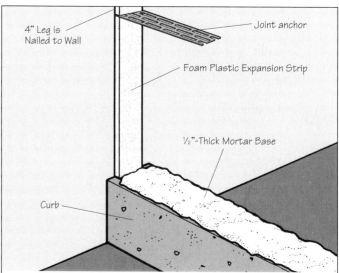

2. *Install joints anchors as appropriate for the glass block you are using, staple expansion strip to the existing wall, then spread mortar 1/2 inch thick on the curb (or floor).*

3. *Use full spacers and spacers cut into "L" and "T" shapes to create the proper spaces for mortar joints between blocks.*

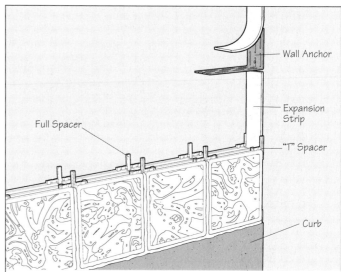

4. *Complete the first course, mortaring a vertical edge of each block before setting that edge against the last block set. Add joint spacers as you go.*

course. Check this course periodically with a level to make sure all blocks are level and the glass wall is plumb. When the first course is done, put a layer of mortar on top of it and continue the wall.

Step 5. *Install Joint Reinforcing.* When you come to a course with wall anchors, slip the end blocks under the long arm of the anchor. Lay down mortar atop the entire course. Then gently embed wire reinforcing in the mortar. If you need more than one piece of the wire reinforcement, overlap the pieces by 6 inches.

Step 6. *Set the Top Course.* Because it meets an expansion strip, the top course gets no mortar on top. Apply mortar to one vertical edge of each top course block and install it with "L" and "T" spacers as shown.

Step 7. *Smooth the Joints.* When the mortar has set for about an hour, use a plastic jointing tool to smooth the joints into a concave profile.

Step 8. *Caulk around the Glass Block Wall.* Caulk the joint between the glass block wall and the original wall and top plate or ceiling with silicone caulk. Tool the joint to a smooth, concave shape with your finger. Then buff the dried mortar film with an old towel.

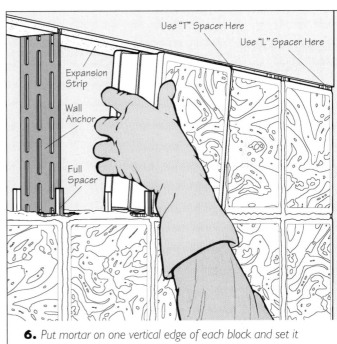

5. *Slip a block under the wall anchor, spread mortar atop the entire course, then embed wire reinforcement in the mortar.*

6. *Put mortar on one vertical edge of each block and set it against the preceding block with "T" and "L" spacers.*

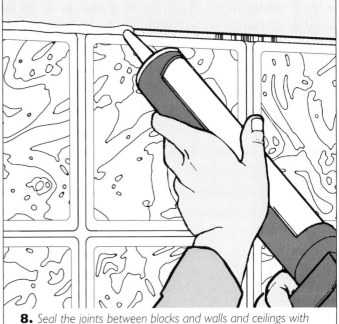

7. *Smooth the mortar joints with a plastic jointing tool.*

8. *Seal the joints between blocks and walls and ceilings with silicone caulk.*

11

Installing Plumbing Fixtures

Bathroom plumbing improvements can be as simple as replacing a leaky faucet or as complicated as rerouting piping in the walls or floor and installing a new whirlpool. If you have ventured beyond fixing a leaky tap, you have an idea of what you can do and when to call in a plumber. If you are new to plumbing, you should get a good idea of what is required from the step-by-step instructions in this section.

Because building codes differ from place to place, before beginning any plumbing project you should check with your plumbing inspector to see how your local codes could affect your plans. Codes specify both the design of piping systems and the acceptable materials for a particular application. Local regulations determine who can do certain kinds of work and how the work will be inspected. Plumbing work is unforgiving, and even minor mistakes can result in leaks, which will have to be repaired at a greater cost in the long run. So it pays to know what you're doing.

It's also important to understand the hazards involved in plumbing work, and to take appropriate measures to protect yourself and your home. You can be burned. Flying particles can injure your eyes. Using power tools around pipes poses the risk of electrical shock in addition to the usual hazards. Flame from a soldering torch can ignite a fire in the floor or wall. Anticipate and prevent these problems by shutting off electrical circuits, wearing goggles and gloves, shielding combustible materials from soldering torches, having adequate battery-powered lighting, and using common sense.

Bathroom Plumbing Basics

Bathroom plumbing has to do three things:

♦ Deliver hot and cold water to the fixtures

♦ Remove waste to the sewer or septic system

♦ Vent the waste piping to outside air

Here's what's required to achieve each of these goals:

Getting Water to the Fixtures

Every fixture except the toilet requires a separate hot and cold water supply pipe (the toilet requires only a cold water supply). At the first convenient location below the point of use, there should be a shutoff valve to enable you to repair the fixture without shutting down the water to the entire house. By shutting off the main valve, not only will every fixture be out of commission for hours (or even days), but you'll have to run back and forth between the master shutoff valve in the basement and the bathroom.

Hot and cold water piping used to be made of galvanized steel, joined with threaded connectors. Cutting and threading pipes were difficult and required specialized tools. Little wonder this work remained firmly in the domain of plumbers. Today, do-it-yourselfers can install their own hot and cold piping, thanks to rigid and flexible copper piping alternatives that are far simpler to work with and more economical to install (and to rework, when mistakes are made). Polybutylene and CPVC plastic are also used for supply piping, but because these materials are not as widely accepted by building codes as is copper, they will not be discussed here.

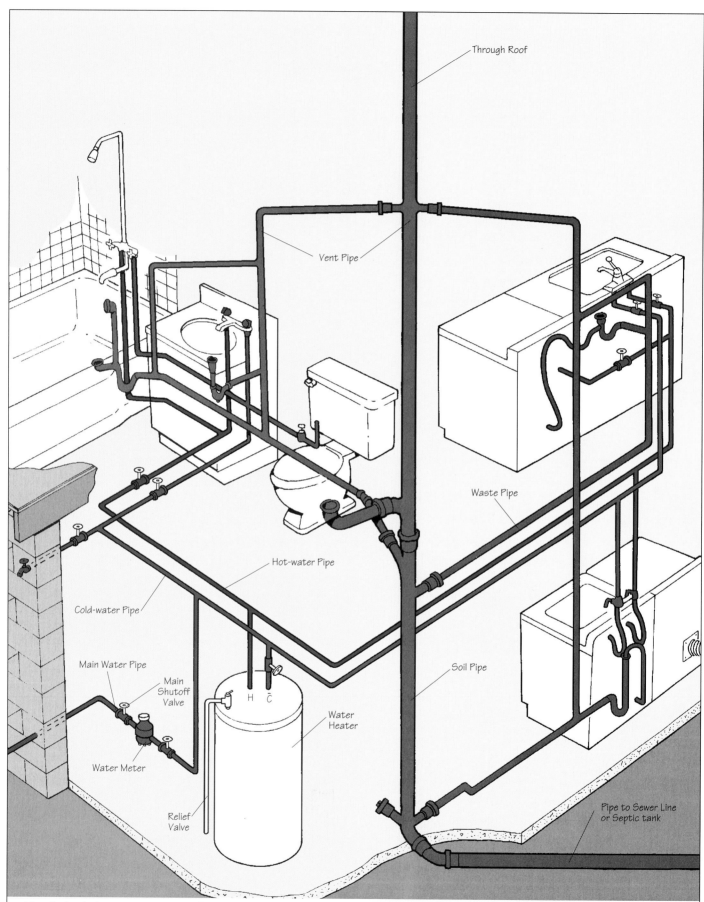

Through Roof

Vent Pipe

Waste Pipe

Hot-water Pipe

Cold-water Pipe

Soil Pipe

Main Water Pipe

Main Shutoff Valve

Water Meter

Relief Valve

Water Heater

H   C̄

Pipe to Sewer Line or Septic tank

Here is the drain-waste-vent system for a typical home. Note the vent line between the sink and toilet. The toilet itself is vented through the soil stack, which extends through the roof.

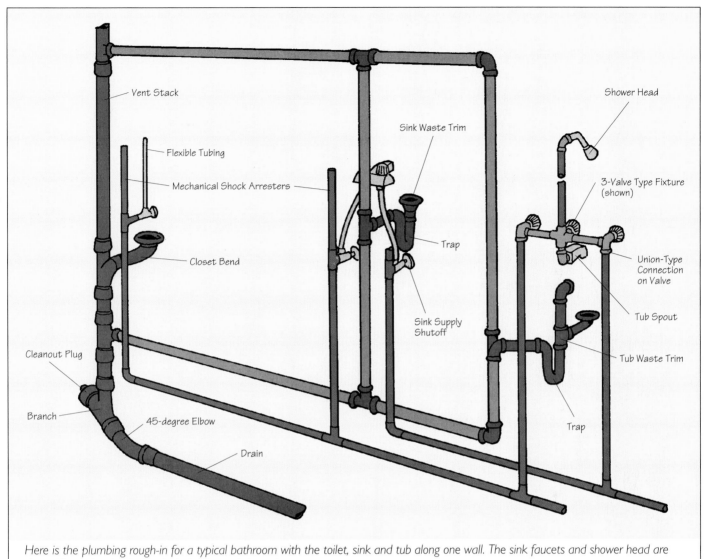

Here is the plumbing rough-in for a typical bathroom with the toilet, sink and tub along one wall. The sink faucets and shower head are shown for clarity; they're not included in rough-in work.

Waste and Vent Piping

The pipes that remove wastes to the sewer, and vent fixtures to outside air, work together as a drain-waste-vent (DWV) system. Waste pipes carry off water, while vent pipes allow outside air into the pipes. The soil stack is a single large-diameter pipe that carries waste down to the sewer and vents air through the roof. Getting water to the fixtures requires piping that is 1/2 or 3/4 inch in diameter; home waste lines are 3 or 4 inches in diameter, depending on the number of fixtures served. As with water supply piping, installing DWV systems was pretty much a plumber's realm in the past. Cutting heavy cast-iron sections and then uniting them by pouring melted lead into bell and spigot joints were beyond the capabilities of most homeowners. By contrast, plastic piping can be installed by anyone with moderate skills and ability. What could be simpler than cutting pipes with a handsaw and joining them with solvent cement? But first a few basics.

The waste lines in the DWV system consist of pipes that are sloped to drain to the sewer. Like branches of a tree, small-diameter pipes from sinks, showers, and tubs feed into a large trunk

(the soil stack), which usually sits in the wall just behind the toilet. Each of the branches contains a curved portion near the fixture drain to trap water, preventing odors and sewer gasses from entering the room. To allow the trapped water to refill each time instead of being sucked into the sewer, a vent is provided between the trap and the sewer.

In a simple arrangement with a sink, toilet, and tub on the same wall, the soil stack is simply extended up through the roof to provide a vent. When plumbing fixtures are on more than one wall, set apart from each other, or more than a few feet away from the main vent, it is often more practical to provide a separate vent.

When planning to relocate fixtures or add new ones, try to use as much of the existing waste and vent piping as possible. Snaking small-diameter water pipes through existing floors and walls is much easier than dealing with large DWV piping. In this chapter we'll begin with the simplest projects—which generally involve sinks and then move on to more ambitious ones such as installing toilets, tubs, showers, and whirlpools.

Basin Wrench

Standard Screwdriver

Phillips Screwdriver

Spud Wrench

Monkey Wrench

Tube Bender

Strap Wrench

Nut Driver

Adjustable Pliers

Bulb-Type Toilet Plunger

Allen Wrenches

Pipe Wrench

Tubing Cutter

Adjustable Wrench

Solder & Flux

Emery Cloth

Hacksaw

Backsaw

Chain Wrench

Reamer

Propane Torch

Die

Open-End/Box Wrench

Standard Pliers

Tap

Needle-nose Pliers

Volt-Ohmmeter

The plumbing tools shown here will suffice for most of the plumbing tasks in this book.

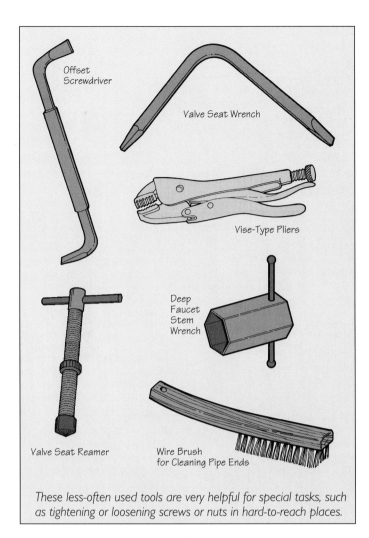

These less-often used tools are very helpful for special tasks, such as tightening or loosening screws or nuts in hard-to-reach places.

Basic Plumbing Tools

Most of the projects in this chapter will require basic plumbing tools, which are listed below (some of these tools belong to the basic carpentry tool list, page 13). Tools that are used to cut and join copper, ABS, and CPVC plastic pipe are listed, but specialized tools that are used for cast-iron waste lines and galvanized steel pipes are not.

- ☐ Adjustable wrench (or a set)
- ☐ Spud wrench
- ☐ Adjustable pliers
- ☐ Needle-nose pliers
- ☐ Propane canister
- ☐ Backsaw
- ☐ Tubing cutter
- ☐ Tube bender
- ☐ Phillips screwdriver
- ☐ Basin wrench
- ☐ Allen wrenches
- ☐ Standard pliers
- ☐ Solder flux
- ☐ Hacksaw
- ☐ Miter Box
- ☐ Reamer
- ☐ Standard screwdriver
- ☐ Utility knife
- ☐ 1-inch wide roll of emery cloth
- ☐ Pipe wrenches (one 10-inch, one 14-inch)
- ☐ Lead-free wire solder (as required for potable water)
- ☐ Propane torch (the type that screws onto a propane canister)
- ☐ 12x12-inch piece of sheet metal (to use as a shield when soldering)

Cutting and Joining Plastic Pipe

Difficulty Level: 🔩 🔩

Tools and Materials

- ☐ Basic plumbing tools
- ☐ Primer (PVC piping)
- ☐ Solvent cement
- ☐ Compression clamp fittings (if joining to cast iron)

Lightweight plastic pipe ranges in diameter from 1½ to 6 inches. Most plastic DWV lines can be installed with just a few simple tools. Making connections is easy and straightforward, but requires a little practice to do with ease. After cutting the pipe with a handsaw, clean the ends to be joined, apply solvent cement, and join the pieces. Be sure to match the solvent cement to the type of plastic used in the pipe (PVC, or ABS). You can even join a new section of plastic pipe to an existing cast-iron waste line with compression clamp fittings (consisting of flexible gaskets and metal rings that screw-tighten).

Plastic waste piping is made of ABS (black) or CPVC (white) plastic. Check with your local plumbing inspector to find out which type is acceptable for your project. Make sure to match the solvent to the type of piping material.

Step 1. *Cut the Pipe.* Measure the lengths required, allowing for the fittings (assume the pipe will fit all the way inside the sleeves of the fittings). Unless you are cutting piping already in place, put the lengths to be cut in a miter box. Cut the pipe with a backsaw or hacksaw. Use a utility knife and/or emery cloth to remove burrs from the cut ends and to dull the outer cut edge so that it will slide smoothly into the fitting.

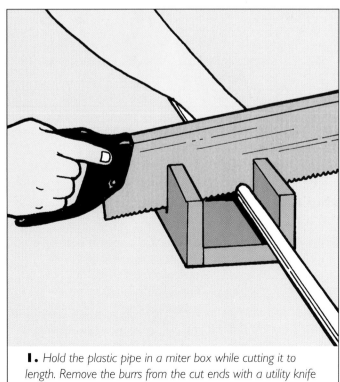

1. *Hold the plastic pipe in a miter box while cutting it to length. Remove the burrs from the cut ends with a utility knife or emery cloth.*

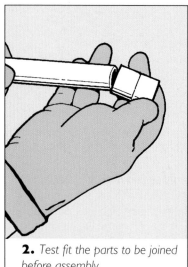

2. *Test fit the parts to be joined before assembly.*

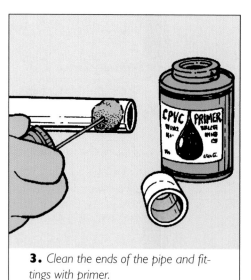

3. *Clean the ends of the pipe and fittings with primer.*

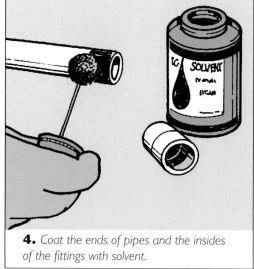

4. *Coat the ends of pipes and the insides of the fittings with solvent.*

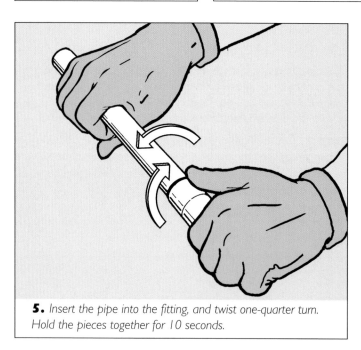

5. *Insert the pipe into the fitting, and twist one-quarter turn. Hold the pieces together for 10 seconds.*

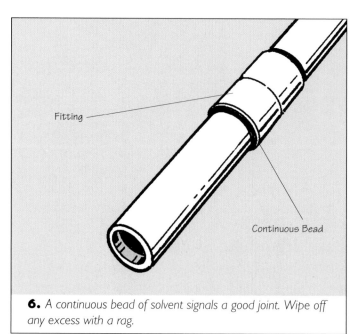

Fitting

Continuous Bead

6. *A continuous bead of solvent signals a good joint. Wipe off any excess with a rag.*

Step 2. *Test the Fit.* After cutting the pipes, test fit the parts that are to be joined. If the new pipe is too long, simply trim to the correct size. If the pipe is too short to fit completely in the fittings, cut another piece of pipe, which can be added to the first piece, or start over with a new section of pipe.

Step 3. *Clean the Ends of the New Pipe.* Use PVC primer to clean the ends of PVC pipe and fittings.

Step 4. *Apply the Solvent Cement.* Thoroughly coat the ends of each pipe and the insides of the fittings with the solvent cement. Be sure to use the type of solvent cement intended for the type of plastic pipe you are using.

Step 5. *Join the Pipe to the Fitting.* Immediately after applying solvent cement, insert the pipe into the fitting, and twist the two parts against each other about one-quarter turn. Hold the pieces together for about 10 seconds.

Step 6. *Wipe Off Any Excess Solvent Cement.* If the joint is formed properly, the solvent cement will form a continuous bead

around the joint. Wipe off any excess cement around the pipe and fitting with a cloth.

Installing Faucets in Basins

A visit to a home center will give you a good idea of the wide array of faucets available. In addition to the old tried-and-true dual-lever faucet with replaceable washers, you'll see single-lever types in a variety of styles. You can have handles that incorporate wood or ceramic. Spouts and bases come in polished or dull-finish chrome, brass, and nickel as well as many colors of enameled metal. Naturally, prices range to suit the level of luxury. To find your way through the options, it will help to have some idea of the basic faucet types.

Your first decision is whether to select a dual- or single-lever faucet. Both are available with or without drain control levers. Faucets control water flow in various ways. Compression-type faucets depend on rubber washers or diaphragms to open or

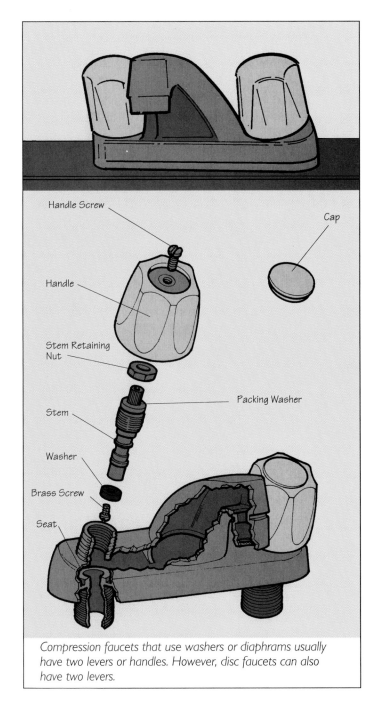

Compression faucets that use washers or diaphrams usually have two levers or handles. However, disc faucets can also have two levers.

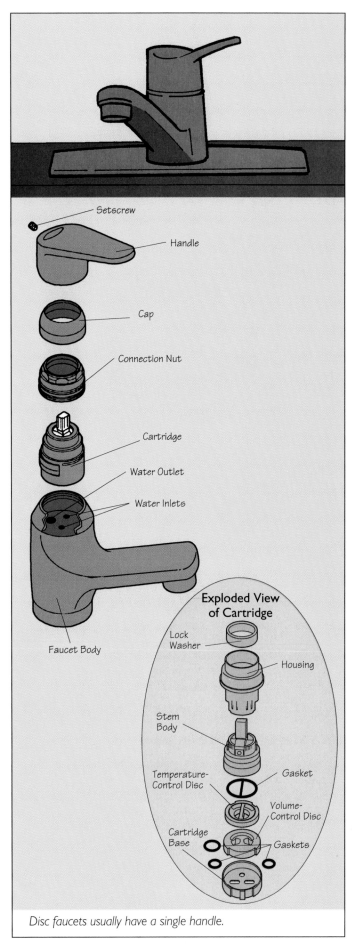

Disc faucets usually have a single handle.

close down the water flow. Newer types use other means than compression to control the water flow, such as cartridges, balls, or discs. Cartridge faucets regulate water flow with a movable cartridge and rubber O-rings. Ball faucets use a slotted plastic or brass ball atop a pair of spring-loaded rubber seats. The single lever rotates the ball to adjust the water temperature and flow. Disc faucets contain a pair of plastic or ceramic discs that slide back and forth to regulate the volume of the flow and rotate to control the temperature.

The following steps describe how to replace an old faucet or install a new one. Before you buy a faucet set, be sure its offset (the distance, center to center, between the hot and cold taps) matches the spacing of the holes in the basin. Check this by measuring the distance between the center of the hot and cold supply risers from under the basin.

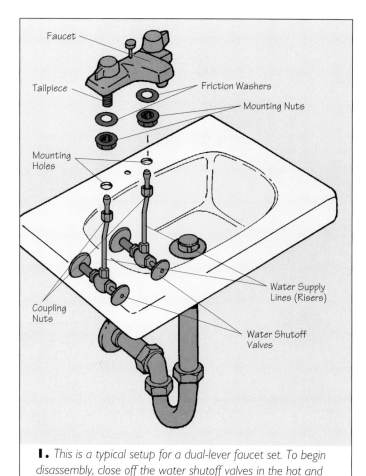

Faucet

Tailpiece

Friction Washers

Mounting Nuts

Mounting Holes

Coupling Nuts

Water Supply Lines (Risers)

Water Shutoff Valves

1. *This is a typical setup for a dual-lever faucet set. To begin disassembly, close off the water shutoff valves in the hot and cold supply risers below the basin.*

Removing the Old Set

Difficulty Level: 🔩 **to** 🔩🔩

depending on the accessibility of the faucet mounts

Tools and Materials

☐ Basic plumbing tools

☐ Plumber's putty or silicone sealant

☐ Braided stainless-steel risers

☐ Putty knife

☐ Flashlight

☐ Caulking gun

Step 1. *Close the Shutoff Valves.* Begin by shutting off the valves in the hot and cold supply pipes below the basin. If there are no valves, shut off the water supply at the main, which is probably in the basement.

Step 2. *Disconnect the Tailpieces from the Risers.* Set up a flashlight to shine on the piping below the basin, then use a basin wrench to disconnect the faucet tailpieces from the supply risers.

Step 3. *Remove the Drain Controls.* If the faucet contains a drain control, it must come out before you can remove the faucet. Loosen the clevis screw with a pair of pliers to free the lift rod from the clevis. Then use adjustable pliers to free the pivot rod from the drain. Finally, disconnect the pivot rod from the pop-up plug and remove both (your new faucet set should come with replacement drain parts).

Step 4. *Remove the Mounting Nuts and Washers.* Remove the faucet mounting nuts and washers by turning them counter-clockwise. On single-lever faucets, the supply piping converges at the center and the unit is held in place by mounting nuts at the

Compression Fitting

Compression Slip Nut

Hot-water Supply Tube (Riser)

Cold-water Supply Tube (Riser)

Basin Wrench

Hot Water Shutoff

Cold Water Shutoff

2. *Disconnect the faucet tailpieces from the supply risers with a basin wrench.*

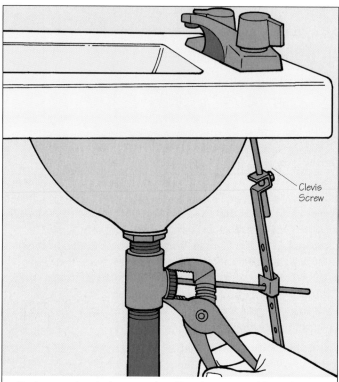

Clevis Screw

3. *Loosen the clevis screw, then free the pivot rod from the drain. Separate the pivot rod from the pop-up plug; remove both pieces.*

sides and a nut and retaining ring in the center. Use whichever tool fits: adjustable pliers, adjustable wrench, or basin wrench.

Step 5. *Pry the Faucet Off the Basin.* If the faucet won't budge easily, coax it by inserting a putty knife under the baseplate. Then use the putty knife to remove any caulk or adhesive from the basin.

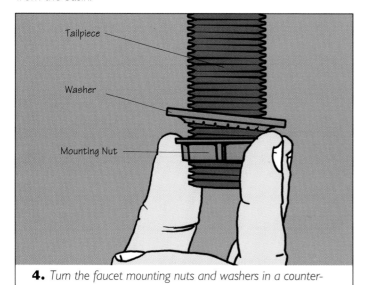

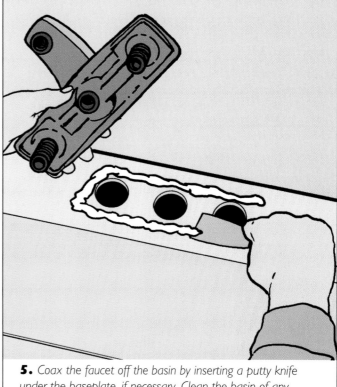

4. *Turn the faucet mounting nuts and washers in a counterclockwise direction and remove.*

5. *Coax the faucet off the basin by inserting a putty knife under the baseplate, if necessary. Clean the basin of any remaining caulk or adhesive.*

Installing the New Faucet Set

Step 1. *Install the Gasket or Sealant.* After cleaning the surface of the basin in the area in which the new faucet will sit, install the gasket. If your faucet set came without a gasket, put down a bead of silicone sealant or plumber's putty around the

lip of the faucet baseplate. Insert the faucet tailpieces into the mounting holes of the basin and press the faucet down into the sealant, if used. Wipe off any excess sealant with a rag.

Step 2. *Tighten the Mounting Nuts.* Put the washers and mounting nuts (if any) onto the tailpieces and tighten. Do not overtighten.

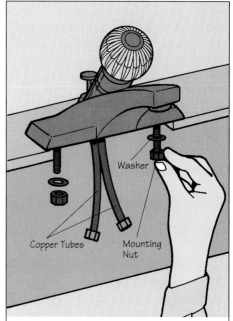

1. *If the faucet comes with a gasket, put the gasket on the basin, below the faucet (left). For faucet sets without gaskets, place a bead of silicone sealant around the lip of the faucet baseplate (right).*

2. *If the new faucet has copper tubes attached, set the faucet into the sink and tighten the mounting nuts.*

Step 3. *Attach the Risers.* Attach braided stainless-steel risers to the faucet and to the water shutoff valves (this type is flexible, unlike chrome-plated copper, making it easier to adjust when connecting). Tighten the nuts, avoiding overtightening.

Step 4. *Install the Drain Fittings.* Insert the lift rod control through the top of the faucet. Next link the lift rod and spring clip with the ball assembly inside the drain. Insert the pop-up stopper into the drain hole, and engage it with the pivot rod. Adjust the elevation of the stopper by selecting the appropriate hole in the clevis.

Finishing Up. When all the parts are assembled, turn the shut-off valves on and check all the connections for leaks. If a connection is leaking, turn the nut a little at a time until the leak stops.

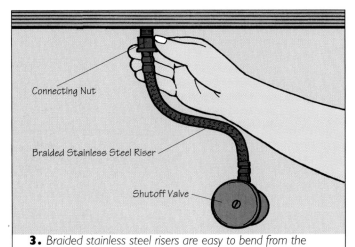

3. *Braided stainless steel risers are easy to bend from the shutoff valve to the faucet. Tighten the compression-type nuts first by hand, then with a wrench.*

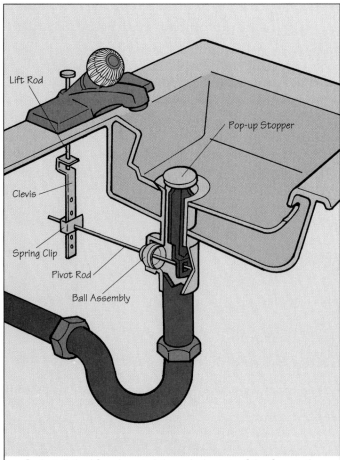

4. *Install the lift rod control through the top of the faucet, then link the lift rod and spring clip with the ball assembly. Insert the pop-up stopper, and engage it with the control rod.*

Installing a New Toilet

Installing a new toilet in the same location requires careful removal of the old unit, and mounting and connecting the new one. If you are installing the toilet in a new location, you will need to modify the existing piping system.

Difficulty Level: 🔨🔨🔨

Tools and Materials

☐ Basic plumbing tools
☐ Measuring Tape
☐ Plumber's putty
☐ New toilet
☐ Extension piping for drain
☐ Braided stainless-steel riser
☐ Extension piping and fittings for water supply
☐ Threaded compression union (if needed to join to steel)
☐ Drill (electric or hand) with 3/4-inch bit
☐ Closet bend flange (the transition piece between the soil stack and toilet)
☐ Coupling nut and compression ring (if needed for chromed copper pipes

☐ Framing square
☐ Saber saw
☐ Teflon tape
☐ Shutoff valve
☐ Wax seal ring
☐ Spud Washer

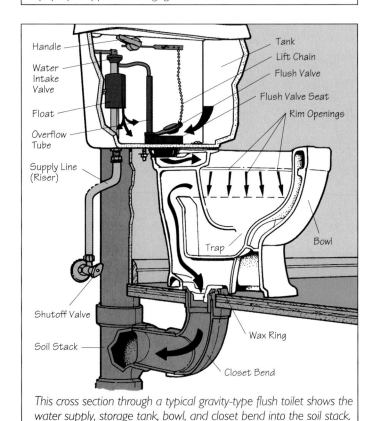

This cross section through a typical gravity-type flush toilet shows the water supply, storage tank, bowl, and closet bend into the soil stack.

Removing the Old Toilet

Step 1. *Turn off the Water Supply and Disconnect the Riser.* Shut off the water supply at the home's main valve, even if the toilet has a separate shutoff valve. This is necessary because you'll be removing the old valve. Disconnect the riser, shutoff valve, and escutcheon with an adjustable wrench.

Step 2. *Disconnect the Toilet from the Floor.* Remove the protective caps (if any) from the bolts that hold the toilet to the floor, then unscrew the nuts with a wrench. If the bolts are too corroded to come loose, cut them with a hacksaw.

Step 3. *Remove the Toilet from the Drain.* Rock the bowl back and forth to free it from the floor; then lift it straight up off the drain. Next, stuff a rag into the drain hole to keep sewer gas from escaping into the house. If any residue from the wax ring that seals the toilet to the drain remains behind, scrape it off the drain.

Caution: *Lifting the toilet can put stress on your back, so keep your knees bent while maneuvering the bowl.*

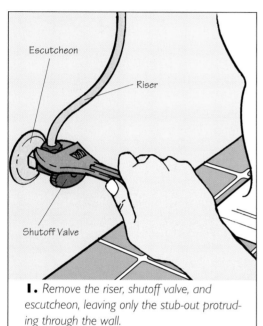

1. *Remove the riser, shutoff valve, and escutcheon, leaving only the stub-out protruding through the wall.*

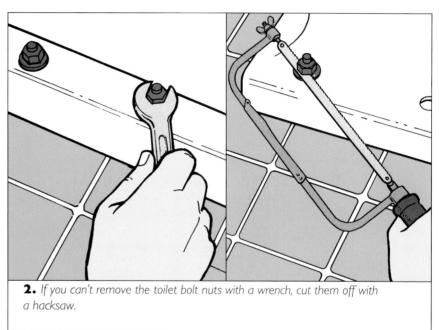

2. *If you can't remove the toilet bolt nuts with a wrench, cut them off with a hacksaw.*

3. *After all connecting parts have been removed, rock the bowl from side to side to remove it from the drain. Bend your knees to avoid harming your back.*

Adapting the Piping System for a New Toilet Location

Begin by checking out the requirements of your municipal plumbing code (ask your building inspector for this information). The code might specify things such as the allowable maximum distance between the toilet's drain and soil stack and vent. Every fixture needs to be vented somehow, and a separate vent is usually required when the toilet is more than 6 feet away from the existing vent. Getting a new vent up through the roof might be more than you want to undertake, so be sure to think through your proposed layout. The following steps describe how to install a toilet in a new location but still tap into the existing soil stack. Relocating a toilet usually requires removing part of the subfloor and wall finish material to get access to the water supply and waste piping, unless you can get to the piping from open joists in a basement.

Step 1. *Extend the Water Supply Pipe.* Cut the pipe that supplied the previous toilet and extend it with straight piping and elbows that terminate in a hole in the floor or wall to the rear of the new toilet. If the existing supply line is copper tubing, extend the line by tapping into it at a convenient place with a Tee fitting and copper piping of the same size. If the existing pipe is steel, use a threaded compression union at the old pipe's

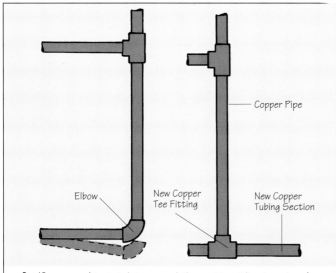

1. *If you need to tap into an existing copper pipe to extend a supply line, melt the solder at an elbow. Then break the elbow free. Install a new connection and solder all joints.*

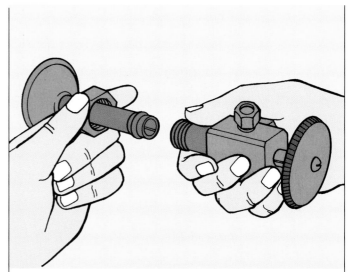

2. *Slide the escutcheon over the pipe stub and press it to the wall. Then slip on the nut and compression ring. Slide on the shutoff valve and tighten the nut.*

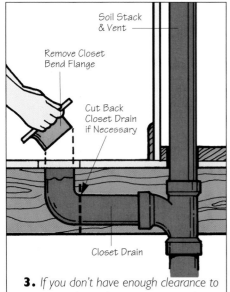

3. *If you don't have enough clearance to tie a new closet drain extension to the existing drain, cut the pipe as shown here and add a new section.*

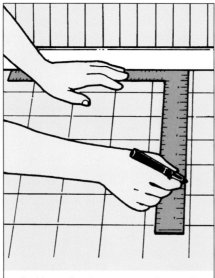

4. *Use a framing square to locate the center of the toilet drain on the floor.*

5. *Measure the distance from the center of the toilet's drain hole to the outside edge of its base.*

threaded end and add a new section of copper tubing to other side of the union (see "Working with Copper Tubing," page 124).

Step 2. *Connect the New Shutoff Valve.* Select a shutoff valve with a compresion ring connection that matches the diameter of the pipe stub. Insert the nut over the end of the pipe stub, then the compression ring, then the valve. Tighten the nut, taking care not to overtighten it.

Step 3. *Adapt the Drainpipe.* Remove the closet drain flange from the floor. The bent part is called the "closet bend" and the straight part, the "closet drain" (these names are derived from the term "water closet," which is the formal title of the toilet). If necessary, cut the drain at the elbow and stuff a rag inside it to temporarily cap it until you finish the piping and install the toilet. Place a board over the hole until you finish the floor. Extend the

drainpipe to the new location with plastic piping of the same type and diameter as the existing piping. ABS plastic is commonly used for this, but your local code may permit CPVC piping (see "Cutting and Joining Plastic Pipe" page 115).

Step 4. *Locate the New Drain on the Floor.* Use a framing square to draw a centerline on the floor perpendicular to the wall. From the fixture instructions determine the required distance from the wall to the center of the drain hole and mark it on the floor.

Step 5. *Mark the Position of the Toilet Base.* Turn the toilet upside down and measure the distance from its drain hole to the sides and front of the base. Mark these dimensions on the floor and position the toilet right side up over the marks. Trace the outline of the base onto the floor.

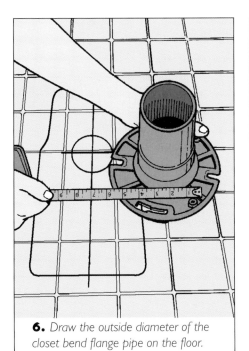

6. *Draw the outside diameter of the closet bend flange pipe on the floor.*

7. *Cut the hole with a saber saw or keyhole saw.*

8. *Connect the elbow and drain sections to the soil stack.*

Step 6. *Mark the Flange's Location on the Floor.* Measure the outside diameter of the pipe of the closet bend flange and scribe a circle of this diameter on the floor.

Step 7. *Drill a pilot hole at a point on the circle and use a saber saw to cut out the hole in the subfloor.* Insert the closet bend flange in the hole and screw it to the floor.

Step 8. *Join the Closet Bend Flange to the Waste Line.* Use both an elbow and a straight piece of pipe of the proper diameter and length to join the tailpiece of the closet bend flange to the main drain. (See "Cutting and Joining Plastic Pipe," page 115).

Mounting the New Toilet

Step 1. *Attach the Mounting Bolts to the Flange.* Slip the heads of the mounting bolts into the slots of the closet bend flange.

Step 2. *Put the Wax Seal on the base of the Toilet.* With the toilet turned on its side or upside down, press the wax seal ring over the horn at the base of the bowl. The horn is the protruding lip around the drain hole in the base of the toilet.

Step 3. *Position the New Toilet.* Remove the rags from the drain hole, then turn the toilet right side up and lift it into position, aligning the bolt holes in the base with the bolts in the flange. Lift the bowl and slowly coax it to the floor, twisting it slightly to seal the wax ring. Place a level over the rim, side to side. Pour some water into the bowl to check for leaks. Re-mold the wax ring if leaks occur. When set, install the washers and nuts on the bolts. Do not overtighten the nuts, or they may crack the bowl.

Step 4. *Install the Tank.* If the tank is separate from the bowl, place the spud washer (a large rubber ring) over the drain hole

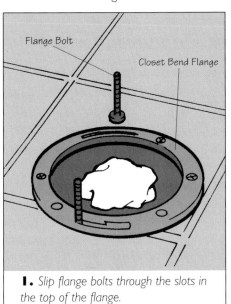

1. *Slip flange bolts through the slots in the top of the flange.*

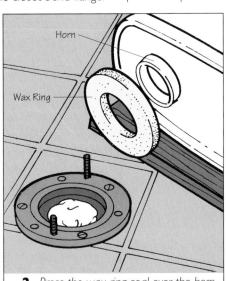

2. *Press the wax ring seal over the horn of the toilet drain hole.*

3. *Lift the toilet into position, aligning the holes in the base with the bolts in the flange.*

4. *If the tank is a separate unit from the bowl, sandwich a spud washer between drain hole and the tank. Fasten the tank to bowl's rim.*

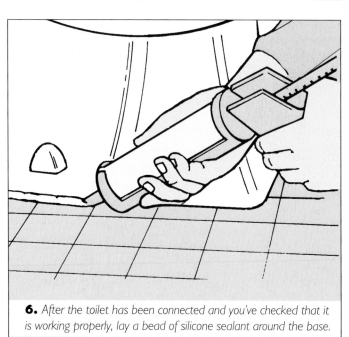

6. *After the toilet has been connected and you've checked that it is working properly, lay a bead of silicone sealant around the base.*

in the lower section, then place the tank over it. Attach the tank to the bowl rim with washers and nuts from below.

Step 5. *Connect the Tank to the Shutoff Valve.* It is best to use a braided-stainless steel riser, but a chromed copper riser could also be used. The pipe should be of the diameter recommended by the toilet manufacturer. If using a braided riser, fit one end into the shutoff valve and the other into the tank's threaded inlet, hand tighten the nuts, then tighten with an adjustable wrench. For chromed copper pipes, measure the distance from

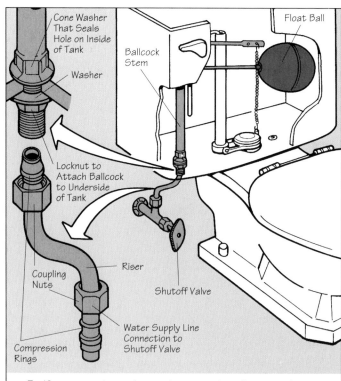

5. *If you are using a chromed copper pipe, slip a coupling nut and compression ring over both ends before inserting it into the shutoff valve and toilet inlet, then tighten the nuts.*

the toilet connection to the shutoff valve, and allow enough extra length for for the fittings, then cut the pipe with a tube cutter. Slip a coupling nut and compression ring over both ends of the pipe before inserting it into the shutoff valve and toilet inlet, then tighten the nuts. Take care not to make a sharp bend or kink in a copper tube. Turn on the water supply and check for leaks. If you can't stop a leak by a bit more tightening, disconnect the riser and apply plumber's putty or Teflon tape to the threads.

Step 6. *Seal the Base of the Toilet.* Use a caulking gun to place a bead of silicone sealant around the base of the toilet.

Working with Copper Tubing

Copper tubing is much easier to install than galvanized steel. You can choose between 20-foot-long lengths of rigid tubing or coils of flexible tubing. The advantage of flexible tubing is that you can bend it to snake through curves in existing walls and floors without making joints. The downside is that curves have to be gentle and without kinks; making the bends requires a little practice. By contrast, each turn in rigid tubing requires a joint with a soldered or threaded coupling, which can be easily made if you can get access to the joint, but hard to make in places with cramped access.

Copper tubing is made in four grades, according to the thickness of the walls: K, L, M, and DWV. Find out which types your local code accepts. Very likely, they will be type M or L for water supply piping. Both type M and type L are available in rigid and flexible tubing.

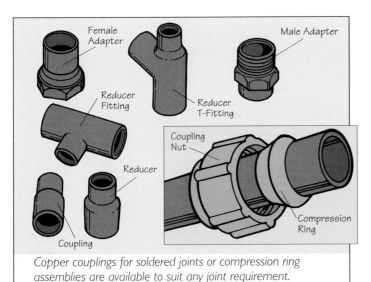

Copper couplings for soldered joints or compression ring assemblies are available to suit any joint requirement.

Couplings

You can join both rigid and flexible copper tubing with soldered joints or compression couplings. Soldered connections may be less prone to leakage over time, but they can't always be made. Joining copper tubing to a pipe or fitting of another material, such as brass, has to be made with compression couplings. Compression couplings become watertight when you tighten the threaded nut, drawing a flange against the end of the pipe. Couplings are available with threaded nuts on both ends or with one end threaded and the other straight, to be soldered.

Cutting Copper Tubing

Difficulty Level: 🔧

Tools and Materials

☐ Basic plumbing tools   ☐ Wire brush
☐ Emery cloth or multipurpose tool

Step 1. *Cut the Pipe.* Cut the pipe with a tubing cutter or hacksaw. If using a tubing cutter, gradually tighten the cutting blade

against the pipe as you rotate the tool several times (until the pipe snaps apart). If using a hacksaw, place the pipe in a grooved board or miter box, for easier cutting.

Step 2. *Remove the Burrs from Inside the Pipe's End.* After cutting, remove the burrs from the inside of the pipe. Some tubing cutters contain a burr remover. Use a wire brush to clean the insides of the pipe and fitting that the pipe will be joined to.

Step 3. *Clean the Outside of Pipe's Ends.* Before soldering, clean the ends of the pipe with emery cloth or a multipurpose tool that contains an abrasive for cleaning the outside of the pipe and a brush for the inside.

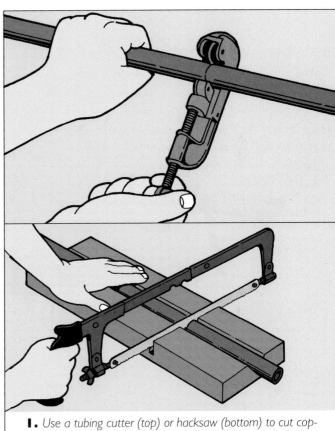

1. *Use a tubing cutter (top) or hacksaw (bottom) to cut copper pipes.*

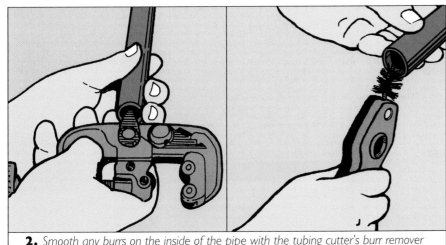

2. *Smooth any burrs on the inside of the pipe with the tubing cutter's burr remover (left) or a wire brush (right).*

3. *Clean the ends of the pipe with emery cloth or a multipurpose tool before soldering.*

Soldering Connections

Difficulty Level: 🔩🔩

Tools and Materials

- ☐ Basic plumbing tools
- ☐ Solder
- ☐ Small brush
- ☐ Flux

From a home center or hardware store, get a small torch that screws to a disposable propane canister. Also buy a good self-cleaning flux and solder. Use only lead-free solder (nickel or silver) for pipes that carry potable water. When soldering with a torch you can endanger both your body and your house. Protect your eyes with goggles and your hands with gloves. Get a 12x12-inch piece of sheet metal to insert between the joint to be soldered and any nearby wood, to protect your house from catching on fire.

Step 1. *Apply the Flux.* Use a small brush or toothbrush to coat the joint ends with flux.

Step 2. *Join the Pipes to the Fittings.* Slide the fitting over the pipes' ends so that half of the fitting is on each pipe.

Step 3. *Apply the Solder.* Light your torch and heat the joint by running the flame over the pipe and fitting, taking care to avoid burning the flux. When the pipe is hot enough to melt the solder, take the torch away and feed solder into the joint until it won't take any more. Heat the pipe for about 5 seconds. Then move the torch to the fitting as you feed more solder into the joint. Continue until the joint stops drawing the solder in and there are no gaps in the solder. If the solder around the rim of the joint stays puddled and does not draw in as it cools, reheat until the solder liquefies, then try again. Practice with some scrap pipes and connectors, until you feel confident to solder your new supply lines.

Step 4. *Protect Surfaces.* If soldering near wood or other combustible materials, place a piece of sheet metal between the soldering area and the material to prevent fire.

Step 5. *Clean the Joint and Test for Leaks.* Cool the pipe with a wet rag, then test the joint for leaks. If more solder doesn't stop the leaks, melt the joint apart and start over.

1. *Coat the pipe ends with flux.*

2. *Insert the fitting over pipes' ends.*

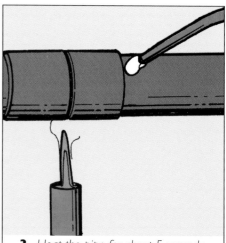

3. *Heat the pipe for about 5 seconds. Then move the torch to the fitting as you feed solder into the joint. Continue until the joint stops drawing the solder in.*

4. *To prevent fire, place a piece of sheet metal between the soldering area and any combustible material.*

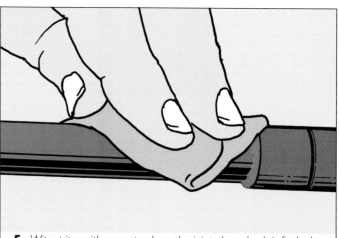

5. *Wipe pipe with a rag to clean the joint; then check it for leaks. Stop leaks with more solder; if that doesn't work, redo the joint.*

Putting in a New Bathtub

If you are new to plumbing, you may not realize that hooking up your new tub may be the simplest part of the job—most of the hard work involves removing the old one. Here's how to replace an old tub with a new one, using the same supply and drain piping, but new fittings.

Difficulty Level: 🔩🔩🔩

Tools and Materials

- ☐ Basic plumbing tools
- ☐ Putty knife
- ☐ Basic carpentry tools
- ☐ Pipe joint compound
- ☐ Sledge hammer or mason's hammer
- ☐ New fittings
- ☐ Wood shims
- ☐ Brass nipple
- ☐ Spout
- ☐ New bathtub

Removing the Old Tub

Step 1. *Remove the Overflow Fittings.* Shut off the water supply to the tub. Next, open the taps to relieve any back pressure. Remove the overflow cover and slowly pull the linkage rod coil assembly out. To remove a plunger-type tripwaste, pull the mechanism out through the overflow hole.

Step 2. *Remove the Drain Fittings.* Remove a pop-up-type tripwaste from the tub drain.

Step 3. *Free the Tub from the Wall.* Separating the old tub from the wall may be as simple as running a putty knife around the edge to break the bond between the tub and a caulked joint. Or you may have to gut a portion of the wall and remove tiles.

Step 4. *Free the Tub from the Floor.* Separate the tub from the floor, trying to protect the existing floor as much as possible, unless you intend to replace the flooring anyway.

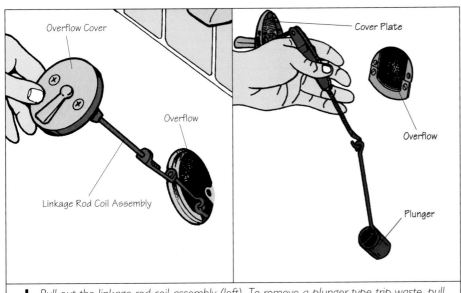

1. *Pull out the linkage rod coil assembly (left). To remove a plunger-type trip-waste, pull the mechanism out through the overflow hole (right).*

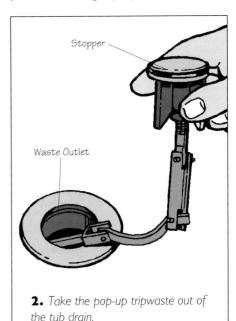

2. *Take the pop-up tripwaste out of the tub drain.*

3. *Separating the old tub from the wall may require gutting a portion of the wall.*

4. *To remove the tub you may have to take up a portion of the floor.*

5. *If you have to remove a tub in one piece, get another person to help you (top). Turn it sideways or on end to move it through doorways and down any stairs. Break up the tub if you have to (bottom). Use a mason's hammer or sledge hammer, and be sure to wear eye and ear protection.*

Step 5. *Remove the Tub.* If the tub is steel, you'll have to remove it in one piece. A standard-size tub (30x60 inches) will fit through doorways, when turned on its side. Larger tubs may require you to remove them through windows or openings in walls (see "Getting a Tub or Shower Inside or Outside the House," at right).

Tubs that can't be removed in one piece, may be broken up into shards if they are made of cast iron, as are many old tubs. First protect yourself with eye goggles, gloves, and ear plugs (and make sure no babies are sleeping nearby). Use a mason's hammer or sledge hammer, applying only as much force as necessary.

Getting a Tub or Shower Inside or Outside the House

When you are planning the space and selecting fixtures, you should also construct a plan for removing your old tub or shower and installing the new unit. If you simply can't get the old unit out without more expense and hassle than you want, you will probably opt to leave it in place. When choosing a new fixture you may want to make sure that you can carry it through the house to the bathroom. But if you have your heart set on a unit that cannot be moved into the bathroom through existing hallways or doors, consider ways to move it through the outer wall. The process can be as easy as removing a first-floor window to as complex as removing an entire wall on the second or third floor.

Using a Window Opening

Can you move the unit through a window? Test the measurements of the tub or shower unit to the net width and height of the window, minus the sash. If clearance is adequate, remove the storm windows from the outside (if any) and the stops that hold the sash units in place. See "Installing a New Sash in an Old Frame," page 93. After moving the bath unit through the opening, replace the pieces in reverse order.

Making an Opening to Fit

If removing the window sash from the frame won't yield a big enough opening, remove the entire window, sash

and frame, as a last resort. You may also have to remove portions of the wall surrounding the window to get the unit inside. See "Enlarging the Rough Opening in a Bearing Wall," page 97.

Installing the New Tub

Step 1. *Position the New Tub.* Place the new tub into position and use a carpenter's level to check that the unit is level in both directions. Shim, as needed, between the base and the floor.

1. *Use a carpenter's level to check the position of the new tub.*

Attach any retaining clips that come with the tub. After any wall and floor finish materials are installed, seal around the tub edges at the walls and floor with silicone caulk.

Step 2. *Connect the Drain Fittings.* Place the large beveled washer between the back of the tub and the overflow pipe. Place the large flat washer between the drainpipe and the bottom of the tub. Position the assembly and tighten the slip nuts to lock it into place. Press plumber's putty around the underside of the crosspiece, then screw it into the tub drain hole and tighten it with pliers handles and a screwdriver. Then screw down the strainer cap.

Step 3. *Adjust the Linkage.* The linkage assembly allows you to open and close the drain with a lever in the tub's wall. Loosen the locknut to turn the threaded rod that adjusts the linkage to the proper length. After adjusting, tighten the locknut and slip the linkage into the overflow hole. Finally, attach the overflow plate.

Step 4. *Attach the New Fittings.* After restoring the wall finish, slide the escutcheons and sleeves onto the protruding faucet stems and screw the handles on (for single-lever controls, follow the manufacturer's instructions). Stick your measuring tape into the wall to measure the distance from the pipe ell to the face of the tile or other finish. To this measurement, add the depth of the spout, from threaded end to wall end. Add another 3/4 inch to get the total length of the nipple you'll need. Get a brass nipple

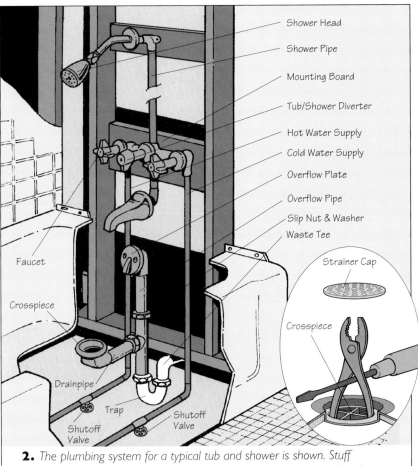

2. *The plumbing system for a typical tub and shower is shown. Stuff plumber's putty around the underside of the crosspiece, then install with pliers and a screwdriver.*

3. *Adjust the linkage length by loosening the locknut and turning the threaded rod. Then slip the linkage into the overflow hole and attach the overflow plate.*

4. *After the faucet stems are attached, slide on the escutcheons and sleeves, then screw on the handles. Follow the manufacturer's instructions for installing single-lever faucets (top). Before screwing on the spout, measure its depth and add 3/4 inch to get the required length of the pipe nipple (bottom).*

from your plumbing supplier and coat the threaded ends with pipe joint compound, then screw it into the wall ell. Finally screw on the spout.

Mounting a Door on a Bathtub

Do you mind being caressed by shower curtains that somehow waft into the cramped compartment when you are showering? Are you tired of the water that always seems to spill out on the floor, even when you think you have closed the curtains tight? If so, it's time to consider replacing the curtain with a more substantial barrier, such as a bifold or sliding door. Keep in mind though, it's easier to dodge a curtain than a door when bathing small children. Here's how to install a simple sliding door kit:

Difficulty Level: 🔨

Tools and Materials

☐ Electric drill with 3/16-inch bit (carbide-tipped, if wall is tiled)
☐ Screwdriver to match type of screws used
☐ Hacksaw and miter box
☐ Door enclosure kit   ☐ Carpenter's level
☐ Masking tape   ☐ Caulking gun
                             ☐ Silicone sealant

Step 1. *Position the Bottom Channel.* Center the bottom channel from the kit along the front edge of the tub. When it is positioned, tape it to the tub with masking tape. Mark the inside edge along the tub with a pencil.

Step 2. *Position the Side Channels.* Hold one of the side channels in place perpendicular to the bottom channel and use a carpenter's level to make it plumb. Mark the screw holes on the wall and repeat for the other side.

1. *Tape the bottom channel to the front edge of the tub and mark its position with a pencil.*

2. *Hold a side channel plumb against the wall then mark it for screw holes. Repeat process for other side.*

3. *Drill screw holes for the side channels using a carbide-tipped bit for tile.*

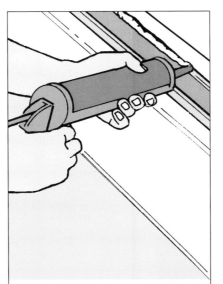

4. *Apply silicone caulk to the outside bottom edge of the bottom channel then position it on the line you drew.*

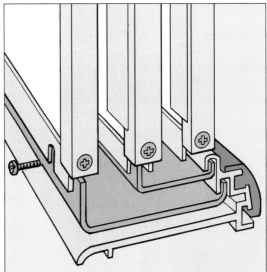

5. *Install the guides in the bottom channel. This shows how the doors fit into one type of channel, although the doors are not yet installed.*

6. *Screw the side channels into place.*

7. *Lay the top channel in place, then test-fit the doors. Adjust the fit if necessary, then apply silcone to the side channels before screwing them to the wall. Install top and door panels.*

Step 3. *Drill the Wall Holes.* Remove all the channels and drill the wall holes with a 3/16-inch bit. Use a carbide-tipped bit for tile.

Step 4. *Install the Bottom Channel.* Apply a bead of silicone sealant to the outside bottom edge of the bottom channel, and press the channel into place on the tub's rim, using the lines you drew as a guide.

Step 5. *Assemble the Door Guides.* When the sealant has set firmly, install the guides into the bottom channel.

Step 6. *Attach the Side Channels.* Put the side channels into place and tighten the screws just enough to hold the channels but loose enough to allow you to adjust their position.

Step 7. *Attach the Top Channel.* Lay the top channel across the side channels. Hang the doors in the rails to test the fit. If the side channels need to be cut, place them in a miter box and cut them with a hacksaw. When everything fits, remove the doors and the top and side channels. Apply silicone to the side channels and then screw them to the wall. Then install the top channel and door panels.

Installing a Whirlpool or Spa

The simplest way to replace a tub with a whirlpool is to select a whirlpool of the same size as the tub. That way, you can reuse much of the supply and drain piping. The problem is, you are probably attracted to a whirlpool for the luxury, and small units don't provide much.

Before settling on a particular model, carefully plan where it will go and how you will get it into position. You can mount whirlpools into various kinds of surrounds built on top of the floor or you can recess them into the floor. Recessing isn't usually possible, though, unless the whirlpool will sit over a crawl space or basement.

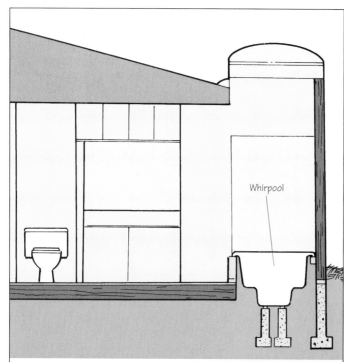

A whirlpool can be installed over an existing crawl space or a new crawl space addition (as shown). Concrete blocks set on concrete footers support this unit.

Recessing also means that you have to build the floor structure to provide adequate support. Although whirlpools are available with one or two finished sides, most are made to be set into a base, at floor level or raised up. You can make the platform as high as you like, but you will have to provide steps for any rim height above about 16 inches, and steps can be hazardous when wet.

If the whirlpool will rest on a wood floor, ask the supplier how much it weighs when full and the best way to support the load. If the unit is taller than your present tub, you will probably have to reinforce the existing joists to support the additional weight (see "Reinforcing the Floor Joints," page 70).

Difficulty Level: ⚚⚚⚚

Tools and Materials

☐ Basic plumbing tools   ☐ Electric drill
☐ Basic carpentry tools   ☐ Crowbar
☐ 3/4-inch plywood (for subfloor)   ☐ 2x4 framing lumber
☐ 1/4-inch x1/2-inch panel edge trim   ☐ Junction box
☐ Bolts and washers   ☐ Sheet metal shims
☐ Waste and drain piping   ☐ 10d galvanized nails
☐ 8d nails or 3-inch drywall-type screws
☐ Water supply piping and accessories
☐ Power cable and wire connectors
☐ Cement board and cement board screws (if needed)
☐ 2 hinges or six 1-inch flathead wood screws with washers
☐ 1/2-inch AC grade plywood (for access panel and support platform)

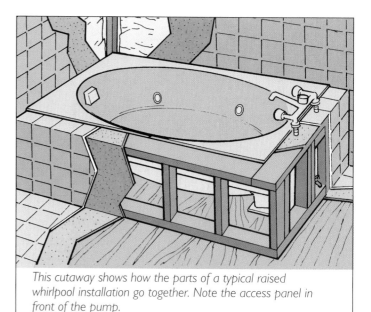

This cutaway shows how the parts of a typical raised whirlpool installation go together. Note the access panel in front of the pump.

Step 1. *Rough In the Plumbing.* If you are retrofitting the whirlpool into an existing bathroom, you will have to remove enough subfloor to allow you to rough in the hot and cold water piping and the drain and vent system. You can use 1/2-inch copper piping for water supply, but will get speedier filling with 3/4-inch pipes. Use ABS or CPVC plastic piping (as required by your local code) for drain and vent piping. If you need to cut joists to run pipes through, cut the holes in the center portion of the joist. Notching the top or bottom of a joist will weaken it.

Step 2. *Install the Subfloor and Support Platform.* Mark the cutouts for the drain and water supply stubs on the subfloor. Cut and drill these holes; then secure the replacement subfloor or new subfloor with 8d nails or screws. Lay a piece of 1/2-inch ply-wood over the floor to serve as a support platform. After cutting

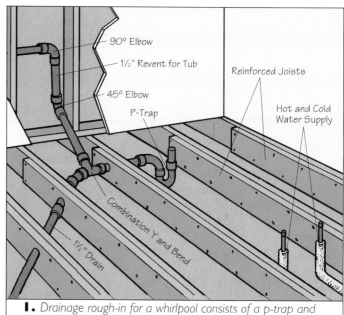

1. *Drainage rough-in for a whirlpool consists of a p-trap and vented drain. Use 1 1/2-inch plastic waste and vent piping. Select 3/4-inch copper water pipes for speedy filling. Insulate the hot water supply line to ensure hot water and save energy.*

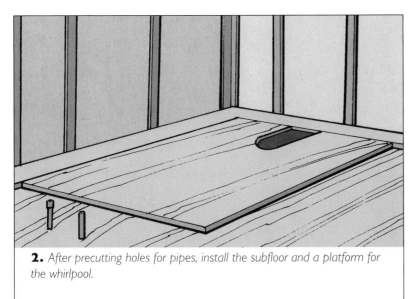

2. *After precutting holes for pipes, install the subfloor and a platform for the whirlpool.*

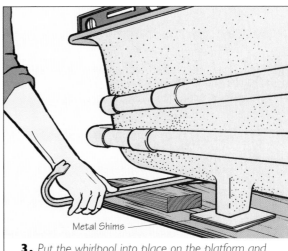

Metal Shims

3. *Put the whirlpool into place on the platform and check to see if it lies level. If adjustment is needed, lever up the unit and insert metal shims where necessary.*

4. *Close the walls around the sides with cement board before finally installing the whirlpool.*

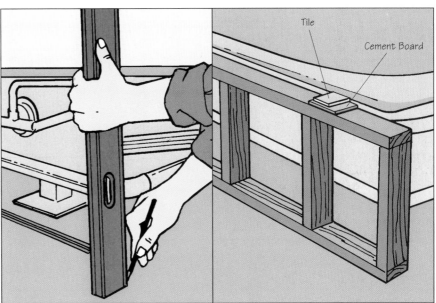

Tile

Cement Board

5. *Mark the outline of the base enclosure on the floor by using a carpenter's level from the top edge (left). Put the enclosure framing into position to test the fit of the cement board and tile finish to the fixture rim. If the enclosure fits, nail it to the floor (right).*

out holes for pipes to pass through, secure the platform piece to the subfloor with 8d nails or screws.

Step 3. *Position the Whirlpool on the Platform.* Lift the whirlpool onto the platform and check that it is level. If necessary, lever up the base with a crowbar set against a piece of 2x4 and insert pieces of sheet metal for shims.

Step 4. *Attach the Wall Substrate.* If you will be tiling the walls around the whirlpool, now is the time to attach the cement board. See "Putting Up Cement Board," page 90.

Step 5. *Build the Base Enclosure.* Frame up the base enclosure with 2x4s. Starting at a corner, draw the outlines of the base enclosure on the subfloor, using a level from the top edge. Then cut the headers (top horizontal pieces) and sills (floor horizontal pieces). Cut enough studs for a 16-inch spacing. Nail the headers

and sills to the studs with the assembly laid flat, then tip it up into place. Put a piece of cement board and a piece of tile on the frame to make sure it fits. If it does, nail the sills to the subfloor

Step 6. *Build an Access Panel.* All whirlpools require a removable panel to provide access to the electrical and mechanical equipment. The instruction sheet provided by the manufacturer will specify the required size and location of this panel. Try to place it, if possible, on a wall behind the whirlpool. To make a simple panel, frame the opening all around with 2x4s, then attach a panel, sized to overlap the rough framing by at least 1 inch. If the surrounding wall is 1/2-inch drywall, trim the edge of the drywall around the opening with metal J-mold (a metal edge trim shaped like a "J"). Make the access panel of 1/2-inch plywood (grade A/C), edged with a solid-trim strip, 1/4x1/2 inch. Attach the panel to the frame with two hinges mounted at the side or

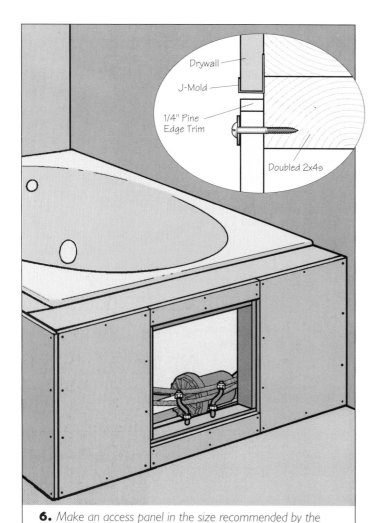

Drywall
J-Mold
1/4" Pine
Edge Trim
Doubled 2x4s

6. *Make an access panel in the size recommended by the manufacturer. Read the instructions to determine the best location for this panel.*

7. *Attach the cement board to the frame with cement board screws. Then drill holes for the water faucet supply lines.*

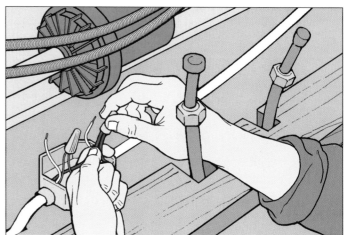

8. *Run wiring to the whirlpool equipment as recommended in the manufacturer's instructions and the electrical codes in your locale.*

9. *Tile is one of the best surfaces for around a whirlpool.*

six 1-inch wood screws with washers. Later, you can paint the panel to match the surrounding wall.

Step 7. *Attach the Plumbing.* Using an ordinary trap, connect the waste outlet to the drain and overflow. Use plastic pipe for the drain and waste lines if your local code allows it. When all piping is installed below the unit, attach cement board to the sides of the enclosure frame with 1½-inch cement board screws. Measure the water supply lines and drill the holes through the cement board. Bring the lines to the faucet, but don't install the faucet until the wall finish has been applied.

Step 8. *Complete the Electrical Wiring.* Install a junction box to connect the house's main service panel to the whirlpool motor. Follow the wiring instructions supplied with the whirlpool, but ground the installation to conform to your local building code. If you are not confident working with electricity, hire an electrician for this part of the work.

Step 9. *Finish the Base Enclosure.* Tile or solid-surface plastic make terrific finishes for the surfaces around a whirlpool. You can even apply wood if you seal it adequately. If you want to tile the base, do it when you do the walls, as described in Chapter 14.

Replacing a Shower Head

Today's shower heads conserve water, which is good, but the resulting flow doesn't feel anywhere near as luxurious as the older wasteful ones. Having a choice of spray patterns helps make up for the lack of water volume, and changing over from a water-hogging to water-conserving shower head is one of the simplest bathroom plumbing chores you can do.

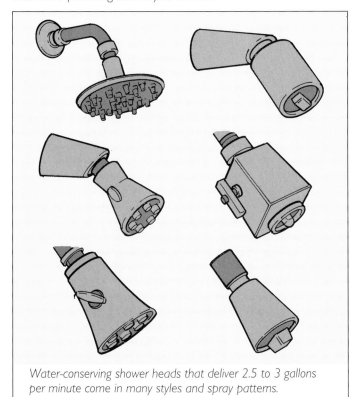

Water-conserving shower heads that deliver 2.5 to 3 gallons per minute come in many styles and spray patterns.

Difficulty Level: 🔧

Tools and Materials

☐ Duct tape (if needed)　　　☐ Adjustable wrench
☐ Adjustable pliers　　　　　☐ New shower head
☐ New shower arm (if needed)
☐ Pipe joint compound or Teflon tape unit

Step 1. *Remove the Old Shower Head.* Grasp the rear of the shower head with an adjustable wrench or adjustable pliers and loosen it by turning the wrench counterclockwise. Don't use too much force; you may twist the shower arm itself and have to replace it. If the head assembly won't budge with mild pressure, wrap duct tape around the shower arm close by and use adjustable pliers (or a pipe wrench) to restrain the arm while you apply more pressure to the head. As a last resort, you can remove the arm and the head and replace both.

Step 2. *Install the New Shower Head.* Make sure that the O-ring that comes with the new shower head is in place, then screw the shower head onto the shower arm by hand until you can no longer turn it. Give it another half turn with adjustable pliers. Turn on the water to check for leakage. Tighten it little by little until there is no leak. If you must replace the shower arm as well, apply

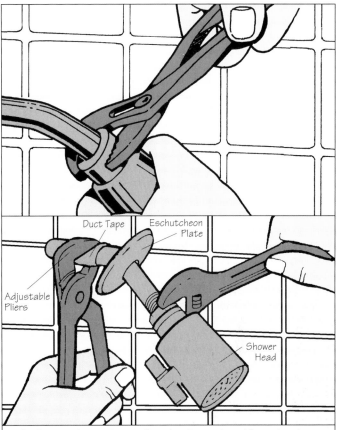

1. *Loosen the retainer to free the shower head from the shower arm (top). If needed, restrain the shower arm with adjustable pliers while you unscrew the shower head retainer. Tape the arm first to prevent scratches (right).*

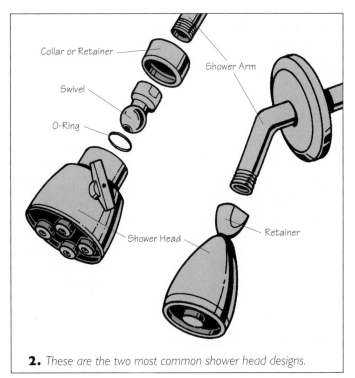

2. *These are the two most common shower head designs.*

pipe joint compound or Teflon tape to the threaded end, wrap the wall end with duct tape to protect it, and screw it into the wall tee with adjustable pliers.

Putting in an Anti-scald Shower Control

Have you ever been jolted out of a peaceful shower by a sudden rush of scalding hot or icy water? This can happen when some- one turns on a tap or flushes a toilet elsewhere in the house, causing the pressure in the hot or cold water line to drop. Stan- dard shower fittings do nothing to control sudden changes in water temperature, but anti-scald valves do. Also called pressure- balancing valves, these single-control fittings contain a piston that automatically responds to changes in line water pressure to main- tain the same temperature, blocking abrupt drops or rises in tem- perature. This is such a good idea that some codes now require anti-scald valves in all new construction.

Installing an anti-scald valve rates a difficulty level of three ham- mers, because it requires tearing into the wall, separating the water supply lines, removing the existing control valves, and sol- dering on the new anti-scald valves to the supply piping. The steps here apply to copper water piping (see "Working with Copper Tubing," page 124.) If you must rework steel piping, refer to more detailed books on plumbing or hire a plumber.

Difficulty Level:

Tools and Materials

- ☐ Basic plumbing tools
- ☐ Anti-scald valve
- ☐ Copper tubing (if needed)
- ☐ Pipe nipples and couplings
- ☐ Dropcloth or other protection for tub
- ☐ Basic carpentry tools
- ☐ Bucket
- ☐ Pry bar

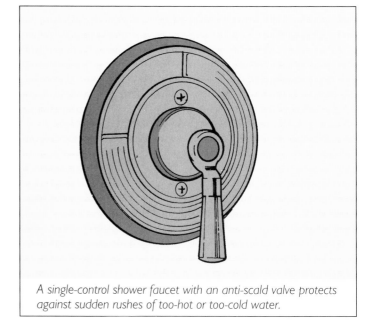

A single-control shower faucet with an anti-scald valve protects against sudden rushes of too-hot or too-cold water.

Step 1. *Shut Off the Water and Open the Faucets.* Shut off the water supply at the nearest valve below the faucets (usually in the basement). Open the bleed valves (be sure to put a bucket underneath), then open the faucets to drain any entrapped water.

Step 2. *Tear Off the Wall Finish.* Protect the tub or shower floor with a dropcloth, then use your carpentry tools to remove the wall surface that is covering the pipes (see "Gutting a Wall or Ceiling," page 81).

Step 3. *Remove the Old Shower Valve.* Separate all the piping from the old valve assembly and remove it. If possible, use a torch to melt the solder joints, holding a piece of sheet metal behind the pipe to protect the wall. As you heat each joint, the solder

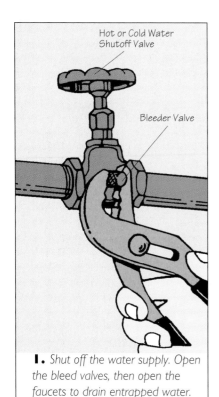

1. *Shut off the water supply. Open the bleed valves, then open the faucets to drain entrapped water.*

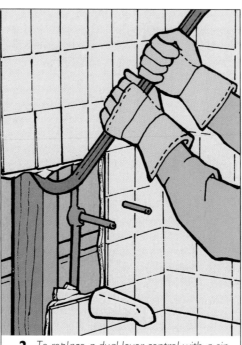

2. *To replace a dual-lever control with a sin- gle-lever control, you need to remove part of the wall finish to get to the existing crossover.*

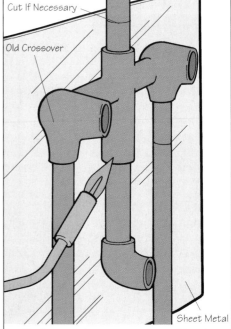

3. *Remove the crossover by melting the solder in the joints, if possible. If not, cut the pipes and install new ones.*

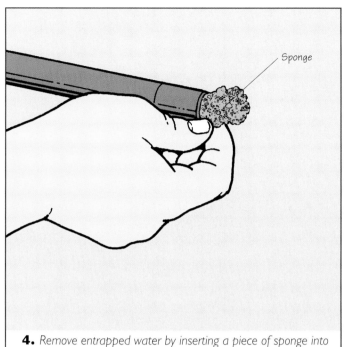

4. *Remove entrapped water by inserting a piece of sponge into the ends of the pipes to absorb as much water as possible.*

will melt. Wearing gloves, pull the pipe out of the joint. If you can't separate the piping from the valve by melting the solder, cut the pipes with a hacksaw or tube cutter about 2 inches back from the joints.

Step 4. *Get Rid of Any Trapped Moisture.* Before you solder in any new items, make sure the pipes are dry. Entrapped water turns to steam and prevents the formation of a watertight connection. One way to dry out the pipes is to stick a sponge into their ends to absorb as much water as possible, then heat the ends of the pipes by moving a torch over them to vaporize drops of water (after removing the sponge).

Step 5. *Install the Pipe Extensions.* If you had to cut pipes to remove the old valve, you will need to add extensions onto the cut ends to restore the pipes to the original length. Cut pieces of copper tubing in the necessary lengths and connect them to the pipe ends with copper sleeves soldered on

Step 6. *Install the New Valve.* Place the new valve into position with the pipe ends inserted into the sockets and solder each joint. When the solder hardens, wipe the joint with a cold wet cloth to cool the pipe. Turn the main water supply valve back on and check each joint for leakage. If a joint is leaking, turn the water supply off again, open the shower valve to drain the water, and add additional solder to the leaking joint. Recheck for leakage. If you are not successful this time, disconnect all the leaking components and start over.

5. *Join pieces of piping to the new valve and use couplings to make an arrangement similar to the one shown.*

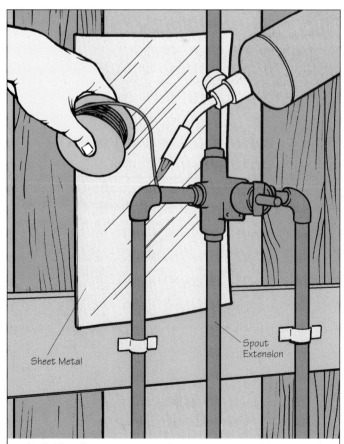

6. *Solder all copper joints in place; use a piece of sheet metal to protect wood against igniting.*

Installing a Hand-Held Shower

Standard shower heads fixed at 72 inches or so above the floor don't always get the water where it's needed and are inconvenient for people who can't stand while showering. A shower head mounted on a flexible hose allows the user to direct the spray to any part of the body. The trade-off is that it keeps one hand occupied. If you want to replace a fixed shower with a hand-held shower you have two options:

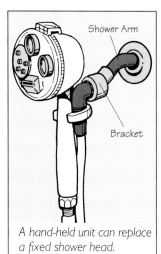

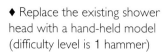

A hand-held unit can replace a fixed shower head.

♦ Replace the existing shower head with a hand-held model (difficulty level is 1 hammer)

♦ Replace the tub spout with a special spout containing a diverter, to which the hand-held shower attaches—if your tub does not already have a shower (difficulty level is 2 hammers)

Here are the pros and cons and installation instructions for each option:

Replace the Existing Shower Head with a Hand-Held Model

The simplest way to install a hand-held shower is to replace the existing shower head. But because the new shower head mounts into a bracket built into the shower arm, it will be out of reach to a person who must sit while showering. To install this type of hand-held shower, follow the same steps under "Replacing a Shower Head," on page 135.

Replace the Tub Spout with Special Spout Containing a Diverter

Although a bit more involved than the first method, replacing the existing tub spout with one containing a special diverter puts the

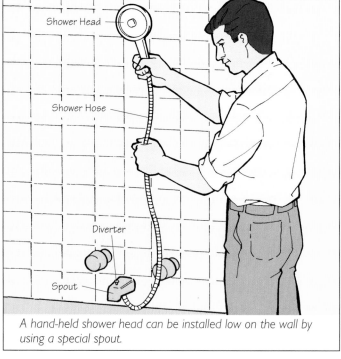

A hand-held shower head can be installed low on the wall by using a special spout.

hand-held shower low enough to be usable while sitting in the tub or on a tub seat.

Difficulty Level:

Tools and Materials

☐ Pipe wrench or adjustable pliers   ☐ Mallet
☐ Drill with carbide-tipped bit   ☐ Expansion anchors
☐ Allen wrench (if existing spout has an Allen set screw)
☐ Hand-held shower kit (the kind that includes the spout)

Step 1. *Remove the Existing Spout.* If the present spout has an Allen set screw on the underside, remove it with an Allen wrench and pull the spout off the pipe. If there is no screw, unscrew it with a pipe wrench (alternatively, you can try inserting something into the spout hole to use as a lever to turn the spout loose).

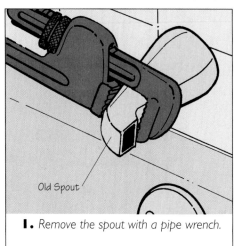

1. *Remove the spout with a pipe wrench.*

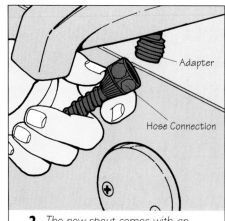

2. *The new spout comes with an adapter that directs water to either the shower head or the tub.*

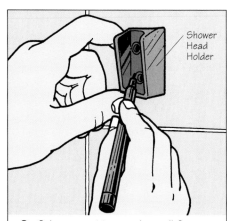

3. *Select a position on the wall for mounting the shower head and position the bracket to mark the screw holes.*

Step 2. *Connect the New Spout.* Screw on the new spout, then attach the shower hose.

Step 3. *Install the Holding Bracket.* Mark the wall where you want to mount the bracket that holds the shower head. For tile, drill holes with a carbide-tipped bit and insert expansion anchors. Then screw on the bracket.

Building a Separate Shower

If you have the space and budget for a separate shower, you can build the stall in several ways. In Chapter 2, we looked at the range of options, from prefabricated one-piece stall units to completely customized stalls with floors and walls built on site.

The instructions that come with prefab shower units will guide your installation work. The following section offers some useful advice to augment the manufacturer's instructions.

Shower Plumbing Basics

Replacing an existing shower won't require you to remodel the basic piping, but installing a new one will mean baring the floor and wall that contain the water supply and drainage pipes.

Hot and cold water lines can be run through the floor, ceiling, or walls to reach the shower valve. The valve should be mounted about 48 inches above the floor. Use 1/2-inch rigid copper tubing if you can make straight runs and 1/2-inch flexible tubing if you have to snake the supply piping around difficult curves. The pipe leading from the shower drain to the soil waste stack can be 2-inch-diameter ABS plastic pipe, joined at ells and tees, as needed, with solvent cement (see "Cutting and Joining Plastic Pipe," on page 115. Building codes usually require the floor drain to be at least 12 inches away from a wall. Just below the drain, there should be a p-trap, then a drain into the main stack that slopes

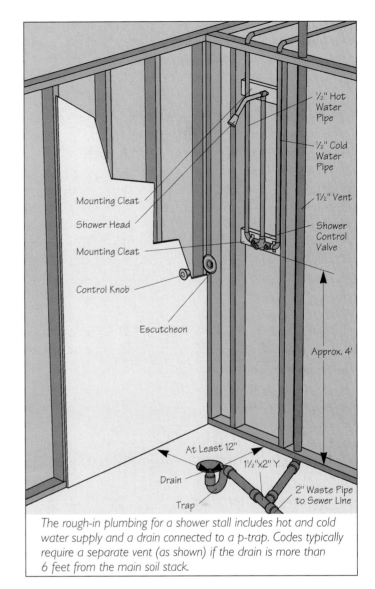

The rough-in plumbing for a shower stall includes hot and cold water supply and a drain connected to a p-trap. Codes typically require a separate vent (as shown) if the drain is more than 6 feet from the main soil stack.

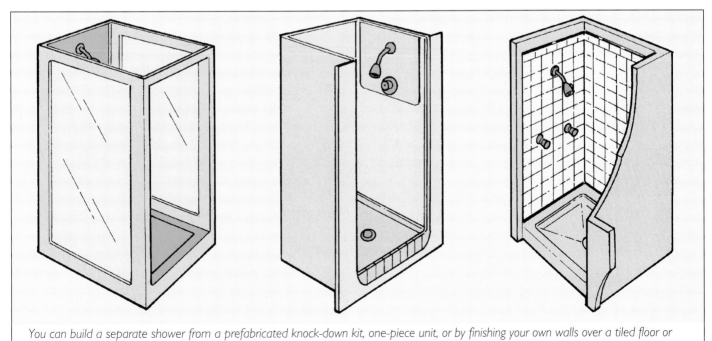

You can build a separate shower from a prefabricated knock-down kit, one-piece unit, or by finishing your own walls over a tiled floor or prefab shower base (right).

at least 1/4 inch per foot. If you are using 1½-inch-diameter vent pipe, it should be within 42 inches of the p-trap. For 2-inch diameter pipe the maximum distance is 60 inches. The vent must rise vertically until it reaches the overflow level of the fixture it serves, then it can run horizontally and/or vertically up through the roof. Because the vent can be a smaller diameter than the drain line, the connecting tee or wye needs to have a reduced opening on the vent side. After installing the drain, seal the joint between the overlapping lip and shower floor with plumber's putty.

Putting in a Prefabricated Shower Stall

Here are the general steps for installing a one-piece or knock-down prefabricated shower stall. When considering a one-piece unit, make sure you can get it through existing doorways or an outside window or be prepared to knock down part of the exterior wall (see "Getting a Tub or Shower Inside or Outside the House," on page 128).

Difficulty Level: ⫠ ⫠ *(if existing plumbing can be used)* **or** ⫠ ⫠ ⫠

Tools and Materials

If existing plumbing can be used:

☐ Electric drill   ☐ Caulking gun
☐ Plumber's putty   ☐ Shower stall kit
☐ Adhesive (for enclosure)   ☐ 2x4s
☐ Shims   ☐ Bricks
☐ Silicone sealant
☐ Saber saw (if hole needs to be cut in side panel)

If plumbing needs to be reworked, add the following:

☐ Basic plumbing tools   ☐ Basic carpentry tools

Prefab shower stalls come with their own watertight walls, so you won't need a special wall substrate such as cement board. You will need to check for any leaks in the plumbing before putting up wall panels or finishing the floor, though. Correcting them afterward will be difficult.

Step 1. *Cut a Hole for the Control.* If the side panel doesn't come with a hole, drill a pilot hole and cut a hole large enough for the control valve with a saber saw equipped with a fine-toothed blade.

Step 2. *Check the Match between the Existing Drain Hole and the Base.* Attach the drain to the base of the unit, then place the base into position to make sure the drain hole coincides with the floor drain nipple.

Step 3. *Assemble the Side Panels.* Remove the base off the drain and put it in the center of the room (to allow you to get to all sides of the unit). Use the clips and screws that come with the kit to join the wall panels to each other and to the base. Do not drill too deeply, and be careful not to penetrate a surface that should not be drilled.

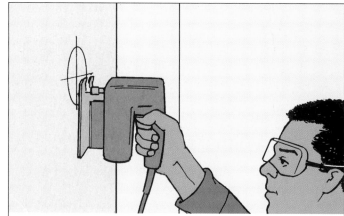

1. *If no hole is provided, cut a hole in the fiberglass panel for the shower control valve.*

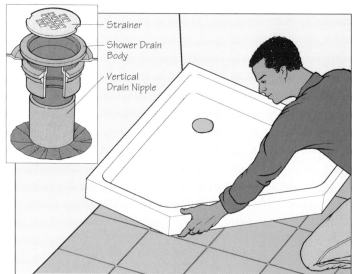

— Strainer
— Shower Drain Body
— Vertical Drain Nipple

2. *Place the shower base into position to mark the center of the drain hole on the floor. Make sure the drain hole lines up with the floor drain nipple.*

3. *Follow the manufacturer's instructions to assemble the sides to the base.*

4. *Test fit the enclosure, making sure it sits level.*

5. *Use the adhesive that is recommended by the manufacturer.*

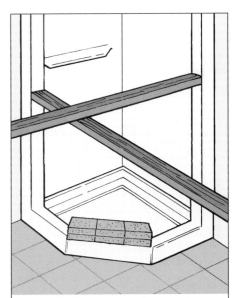

6. *Brace the walls with 2x4s until the adhesive sets.*

7. *Here are two types of glass shower stall doors. At left is a door pivoted off the floor and head brace. The sliding door at right suits wider showers. Follow the instructions provided with your shower kit to install the type of door you have.*

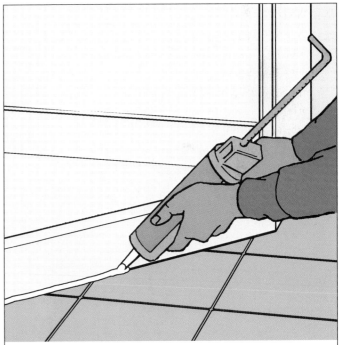

8. *Seal the joints between the bathroom walls and floor and the shower enclosure with silicone.*

Step 4. *Put the Unit into Position.* Place the assembled unit into position and check it for level. Insert shims where needed to adjust the unit. Remove the unit.

Step 5. *Secure the Unit to the Structure.* Spread adhesive (as recommended by the manufacturer) on the floor and wall substrates, then put the unit into place, making sure the drain goes squarely over the opening.

Step 6. *Brace the Side Panels and Base.* Hold the floor and wall panels tight to the substrates, while the adhesive sets, by

weighing the base down with bricks and propping 2x4s up against the walls.

Step 7. *Install the Door.* If the unit comes with a door (instead of a rod for a curtain) follow the instructions to put the door parts together.

Step 8. *Caulk the Joints.* Seal around the door jambs and base with silicone sealant.

12 Remodeling Bathroom Electrical Systems

Bringing your bathroom's electrical system up to current standards when you remodel will make your bathroom safer and more convenient. What should you look for? First, consider safety. Standard electrical outlets should be protected by ground-fault circuit interrupter (GFCI) devices to reduce the hazards of shock present in wet areas. Next consider convenience. You may need additional circuits to power special equipment, such as a whirlpool. If you add a fan to exhaust moisture and odors, you will need both a power source and a switch. New or reworked lighting may require extending the wiring.

Rewiring can be done without tearing off wall and ceiling finishes, but not as easily as when the framing is exposed. Walls stripped to the studs give you an excellent opportunity to replace outdated wiring, outlets, and switches as well as to make any adjustments for your new scheme.

Working with the electrical wiring in a part of your house isn't overly difficult if you take the time and effort to understand what's required and to plan the work. But it is extremely unforgiving. A false connection means all or part of a circuit won't work. More important, if you get caught between a live circuit and a grounding source, your body will take the brunt of the energy passing through the circuit, resulting in injury or death.

Realizing the inherent danger, many homeowners shy away from working with electrical systems. If you are uncomfortable around electricity or are not willing to understand the steps required to do a safe installation, hire a licensed electrician.

Codes, Permits, and Inspections

Your municipality probably requires any new electrical work in your home to conform to the National Electrical Code. Don't rush out to buy a copy, though. Most of the requirements are too dense to be understood by nonspecialists. You'll do better to purchase one of the simplified guidebooks available at most bookstores and home centers.

A permit may also be required to install new electrical work, so after you have an idea of the project's scope, pay a visit to the local building inspection department and ask about the code requirements, how to obtain a permit (if required), and what will be required in the way of inspections.

When you obtain a permit, you can expect at least two inspections: one after rough-in wiring has been completed but before walls and ceilings are closed in and one after completion of the job.

Basic Electrical Tools

Here is a list of basic tools that you will need to do the projects in this book.

☐ Electric drill and bits (3/4 inch for cable holes)

☐ Multipurpose wire-cutting pliers   ☐ Wire stripper

☐ Cable ripper   ☐ Lineman's pliers

☐ Needle-nose pliers   ☐ Standard screwdriver

☐ Phillips screwdriver   ☐ Voltage tester

☐ Fish tape   ☐ Hammer

☐ Utility knife   ☐ Keyhole saw

☐ Accessories   ☐ Electrical tape

☐ Plastic wire caps   ☐ Cable staples

Getting a Power Source

If your house is older than about 50 years, its electrical system is very likely outdated. Chances are that successive owners added bits and pieces over the years in no coherent fashion. Knowing this, you can choose to rewire the whole house or do it as you remodel various rooms. If you go room by room, at least make sure that the main electrical service is up-to-date and capable of carrying additional loads.

The main service consists of wires that come into the house from the outside and a main distribution center inside. If the system is up to current standards, the main service cable will contain three wires—two "hot," or "live," wires that carry 120 volts of electricity and one neutral wire. The cable is probably wrapped until it reaches the inside of the distribution center, or panel box. When you open the panel box, you can see that the cable seprates into the three wires. The two hot wires feed a main breaker switch that shuts down power to the entire house, then goes on to supply power to branch circuits, each with its own cicuit breaker.

A short across any hot wire and a neutral or ground wire causes a sudden current overload. Unchecked, the overload would quickly burn off the wire's insulation and ignite any nearby combustible material. Circuit breakers or fuses protect against overloads by breaking the connection between the incoming electricity and the fault. Very old houses may be protected by a single fuse. When it blows, all power to the house shuts off. Even if your house has several fuses, consider replacing the fuse box with an updated panel and circuit breakers. It's much more convenient to flip the reset switch on a breaker than to replace a fuse.

Another item to consider for replacement is aluminum wiring. Aluminum may be used in the main service wires, but its use in branch circuits has been linked to an inordinate percentage of electrical fires, so if you spot it coming out of the panel, consider replacing it with copper. The National Electrical Code does not permit you to add new aluminum wiring.

Your bathroom lights and power outlets may be wired to a single circuit, protected by a 15- or 20-amp breaker in the panel. If you rewire or change around a few lighting fixtures or power outlets, you won't need to change the power source. If you add new devices, you may stand to overload the circuit, so get the advice of an electrician before proceeding.

Assuming the wiring is sound and you want to leave the wall finishes intact, you can replace a light fixture, switch, or outlet in the same location by simply removing the device and installing the new one. If you want to add an outlet or light, you can tap into the box of a previous fixture or come off of a box containing an outlet. If you tap off an outlet box, you should replace the box with a larger one to contain the additional wiring.

New Wiring in Open Walls

Gutting floors, walls, or ceilings down to the framing gives you the opportunity to replace outdated wiring and to locate electrical fixtures just where you want them. The easiest kind of wiring to snake through the structure is plastic-sheathed, nonmetallic cable, called NM cable or sometimes by the brand name Romex. NM cable contains a black-sheathed (hot) wire, a white (neutral) wire, and a bare (ground) wire. Check with your electrical inspector to see which type and gauge of cable is acceptable for your project and by your local codes. As a rule of thumb, you will probably get by with 14-gauge cable for bathroom lights and outlets. Special equipment such as whirlpools, heaters, and appliances will require 12-gauge or larger (use the product literature as a guide).

Difficulty Level: 🔨

Tools and Materials

☐ Electric drill with 3/4-inch bit	☐ Saw
☐ Cable staples	☐ 5d common nails
☐ Junction boxes, switch boxes	☐ Cable
☐ Metal stud plates (if needed)	☐ Hammer

Suiting the Box to the Task

Each switch, outlet, and light fixture must be installed into a metal or plastic box attached to the structure. Ask your building department which type of box is acceptable. Round or octagonal boxes are usually used for ceiling fixtures or junction boxes (boxes used to contain only wiring). Rectangular boxes usually contain switches or receptacles. You can choose among boxes that come with various types of fasteners, screws, nails, brackets, and clips suited for different conditions of new and existing construction.

The National Electrical Code limits how many wires you can install in any one box and does not permit any wire connections outside a box. A single-switch or duplex (two-plug) outlet will fit into a 2½-inch wide box. More than one device in a box, or more wiring than needed just to serve the device, calls for a wider box. Use the chart below to determine the required box size.

Maximum Number of Wires Permitted Per Box

Type of Box (Size in Inches)	Wire Gauge 14	12	10
Round or Octagonal			
4x1½	7	6	6
4x2⅛	10	9	8
Square			
4x1½	10	9	8
4x2⅛	15	13	12
Rectangular Boxes			
3x2x2¼	5	4	4
3x2x2½	6	5	5
3x2x2¾	7	6	5
3x2x3½	9	8	7

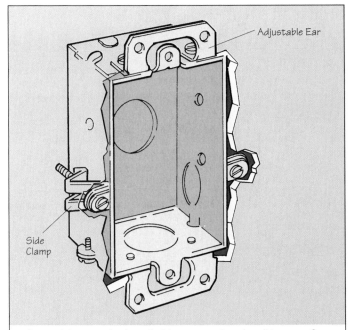

A metal box can be installed into an enclosed wall in one of two ways. First, a hole must be cut through the plaster or drywall and the box inserted. Then it can be secured by screws through the adjustable ears into the lath or by tightening screws at the sides.

Adjustable Ear

Side Clamp

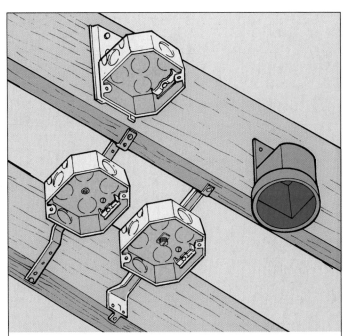

Ceiling boxes intended for fixtures and junction boxes are usually round or octagonal. Mounting methods include side clips (as with the metal and plastic boxes at the top), or offset hanger bars that can be adjusted to span between two joists (below).

Step 1. *Install Boxes.* Before reworking any branch circuit, shut off the power to the circuit at the panel or fuse box. Begin your wiring by figuring out where you want the boxes to go and nailing them to the studs (plastic boxes come with their own nails; use 5d nails for the flanges of metal boxes). Mount them so that the face of the box will be even with the finished wall surface. Switch boxes are usually mounted 48 inches above the floor, while outlets are mounted 12 to 18 inches above the floor. Mount boxes at any convenient height above a counter.

Step 2. *Drill Holes through the Studs.* Drill holes for the cable through the studs at least 1¼ inches back from the facing edge so they won't be punctured by nails or screws. If you can't drill, saw out notches of the same depth.

Step 3. *Run the Cable through the Holes.* Starting from your power source (junction box) run the cable from outlet box to outlet box and run branches to the light fixture boxes. Leave 6 inches or so of cable ends poking out the of the box to give

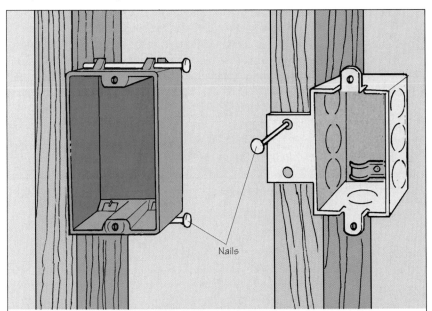

Nails

1. *Boxes for switches and receptacles are made of plastic or galvanized steel, with various attachment options. Two 16d nails are driven through the side tabs of the plastic box (left) into the stud. These boxes come with nails inserted in them. The metal box (right) is nailed through a tab to the face of the stud.*

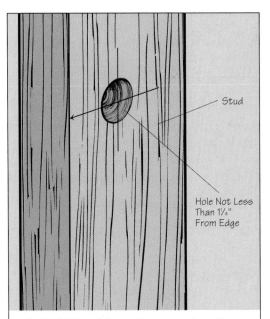

Stud

Hole Not Less Than 1¼" From Edge

2. *Drill 3/4-inch holes (or saw notches, if necessary) at least 1¼ inches back from the stud face.*

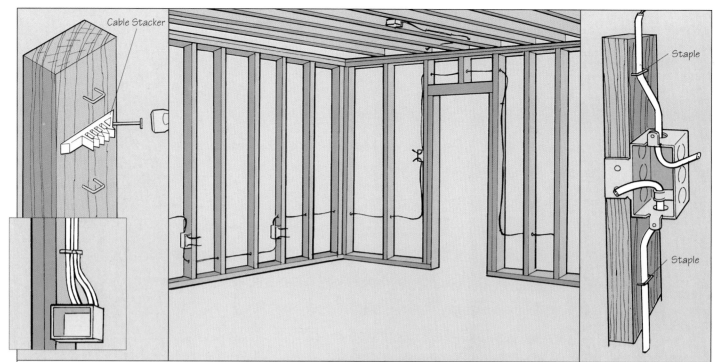

3. *Plastic sheathed cable can be attached to studs by metal cable staples or a more recent development, cable stackers. Made of plastic, stackers allow you to install the fastener first (with a nail) and then push the cable into the holding channels. The one shown is made to hold four cables (left). Run cables through the framing in a straight line, if possible, and secure the cable to the framing with a staple every 48 inches and within 8 inches of a box (right). Attach boxes to studs so that the face of the box is in line with the proposed wall finish (boxes such as the one shown have tabs set back 1/2 inch). Staple the cable to the stud at each side of the box (right).*

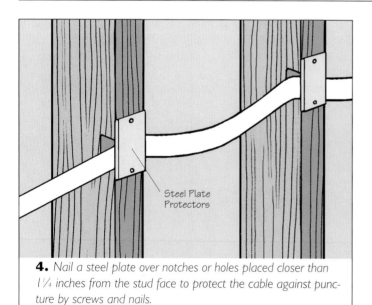

4. *Nail a steel plate over notches or holes placed closer than 1¼ inches from the stud face to protect the cable against puncture by screws and nails.*

you enough wire to connect the devices later. Where cable runs up studs, and just above or below each box, use a hammer to attach cable staples or clips to the studs (use staples made for attaching electrical cable).

Step 4. *Add Plates over the Holes or Notches in the Studs.* Code requires that the cable be protected from punctures, that's why the holes must be 1¼ inches back from the face of the stud. If any cable ends up closer to the stud face, attach a metal plate over the stud at this location. You can get plates made for this purpose at your electrical supplier.

Fishing Wiring through Enclosed Floors and Walls

Snaking new wiring through floors, walls, and ceilings while leaving the surface finishes intact can be somewhat difficult, but it's possible to do. You'll still need to remove the wall finish at key spots. Fish tape is needed for this job. Flexible metallic wire wound in spools, fish tape bends over the end of electrical cable while you fish the other end through enclosed walls and floors. The cable and wire emerge some distance away through a hole that you have opened up in the wall. Then you simply pull the cable through. Make sure to turn off the power at the panel board before beginning. Here's how to run new wiring from a source in the basement to an upstairs bathroom.

Difficulty Level: 🔨 🔨 🔨

Tools and Materials

☐ Electric drill with 3/4-inch bit   ☐ Fish tape
☐ Electrical tape   ☐ Keyhole saw
☐ Electrical boxes   ☐ Metal plates for studs
☐ Electrical cable

Step 1. *Drive a Pilot Nail and Drill a Hole.* If the first box you want to wire is on the first floor, begin by cutting a hole in the wall to fit the box. If you are bringing the wire to the second floor, start by making an access hole in the first-floor wall. Make the access hole near the floor and directly below where the

1. *Drive a pilot nail through the floor below the new box, and use it to help you find the wall from below.*

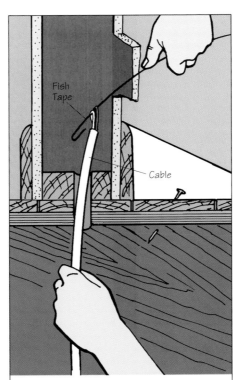

2. *Make a hook in the end of the cable and feed it through the hole while a helper tries to catch the cable with fish tape, fed into the wall from above.*

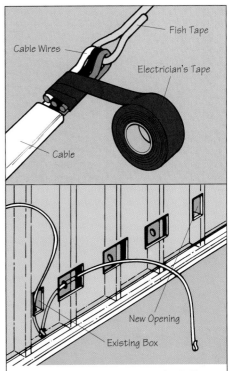

3. *Attach cable to fish tape (top). To route cable across a wall, cut an opening at each stud, drill holes and fish cable through (bottom).*

receptacle will be. Drive a long nail through the floor close to the wall and directly below the first floor receptacle or access hole. From the basement, drill a 3/4-inch-diameter hole up through the ceiling into the wall above, using the pilot nail as your guide.

Step 2. *Insert the Fish Tape.* Take the roll of cable to the basement and bend the ends of the wires over to make a "U" shape. Feed the cable up through the hole in the floor. Have a helper stand upstairs and feed fish tape into the wall through the hole you drilled. Working together, move the cable and tape end around until they hook together, then have your helper pull on the tape to draw the cable up through the wall and out the opening.

Step 3. *Pull the Cable Horizontally.* If you want to run the cable to another point on the wall, try to make the horizontal run in the open basement ceiling. If you can't run cable horizontally below the bathroom floor (as when wiring a second-story bathroom), you can run it through the bathroom's walls by first cutting out access holes along the run, then pulling the cable and fish tape through, from one hole to the next. Begin by taping the cable end to the fish tape to prevent them from coming apart.

Step 4. *Pull the Cable Vertically.* To pull the cable from somewhere inside the wall up to the ceiling, first remove part of the corner above the wall hole, where the wall meets the ceiling. Cut a notch in the framing to make a space for the cable to run. Then thread fish tape from the ceiling opening to the wall/ceiling joint opening then down the wall. Then attach the cable to the tape and pull it back up through the structure and out the ceiling opening. Nail a metal protective plate over the cable in the corner notch before patching the opening. The procedure is similar if you are running cable to a second floor receptacle. Use the notch

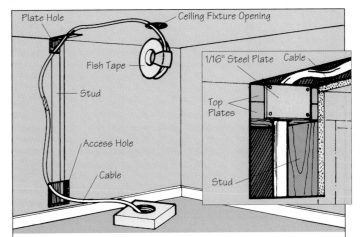

4. *Cut holes in the wall-to-ceiling joint and feed fish tape from the ceiling box to the opening and through the wall below. Use the tape to snag the cable, then pull the cable up through. To pull cable through the ceiling as shown here, the joists have to be parallel to the direction of the cable. If they run the other direction cut holes at each joist. Attach metal protection plates over the cable at the wall/ceiling joint before patching the wall.*

to get into the second-floor wall, then use the cable to snag the tape through the receptacle hole upstairs. Allow at least 6 inches of cable protruding out of the box.

Step 5. *Install the Boxes.* Insert the cable into a box and place the box into the hole in the wall and secure it. How you attach the boxes to the studs depends on the finish of the walls and how much wall you want to remove. If you want to remove a portion of the wall to expose the stud face, you can nail the box

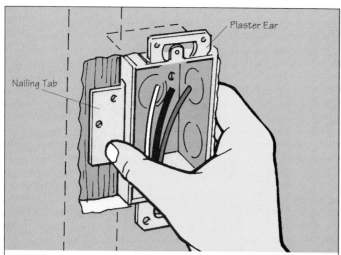

5. *Attach a box inside a finished wall by either screwing the plaster ears to the lath, tightening the side clamps against the backside of the wall material, or cutting away the plaster or drywall at the stud and nailing through the tab into the stud face.*

directly to the stud. You can connect a box to a plaster wall by either screwing through the plaster ears into the lath; by using a retrofit box and tightening the compression connectors to the backside of the lath; or by cutting away the plaster or drywall at the stud and nailing through the tab into the stud face.

Running New Circuits from the Panel

Fixtures such as whirlpools and spas often call for a separate circuit to power a pump and/or heater. Get the power requirements for any special equipment from the manufacturer's instructions. To get an additional circuit you will need to tap into the main panel. If the equipment must be connected to a dedicated circuit, follow the general steps below.

Working on a panel is dangerous, so take all safety measures. If your installation is special in any way or if you are not confident of completing the hookup correctly, have a licensed electrician do the work at the panel after you have done the room wiring. If you do work on your panel, it's a two-hand job so you'll need a helper or some kind of stand to hold your flashlight while you work with the house power off.

Begin by determining how many new circuits you need and the voltage each must carry. A 120-volt circuit usually requires a single breaker of 15- or 20-amp capacity. A 220-volt circuit is wired to a special type of breaker.

Difficulty Level: ☂ ☂ ☂

Tools and Materials

- ☐ Basic electrical tools
- ☐ Flashlight
- ☐ Cable (of type required by the manufacturer and code)
- ☐ 1 or more circuit breakers (of the required amperage and of the same make as your panel)

Step 1. *Run the Wiring to the Panel.* Do the rough wiring of the bathroom first (as described earlier in this chapter) and extend the cables to the panel box.

Step 2. *Shut off the Main Breaker.* Using your flashlight to see, turn off the power to the house with the main breaker switch, which is mounted at the top of the service panel.

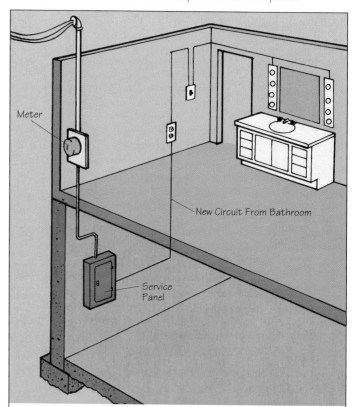

1. *Run the power supply for a new bathroom circuit from the last device (such as an outlet or fixture) or a junction box to the panel along the shortest path. If possible, use the spaces between the exposed joists in the basement to make horizontal runs.*

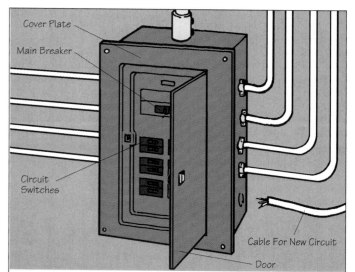

2. *Open the door on the panel box, turn the main breaker to the off position, then unscrew the screws at the corners to remove the cover plate.*

Step 3. *Remove Cover Plate and Note the Breaker Arrangement.* With the house power shut off, remove the panel's cover plate and note the breaker arrangement. Each breaker in use is connected to a circuit cable. A label on the cover plate should identify each circuit. Check to see if there are any breakers not in use (spares) or if there are spare slots for additional breakers. If there are no spare breakers but there are empty slots for breakers, you can add a new circuit. If all slots are in use, you may be able to add a double breaker, which is a device that puts two breakers in the space of one. Or you may have to add a subpanel.

In any case, if you don't see a spare breaker or slot, it's a good idea to get an electrician's advice.

Step 4. *Bring the Cable into the Panel.* Here's how to connect a 120-volt circuit cable to a spare (or new) breaker. Use a screwdriver to pry out a perforated knockout from the side or top of the panel box. Attach a cable clamp and thread 12 or more inches of the cable through the connector, the hole in the box and a locknut. Tighten the two screws against the cable with a screwdriver. Tighten the locknut with a screwdriver. Remove about 8 inches of the outer sleeve of the end of the cable and strip the wire ends.

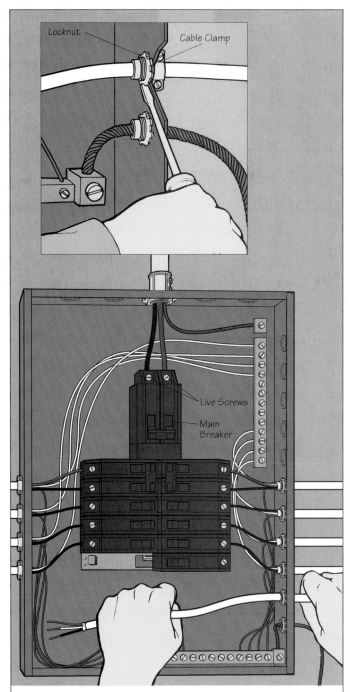

3. *With the main breaker shut off, remove the cover plate and note the breaker arrangement. Check to see if there are any breakers not in use (spares) or if there are spare slots for additional breakers.*

4.*Pry out a perforated knockout from the side or top of the panel box with a screwdriver. Then thread the cable through a cable connector, into the box and then through a locknut. Tighten the cable connector screws and the locknut with a screwdriver.*

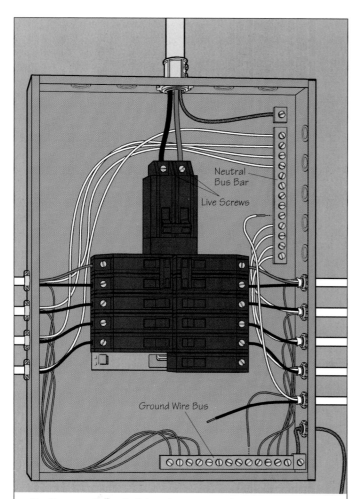

5. *Connect the end of the white wire to the neutral bus bar (where the other white wires are connected). Then connect the ground wire to the ground wire bus, usually near the bottom of the box.*

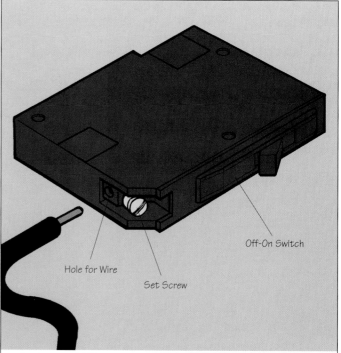

6. *A typical 120-volt circuit breaker comes with a clip in the rear that plugs into the hot bus of the panel and a hole in the side for inserting the black wire of the cable.*

Step 5. *Connect the Neutral and Ground Wires.* Insert the ends of the white (neutral) wire and the bare ground wire into holes along the bus bars intended for these wires at the side or bottom of the panel (note how the other circuits are connected) and tighten the setscrews.

Step 6. *Connect the Hot Wire and Snap the Breaker in the Panel.* If spare breaker is not already in place, snap one into its slot on the panel board. Loosen the screw of the breaker and insert the black wire of the cable into the hole below. Then retighten the screw to secure the wire end.

Step 7. *Replace the Panel Box Cover.* Screw the cover plate back onto the panel box and record the new circuit on the panel door. To prevent a power surge, turn off all the individual breakers, then turn on the main breaker. Now turn the individual breakers back on one by one.

If you need to add a breaker for a 240-volt circuit, such as might be needed for a whirlpool, get a special breaker that occupies two slots in the panel box. The installation is similar to that just described, except the cable will have two hot wires—one black and one red. Insert one of the hot wires into each of the two holes in the double breaker.

7. *Screw the cover plate back onto the panel housing and record the new circuit on the panel door. Turn the main breaker back on.*

Putting in a GFCI Receptacle

Bathrooms pose hazards not found in most other parts of the house because of the presence of two good conductors of electricity: water and metal pipes. If a person is in contact with the piping system while handling appliances or switches, the electrical current may pass through his or her body on its way to the ground. Ordinary receptacles, even when containing a grounding wire, don't completely protect you against the full brunt of an electrical shock. Ground-fault circuit interrupters (GFCIs) do. A GFCI senses an overload and cuts off the current in 1/25 to 1/30 of a second—25 to 30 times faster than a heartbeat.

Code requires that GFCIs be used in fans and lights above tubs or showers, in whirlpool wiring, and in bathroom receptacles. You are required to install a GFCI in an older home any time you're replacing a receptacle in an area that is specified for a GFCI (in old circuits without a ground wire, this requires running a new three-wire cable from the panel). But beyond the code, GFCIs just make good safety sense in the bathroom.

There are three ways to protect circuits with a GFCI. The cheapest and easiest is a portable device that you simply plug into the outlet of the receptacle you want to protect. It protects only that outlet. At slightly more expense and effort, you can replace the receptacle with a GFCI receptacle, which offers the opportunity to protect receptacles downstream from the one you are replacing. Another way to protect all receptacles and devices connected to the bathroom is to wire them to a single circuit and install a GFCI breaker in the panel box (see "Running New Circuits from the Panel," page 148). This is also the most expensive way to achieve protection, as GFCI breakers cost about four times as much as an ordinary 120-volt breaker. The steps below describe how to install a GFCI receptacle. When you buy your GFCI receptacle, it may have four screws at the sides and one below

attached to it. One pair of black and white lugs are marked "line," while the other pair are marked "load." The fifth—green—lug is the ground connection. Another type of GFCI has five color-coded wires instead of lugs.

Difficulty Level: *(tool icon)*

Tools and Materials

☐ Screwdriver   ☐ Voltage tester

☐ Plastic wire connector   ☐ GFCI receptacle(s)

Step 1. *Turn the Power Off.* Go to the main panel box and trip the circuit breaker that controls the outlet receptacle. Make

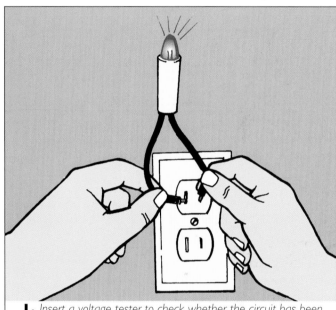

1. *Insert a voltage tester to check whether the circuit has been shut down. If the indicator light comes on, the circuit is live.*

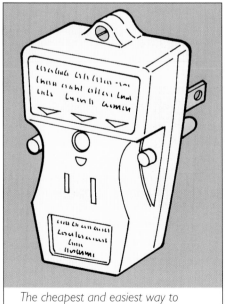

The cheapest and easiest way to protect a single receptacle is a portable GFCI that you simply plug into the outlet.

To protect receptacles downstream, replace a standard one with a GFCI type. The face contains a three-prong outlet at the top and bottom and test and reset buttons in the center.

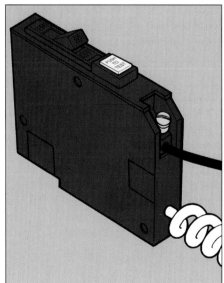

Install a GFCI breaker just as you would any breaker, except that the white pigtail wire must be connected to the neutral bus board in the panel box.

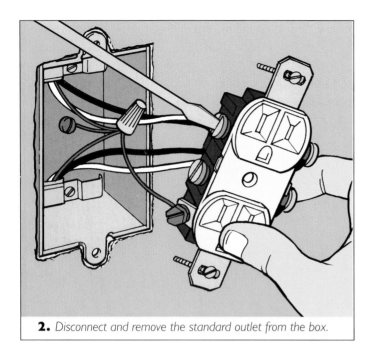

2. *Disconnect and remove the standard outlet from the box.*

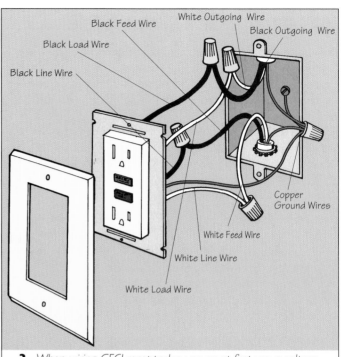

3. *When wiring GFCI receptacles, you must first use a voltage tester to identify which cable is LOAD and which is LINE.*

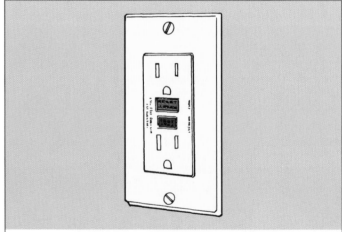

4. *After securing the new receptacle into the box, replace the wall plate and restore the power.*

5. *Press the reset button to test the installation.*

sure you have tripped the right breaker by plugging a voltage tester or lamp into the outlet.

Step 2. *Open the Outlet.* Remove the cover plate and remove the screws that hold the receptacle in the box. Unscrew the hot (black) wires from the brass terminals and the neutral (white) wires from the silver terminals. Disconnect the ground wire and discard the receptacle.

Step 3. *Connect the GFCI.* If there were two cables connected to the old receptacle, you need to use a voltage tester to determine which is feeding power into the box and which is taking power out of the box. Make sure all of the bare ends of the wires are safely away from the walls, well separated from each other. Then turn the power back on. Touch one probe of the voltage tester to a black wire, the other probe to a bare grounding wire. (All of the bare wires should still be connected together.) When the tester lights, that black wire is the feed. Turn off the power. Label the feed black and white wires.

Connect the GFCI black and white leads labeled LINE to the feed wires of the same color. Connect the GFCI leads labeled LOAD to the outgoing wires in the box. If there are no outgoing wires, tape a wire cap onto each GFCI LOAD lead. Connect the green GFCI grounding wire to the other bare grounding wires in the box.

Step 4. *Install the GFCI Receptacle into the Box.* Fold the wires neatly into the box, position the new receptacle inside the box, and secure it with the screws that came with it. Put on the wall plate and restore the power.

Step 5. *Test the Device.* Make sure the button marked "reset" is pressed all the way in. Then, press the button marked "test." The reset button should pop out. If it does, push it back into position. You are all set. But if the device does not work, turn off the power, open up the box, and check the connections.

Installing Receptacles

If you protect all outlets in the bathroom with a single GFCI circuit breaker, you can install standard receptacles intended for 120-volt circuits throughout the room. New receptacles accepted by the National Electrical Code contain three slots: two vertical slots of slightly different length for the hot and neutral wire and a U-shaped slot for the ground wire. You can wire the outlets from the screws on the sides or, more simply, by inserting the stripped end of a wire directly into the proper hole in the back of the receptacle. Some electricians don't consider the holes to be as reliable as screw attachment.

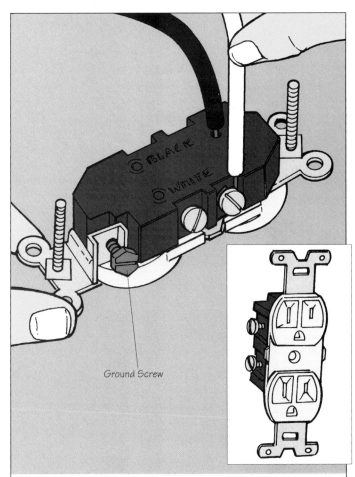

Ground Screw

The currently accepted receptacle design for 120-volt circuits contains two vertical slots of slightly different length for the hot and neutral wires and a U-shaped slot for the ground wire.

Receptacles are installed in the wall according to where they fall in the circuit, as described below.

Wiring Middle-of-the-Run Receptacles

Bring the incoming and outgoing cables into the box through the top or bottom holes. Connect the two hot (black) wires to the two brass-colored screws (or insert the wires into the holes marked "black" on the backside). Attach the two neutral (white) wires to the silver-colored screws (or insert the wires into the holes marked "white"). Connect the ground wires together and to the grounding screw in the box (if metal). Wrap electrical tape

around the sides of the receptacle to protect the terminal screws from contact with ground wires.

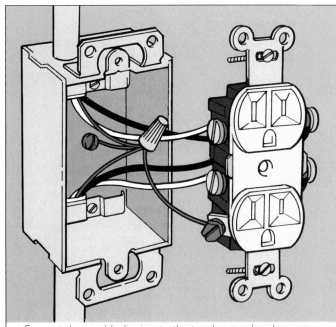

Connect the two black wires to the two brass-colored screws and attach the two white wires to the silver-colored terminals.

Wiring End-of-the-Run Receptacles

Bring the incoming cable into the box through the top or bottom hole. Connect the hot (black) wire to a brass-colored screw (or insert the wire into the hole marked "black" on the backside). Attach the neutral (white) wire to the silver-colored terminal (or insert it into the hole marked "white"). Connect the ground wire to the grounding screw in the box (if metal). Wrap the sides of the receptacle with electrical tape.

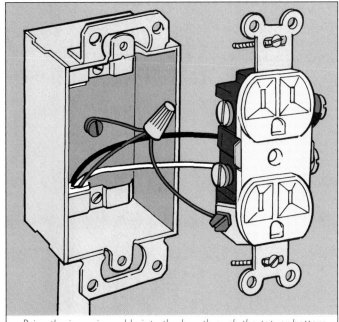

Bring the incoming cable into the box through the top or bottom hole. Connect the black wire to a brass-colored screw and attach the white wire to a silver-colored screw.

Installing an Exhaust Fan

To remove moist air and odors effectively from a bathroom, you need to match the fan capacity to the room's volume. Exhaust fans are sized by the number of cubic feet of air they move each minute (cfm). A fan should change all of the room's air at least eight times each hour, or once each 7.5 minutes. If your ceiling is about 8 feet from the floor, the following formula can help determine the size you need:

Fan capacity (cfm) = Room Width (feet) x Room Depth (feet) x 1.1

If, for example, your room measures 8x9 feet, you'll need a fan capacity of 79.2 cfm. Fans are also rated in "sones" for the amount of noise they produce, and they vary in loudness from 1 to 4 sones. A fan that is rated at 1 sone, the quietest, is about as loud as a refrigerator.

The best place for an exhaust fan is in the ceiling, above a toilet, tub, or shower, although you can also mount them in an outside wall. Once you decide on a fan capacity, you can select a unit that contains just a fan or a unit that comes with built-in features, such as lights, heat lamps, and/or heating elements. The following guidelines are for installing a ceiling-mounted fan.

Difficulty Level: 🔨🔨

Tools and Materials

☐ Basic electrical tools   ☐ Electric drill and bit
☐ Keyhole or saber saw   ☐ Caulking gun
☐ Duct tape   ☐ Duct insulation
☐ Exhaust fan   ☐ 8d common nails
☐ Switch box   ☐ Switch
☐ Silicone caulk   ☐ Roofing cement
☐ Screw clamp (sized to match duct diameter)
☐ 14/2 (or 12/2) NM electrical cable with ground
☐ Flexible aluminum duct vent cap kit (selected for roof, wall, or soffit mounting)
☐ 10-inch-long rigid aluminum duct (in same diameter as the flexible duct)

Positioning the Fan

Step 1. *Drill a Pilot Hole.* The dimensions of the required size of the ceiling cutout should be noted in the manufacturer's instructions. Drill a pilot hole up through the ceiling in the place that you would like to install the fan. Push a length of wire up through the hole to mark the spot.

Step 2. *Mark and Cut Out the Ceiling Opening.* If possible, take the fan housing up into the attic. Find the wire that you pushed through the ceiling below. Try to place the cutout hole near a ceiling joist so that you have something to anchor the fan to. Use the fan housing to mark the cutout, and cut the opening with a keyhole saw.

If you can't (or don't want to) work from inside the attic, begin by cutting a pilot hole in the ceiling large enough to stick your hand up through (so you can determine the location of the ceiling framing). Mark and cut the opening from below.

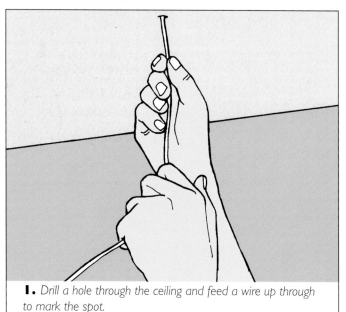

1. *Drill a hole through the ceiling and feed a wire up through to mark the spot.*

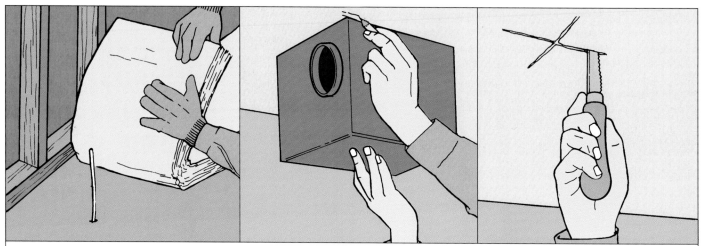

2. *Place the fan opening close to a structural member to provide support (left). Use the fan housing to mark the cutout on the ceiling (center). Cut the opening with a keyhole saw (right).*

Installing the Fan Housing and Duct

You can exhaust a ceiling fan through the roof, as described below, or horizontally through an outer wall or the eaves. Except for wall-mounted fans, you'll need to connect the fan to a length of duct that terminates in the roof or eaves.

Step 1. *Secure the Fan Housing to the Framing.* Nail the extension support brackets that come with the fan housing to the joists or cut lengths of 2x4s to span between two joists as a support.

Step 2. *Cut a Length of Flexible Duct.* In the attic, measure the distance between the fan housing and the roof (or wall) opening where you want the vent. This distance plus an extra 36 inches is the amount of flexible aluminum duct you need. Match the diameter of the duct to the fan (usually 4 inches).

Step 3. *Connect the Fan to the Duct.* Clamp the sleeve of the flexible duct to the discharge opening of the fan housing. Wrap duct tape tightly around the clamp to make the joint airtight. Then pull the insulation over the sleeve and wrap that tightly with duct tape.

Step 4. *Prepare the Exit End of the Duct.* Attach a 10-inch length of rigid aluminum duct to the discharge end of the flexible duct with duct tape.

Step 5. *Cut Out the Roof Opening.* Drill a pilot hole through the spot on the underside of the roof sheathing where you want to place the exit vent. From atop the roof, use a saber saw or keyhole saw to cut an opening to match the diameter of the duct.

Step 6. *Install the Roof Vent Cap.* Pull the duct extension through the roof opening and connect it to the roof cap. Cut away any shingles that keep the roof cap from fitting over the hole. Coat the underside of the roof-cap flashing with roofing cement and press it into place. Nail the flange to the roof. Also apply roofing cement to the undersides of roof shingles.

1. Secure the fan housing to the ceiling framing from above.

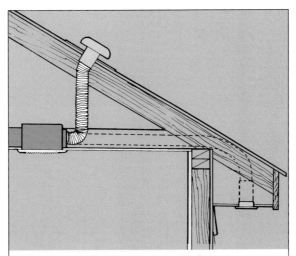

2. Measure the distance from the fan exit port to the vent opening and add 36 inches to get the required duct length. You can mount the vent on the roof or in the soffit of the eaves.

3. Attach the duct to the fan housing with a clamp and duct tape.

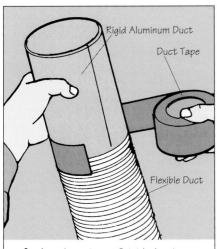

4. Attach a piece of rigid aluminum duct to the end of the flexible duct with duct tape.

5. Use a saber saw or keyhole saw to cut an opening through the roof.

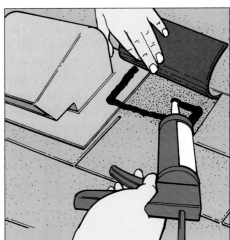

6. Seal each overlapping shingle and the flange of the vent hood with roofing cement.

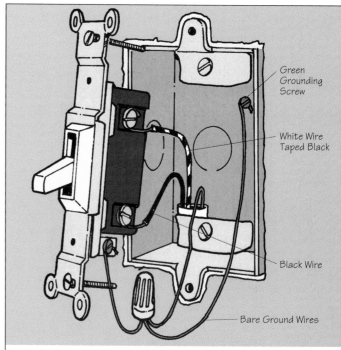

1. *A switch loop brings power into the fan housing, then takes it out to a switch and back to the housing.*

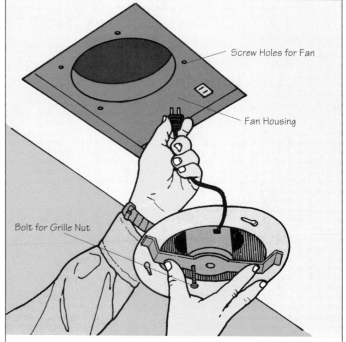

2. *Connect the black wire to one switch terminal and the white wire to the other terminal. Make the grounding connections. Screw the switch into the box and install the cover plate.*

Wiring an Exhaust Fan

The electrical part of this project consists of bringing a power cable to the fan motor and hooking it to a switch. If the power source is closer to the fan than it is to the switch, a switch loop is used. If not, the switch can be wired in-line. Both methods are described below.

Wiring a Switch Loop

Step 1. *Wiring the Fan.* Run two cables into the fan housing; one from the power source and one for the switch loop. Coming from the fan housing itself will be a white wire, a black wire and a green grounding screw. Wrap a piece of electrical tape around the white wire that goes to the switch to code this wire as a black hot wire. Attach the black wire from the power source to this coded white wire. Attach the white wire coming from the fan housing to the white wire from the power source. Attach the black wire coming from the fan housing to the black wire going to the switch. Connect a short piece of bare wire to the green grounding screw in the fan housing. Connect this short bare wire to the bare wires from the power source and from the switch.

Step 2. *Wiring the Switch.* Install a 2½-inch-wide switch box in the wall near the door. Use a standard single-pole switch. Wrap black tape around the white wire coming into the box. Attach this wire to one of the switch terminals and the other black wire to the other terminal. If the box is plastic, connect the bare ground wire to the green grounding screw on the switch. If the box is metal, connect a short piece of bare wire to the green grounding screw on the switch. Connect another piece of bare ground wire to the grounding screw in the box. Connect the

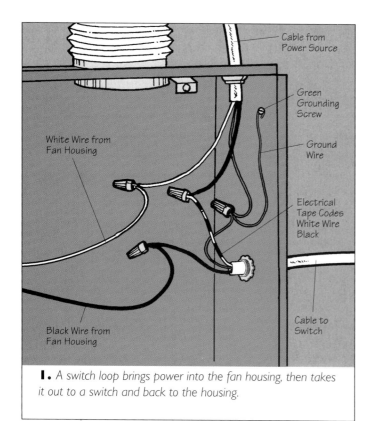

3. *Plug the fan motor into the receptacle and secure the fan to the housing with the screws provided. Then attach the grille.*

two short bare wires to the incoming bare wire with a wire connector. Screw the switch into the box and install the cover plate. Wrap the sides of the switch with electrical tape to protect the terminal screws from contact with the ground wires.

Step 3. *Connect the Fan to the Housing.* Plug the fan into the motor receptacle, secure the fan into the housing, and install the grille.

Wiring the Fan In-Line

If the power source is closer to the switch than the fan, run the power cable from the source into the switch. Then run another cable from the switch to the fan housing. Use cable of the same gauge as the cable that supplies power to the source.

Step 1. *Wiring the Switch.* Run a length of cable from the power source into a 3½-inch switch box in the wall near the door. Run a cable out of the switch box to the fan housing. For a standard single-pole switch, connect one black wire to one switch terminal and the other black wire to the other switch terminal. Connect the white wires together. Connect a short piece of bare wire to the green grounding screw on the switch. If the box is plastic, connect this short bare wire to the two bare wires coming into the box. If the box is metal, connect another short bare wire to the grounding screw in the box. Use a wire connector to connect the two short bare wires to the two bare wires from the cable. Wrap the sides of the switch with electrical tape to protect the terminal screws form contact with the ground wires.

Step 2. *Wiring the Fan.* When the fan is wired in line, there is only one cable coming into the fan housing. Connect the black wire from the cable to the black wire from the fan housing. Connect the white wire from the cable to the white wire in the fan housing. Connect the incoming bare wire to the grounding screw in the fan housing.

Plug the fan into the motor receptacle, secure the fan into the housing and install the grille as you did in step 3 of "Wiring a Switch Loop".

Electrical Lighting Decisions

In Chapter 2, guidelines were given for planning electrical lighting for overall room (general) lighting as well as specific areas (task lighting). Now you need to decide which of these types will give you the kind of lighting you want. Then select the fixtures themselves.

Lamp Choices

First, be sure to have enough lighting capacity. You can determine how much lighting capacity you need by matching the power consumption, in watts, to the floor area to be lit. For general lighting, the National Kitchen and Bath Association recommends the following capacities:

♦ Fluorescent lighting: 1.2 to 1.6 watts per square foot

♦ Incandescent lighting: 3.5 to 4 watts per square foot

Unfortunately, there is no such simple rule of thumb to determine task lighting. Because task lighting must focus on a specific target to be effective, the location of the lamp is as important as the amount of light it yields. The size of the mirror at the main task area can clue you as to the number of lamps you'll need.

To light a mirror with incandescent lamps, figure on at least three bulbs of 15- to 25-watt capacity at each side or a series of strip lights around the sides and top of the mirror (theatrical lighting). Ask your lighting supplier to show you strip lighting fixtures from a catalog. They come in 18, 24, 36, and 48 inches.

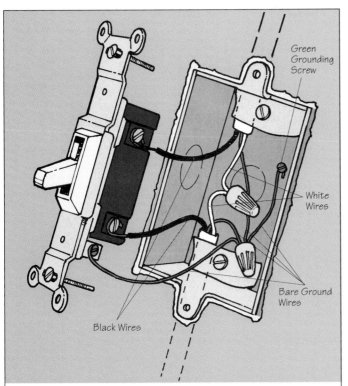

1. *To wire an in-line switch, run cable from power into the switch box. Run another cable from the switch box to the fan. Connect black wires to switch terminals. Connect white wires to each other. Connect bare wires to the grounding screw and to each other.*

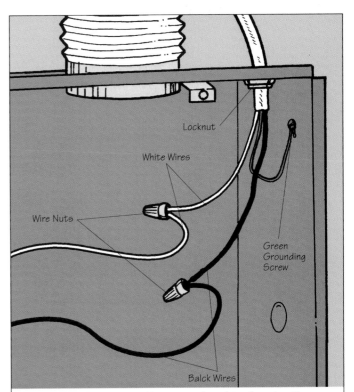

2. *Connect the white cable wire to the white fan wire. Connect the black cable wire to the black fan wire. Connect the bare cable wire. Connect the bare cable wire to the green grounding screw in the fan housing.*

Fluorescent or Incandescent?

You can get both task and general lighting fixtures that employ incandescent or fluorescent lamps. Although incandescent lamps consume up to five times the energy of fluorescent, they have been preferred over fluorescent in homes largely because of the color of their light and their shape.

Whereas incandescent lamps bring out the warm colors in objects, most types of fluorescent lighting feel cool. That's why incandescent lighting makes your skin look healthy, while fluorescent lighting makes it look pallid or gray. One type of fluorescent lighting, deluxe warm white, simulates incandescent lighting, reinforcing the warm tones in the skin.

Until recently, fluorescent lamps came only in tubes of 24-, 48-, and 96-inch lengths and as circles. Today they are increasingly available in compact shapes that screw into ordinary sockets.

You can get the efficiency of fluorescent lighting and the skin-friendly color of incandescent lighting by using fluorescent lamps for task lighting and incandescent for general lighting. If you do this, use the deluxe warm white type of fluorescent lamp.

An enclosed tub or shower is another task area that requires lighting. Choose a recessed vapor-proof fixture with a 60- or 75-watt bulb. For safety, position the switch so it cannot be reached from inside the compartment.

Fluorescent Tube Lamp at Each Side

Mirror Size (w x h, inches)	Designation	Length (inches)	Watts
24x30	T-12	24 or 28	20
24x36	T-12	36 inch	30
30x30	T-12	28 inch	25
30x36	T-12	36 inch	40
30x42	T-12	36 inch	40
30x48	T-12	48 inch	40
36x36	T-12	36 inch	40
36x42	T-12	36 inch	40
36x48	T-12	48 inch	40

Selecting Lighting Fixtures

Once you have an idea of where you want to install the lamps and the kind of lamps to be used, you can select the fixtures that house them. A good way to do this is to visit your local electrical supply store and ask for a catalog. Companies that specialize in residential lighting publish small catalogs that are often available at no cost to retail customers. Inside the catalog, you'll see a variety of styles of surface-mounted and recessed fixtures available to house any bulb or fluorescent tube, and you can select the fixture pretty much by style and cost. But remember that you are selecting fixtures for a small space, so choose fixtures that can be positioned out of the paths of people and swinging doors.

Wiring Fixtures

Wiring lighting fixtures (or any electrical appliance in a permanent location) requires bringing a power supply cable to the fixture, wiring in a switch, and attaching the fixture to the wall or ceiling. You can wire a remote switch by running the power cable through the switch and into the fixture (in-line wiring) or by running the power cable to the fixture first, then taking a "leg" off the hot wire to the switch. Here's how to do both for a wall or ceiling lamp. Use the same steps for any fixture, but be sure to read the manufacturer's instructions. Always shut off power to the circuit at the main breaker before beginning any wiring job.

Difficulty Level: 🔩 🔩

Tools and Materials

- ☐ Basic electrical tools
- ☐ Lighting fixture
- ☐ Switch box
- ☐ 14-gauge cable
- ☐ Switch
- ☐ Plastic wire caps

Wiring a Fixture in Line

Step 1. *Bring a Cable to the Switch.* Bring a power cable from a junction box or receptacle into the switch box. Run an outgoing cable from the switch box into the fixture box. Connect the hot (black) wire from the power cable to the side of the switch marked "hot" or "black" (use the brass-colored screw or push-in hole). Connect the black wire of the outgoing cable to the other

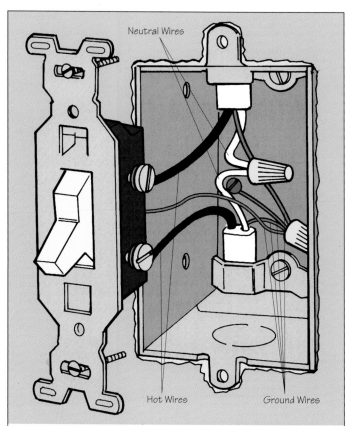

Neutral Wires

Hot Wires   Ground Wires

1. *Bring a power cable from power source (junction box or receptacle) into the switch box. Then run an outgoing cable from the switch box into the fixture box.*

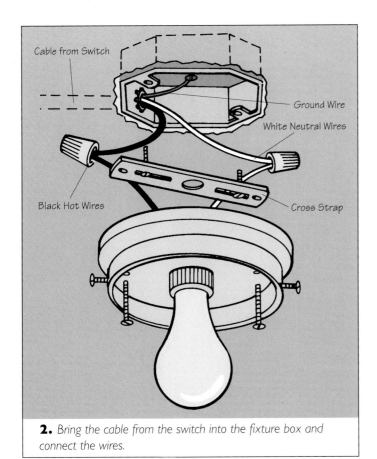

Cable from Switch

Ground Wire

White Neutral Wires

Black Hot Wires

Cross Strap

2. *Bring the cable from the switch into the fixture box and connect the wires.*

hot terminal. Connect the two neutral (white) wires together with a plastic wire cap. Connect the grounding (bare) wires together with a plastic wire cap and attach short lengths to the green grounding screws inside the box (if metal) and on the switch. Insert the connected switch into the box and attach the screws and cover plate. Wrap the sides of the switch with electrical tape to protect the terminal screws form contact with the ground wires.

Step 2. *Connect the Cable to the Fixture.* Bring the cable from the switch into the fixture box and connect the black and white cable wires to fixture wires of the same color with plastic wire nuts. Connect the ground wire to the box (if metal). In plastic boxes, connect the ground wire from the fixture to the ground wire of the cable, if the fixture has a ground wire. Otherwise, do nothing with the bare wire.

Step 3. *Install the Fixture.* Fixtures attach to electrical boxes in various ways. Two common methods for attaching incandescent ceiling and wall lamps are shown below. Begin by screwing a cross strap across the box. If the fixture base has screws at the sides, position the base so that these screws align with the two holes in the cross strap. Insert the screws and install the lamp and lens.

If the lamp has a nipple in the center (instead of side screws), screw the nipple into the center hole in the cross strap of the box. Then place the base and lens over the nipple and install the nuts to hold the parts together.

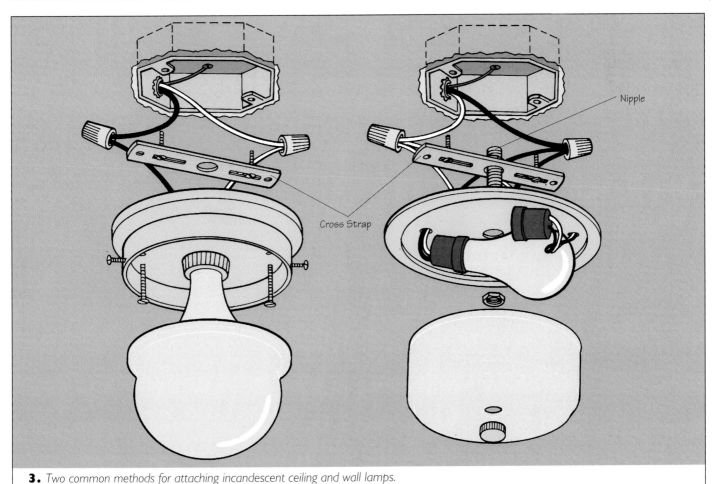

Nipple

Cross Strap

3. *Two common methods for attaching incandescent ceiling and wall lamps.*

13

Installing Cabinets, Mirrors, and Accessories

D on't install cabinetry or mount accessories until the plumbing is roughed in and the walls are faced with drywall, cement board, or plaster. Bars, hooks, and minor accessories go in after the wall finish has been completed.

Removing an Old Basin and Vanity

Difficulty Level: 🔧🔧

Tools and Materials

☐ Basic carpentry tools   ☐ Flashlight

☐ Adjustable wrench   ☐ Adjustable pliers

☐ Basin wrench   ☐ Pipe wrenches

☐ Pail   ☐ Putty knife

☐ Electric drill and bit   ☐ Keyhole saw

☐ Wood chisel   ☐ Penetrating oil

Caution: *Use a flashlight to light the work area below the vanity. If water drips down onto an electrical light and causes a short, you could get hurt.*

Removing the Basin

Step 1. *Shut off the Water.* Turn off the water supply using the water shutoff valves under the basin. If there are no shutoff valves, close the main valve near the water meter (or well pump). Then open the faucets to let any trapped water escape.

Step 2. *Disconnect the Water Supply Risers.* The handles of dual-lever faucets sit above threaded tailpieces that connect the faucets to the water supply risers. Single-lever faucets have two

1. *Shut off water at the shutoff valves under sink or at main valve.*

pre-attached copper tubes that converge under the faucet. Compression fittings attach the copper tubes to the shutoff valves. For a single-lever faucet, use a crescent wrench to

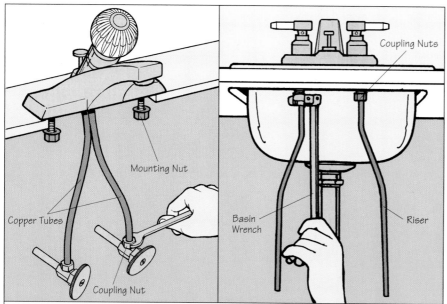

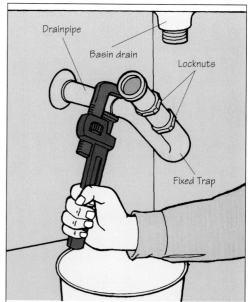

2. *Single-lever faucets come with copper tubes that converge into the faucet valve. Disconnect the coupling nuts (left). Use a basin wrench to access hard-to-reach coupling nuts on dual-lever faucets.*

3. *With a pail placed under the trap, turn the locknuts counterclockwise to loosen. Pour out any water left inside trap.*

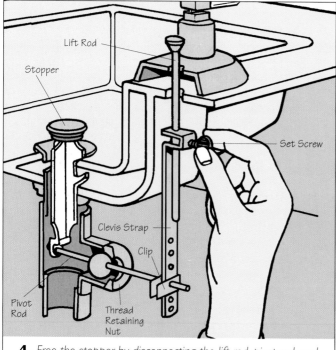

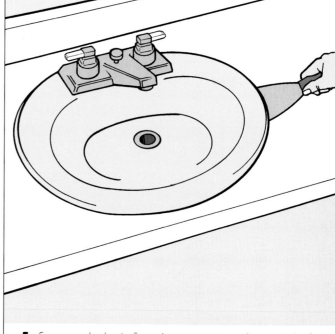

4. *Free the stopper by disconnecting the lift rod, pivot rod, and clevis strap.*

5. *Separate the basin from the countertop with a putty knife. Carefully chip away stubborn sealant with a hammer and chisel.*

disconnect the copper tubing from the shutoff valve. For a dual-lever faucet, you may need a basin wrench to disconnect the risers from the coupling nuts. Basin wrenches let you get at hard-to-reach places. Spray the nuts with penetrating oil if they are hard to turn, then allow the oil to sit a few minutes. When the coupling nuts are free, disconnect the nuts holding the lower ends of the risers to the shutoff valves, then remove the risers.

Step 3. *Dismantle the Drain System.* Place a pail under the trap. Next loosen the locknuts holding the trap by turning them counterclockwise with adjustable pliers or an adjustable wrench.

Turn the locknuts by hand until you can pull the trap free. Pour out any water retained inside the curved section of the trap.

Step 4. *Release the Stopper.* If you want to reuse the basin, you'll need to disconnect the lift rod that controls the stopper to get the sink out of the vanity. Pull off the clip that holds the pivot rod to the clevis strap, then loosen the set screw that holds the clevis strap to the lift rod. Pull out the lift rod and remove the pivot rod and clevis strap.

Step 5. *Remove the Basin.* The basin may be held to the vanity by a sealant, clips, or both. After unscrewing any clips or restraints, use a putty knife to separate the basin from the countertop. If you can't slice through the sealant, chip it away with a hammer and chisel, taking care not to break or chip the basin. Then pull the basin out of the countertop.

Removing the Vanity

Step 1. *Enlarge the Holes in the Back Panel.* Vanities are usually attached to the wall with screws or nails. Begin by enlarging the openings around the water shutoff valves in the back panel, so you can pull the vanity free. Drill a pilot hole, then use a keyhole saw to enlarge the holes. Take care not to damage any parts to be salvaged.

Step 2. *Pull the Vanity away from the Wall.* Remove any nails or screws holding the vanity in place and pull the cabinet away from the wall.

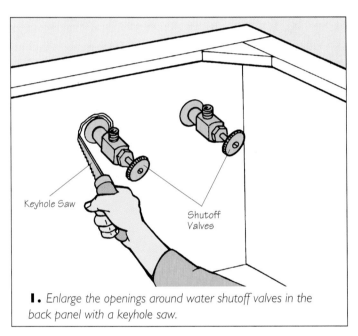

1. *Enlarge the openings around water shutoff valves in the back panel with a keyhole saw.*

2. *Take out the fasteners that are holding the back panel to the wall, and pull cabinet free.*

How to Install a New Prefab Vanity

Difficulty Level: 🔨🔨

Tools and Materials

- ☐ Basic carpentry tools
- ☐ Wood plane
- ☐ Adjustable wrenches
- ☐ 2½-inch wood screws
- ☐ Vanity unit
- ☐ Plumber's putty
- ☐ 1¼-inch wood screws
- ☐ Saber saw
- ☐ Electric drill
- ☐ Caulking gun
- ☐ Wood shims
- ☐ Paint or sealer
- ☐ Construction adhesive
- ☐ Masking Tape

If you want a truly custom vanity cabinet and have a flair for cabinetmaking, consider designing and making your own. Otherwise, check out the selection of prefabricated units available from your building supply or kitchen/bath store. Vanities come as base-only units, a base with an integral basin-countertop, or a base with a countertop for a separate basin. The following steps describe how to install a prefabricated vanity cabinet that comes with a countertop, complete with backsplash and finish, and a cutout for a separate basin (later in this chapter, you'll find instructions for installing a basin into the countertop). Use the same basic procedure to install a multibasin unit. Don't install a vanity cabinet until you have made any necessary alterations to the wall surface, such as putting up new drywall.

Step 1. *Plan the Vanity's Location.* To minimize plumbing work, try to place the vanity so that the basin will align with the existing plumbing. Outline the opening for the water shutoff valves and drainpipe on the back panel of the cabinet. Then, with a saber saw, cut the opening and set the vanity in place against the wall.

Step 2. *Level the Cabinet.* Place a carpenter's level on the top of the cabinet to see if it is level, front to back and side to side. If not, put wood shims under the base, tapping them in gently, a little at a time, until the cabinet is level in both directions. For a tight fit without shims, mark and plane the vanity so that it hugs the floor. (While the vanity is turned upside down, coat any exposed wood with paint or sealer to protect against water damage.)

Step 3. *Secure the Cabinet to the Wall.* Locate the studs in the wall behind the cabinet. Drive two 2½-inch wood screws, one near the top and one near the bottom, through the back panel or mounting rail and into the two studs closest to the ends of the cabinet.

Step 4. *Attach the Countertop.* Have a helper hold the counter firmly down and against the wall while you drill pilot holes up through the corner braces and into the particleboard of the countertop. Then drive 1¼-inch wood screws through the braces.

Step 5. *Caulk the Backsplash.* After the top is secured, attach a strip of masking tape along the wall, 1/4 inch above the backsplash, and another strip on the top of the backsplash, 1/4 inch away from the wall. Run a bead of silicone caulk (white is usually preferred) along the joint between the backsplash and the wall inside the two strips of tape. Tool into a smooth, concave profile with your finger. Then carefully strip off the masking tape.

1. *Cut a triangular opening in the back of the new vanity large enough for the faucet valves and basin drain to fit through.*

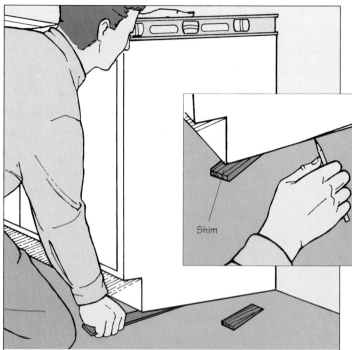

2. *Check that vanity is level front to back and side to side. Use shims or mark the high portion of the vanity and then plane it down as necessary to get a snug fit to the floor.*

3. *Secure vanity to wall by screwing it to wall studs.*

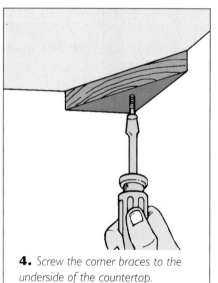

4. *Screw the corner braces to the underside of the countertop.*

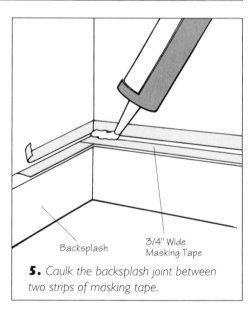

5. *Caulk the backsplash joint between two strips of masking tape.*

Installing a Solid-Surface Countertop

For the simplest installation, choose a prefabricated countertop that contains an integral basin. If your top must have a shape not available in stock sizes, make a sketch of your proposed countertop, including the dimensions, and order the pieces precut and predrilled. The steps for installing a precut countertop are described on the next page. If the basin is to be a separate unit, see "Installing a Basin in a Plastic Laminated Countertop," page 168.

Difficulty Level: 🔨🔨

Tools and Materials

- ☐ Saber saw with carbide-tipped blade
- ☐ Respirator or dust mask
- ☐ Sandpaper
- ☐ Solid-surface countertop
- ☐ Bar clamps
- ☐ Electric drill with hole saw attachment
- ☐ Cement (as recommended by supplier)
- ☐ Adhesive (as recommended by supplier)
- ☐ Belt sander
- ☐ Solvent alcohol
- ☐ Scotch-Brite pad
- ☐ Caulking gun
- ☐ Cornstarch

Step 1. *Sketch Out the Countertop.* Sketch out the countertop, showing the dimensions of the top and backsplash. Allow an extra 1/4 inch at each side of the top if it is to fit between two walls. Dimension any trim pieces, such as aprons. If the basin is to be installed into the top separately, give the dimensions from each side to the center of the drain hole and the positions of the faucet holes. Take the sketch to your supplier and order the pieces to be cut and drilled according to the sketch. If you want rounded edges on the front or exposed sides, include this in your specifications.

Step 2. *Smooth the Edges.* Smooth the edges of the pieces with a belt sander and 100-grit paper. Finish sanding them by hand with 120- and 220-grit sandpaper.

Step 3. *Attach the Countertop.* Using a caulking gun, apply a bead of adhesive to the cabinet and place the top in its final position.

Step 4. *Attach Backsplash and Trim.* Use the cement recommended by the supplier to join the backsplash to the countertop and attach any trim pieces, such as a front or side apron, following the manufacturer's directions. Clamp the pieces together until fully set. Clean any excess cement off the material with solvent alcohol.

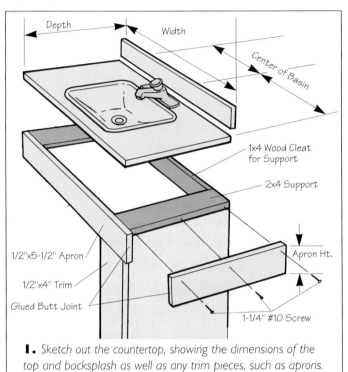

1. *Sketch out the countertop, showing the dimensions of the top and backsplash as well as any trim pieces, such as aprons.*

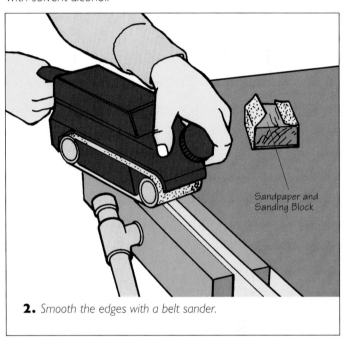

2. *Smooth the edges with a belt sander.*

3. *Position the countertop on the base cabinet and check the overhangs. Then set it in a bead of adhesive.*

4. *Attach the backsplash and trim with the cement recommended by the supplier. Clean excess cement with solvent alcohol.*

Tiling a Countertop

You can apply ceramic tile to old tile, plastic laminate, or plywood (but not over particleboard or fiberboard). Roughen old tile and plastic laminate by sanding the surface with 200-grit wet/dry sandpaper before beginning.

Difficulty Level: 🔨 🔨

Tools and Materials

☐ Framing square
☐ Tile cutter (rent from supplier)
☐ Tile nippers (rent from supplier)
☐ 2x4x12 wrapped with carpet
☐ Masking tape
☐ Plastic spacers
☐ Solvent (as recommended for the adhesive)
☐ Adhesive (type and quantity as recommended by supplier)
☐ Notched trowel (notch size as recommended for the tile and adhesive you want to use)

☐ Sponge
☐ Tape measure
☐ Hammer
☐ Rubber float
☐ Tiles
☐ Grout
☐ Squeegee

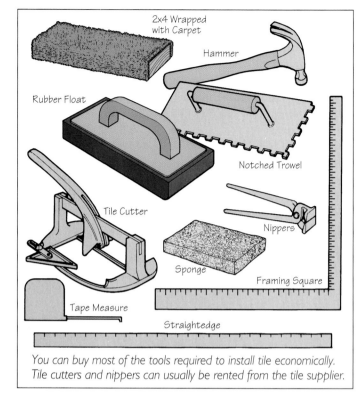

You can buy most of the tools required to install tile economically. Tile cutters and nippers can usually be rented from the tile supplier.

Step 1. *Support and Lay Out the Tiles.* If you are making a new countertop, build a solid base out of two layers of 3/4-inch plywood that have been glued and nailed together.

Arrange the tiles on the countertop in the desired pattern. Try to position them so that the amount of cutting is minimized, and you avoid having to make narrow cuts. If your tiles do not come with self-spacers, insert plastic spacers in each corner to set the proper grout-joint widths (they stay in place when tiles are permanently set). Draw joint lines near the center of the top, front to back and side to side, as reference (work) lines. Mark them in with a pencil, using a framing square for alignment.

Step 2. *Cut the Tiles.* Use a tile cutter and nipper to cut tiles to the required size and shape. Cut whole tiles by first scoring the tile with the cutter, then pressing down on the handle to snap the tile in two. Use the nipper to make small cuts and to cut corners and irregular lines, working from the ends toward the middle. Make small nibbles until you get the shape you need.

Step 3. *Install the Trim Tiles.* With the dry-laid tiles on the top still in place, adhere the tiles to the front and side edges. Apply adhesive with the smooth side of the notched trowel, then

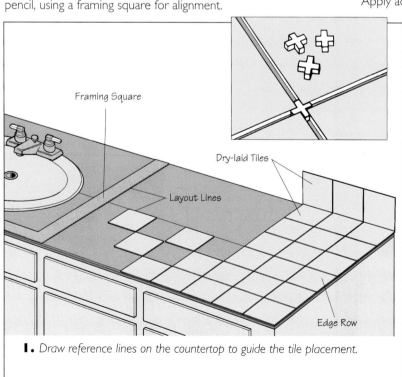

1. *Draw reference lines on the countertop to guide the tile placement.*

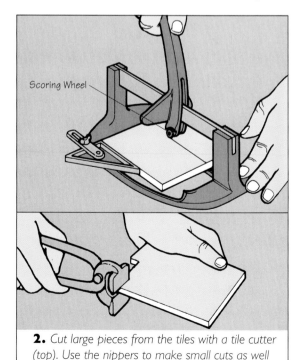

2. *Cut large pieces from the tiles with a tile cutter (top). Use the nippers to make small cuts as well as to cut corners and irregular lines (bottom).*

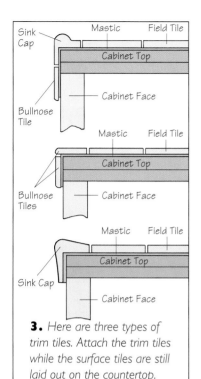

3. *Here are three types of trim tiles. Attach the trim tiles while the surface tiles are still laid out on the countertop.*

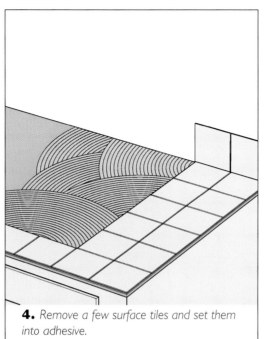

4. *Remove a few surface tiles and set them into adhesive.*

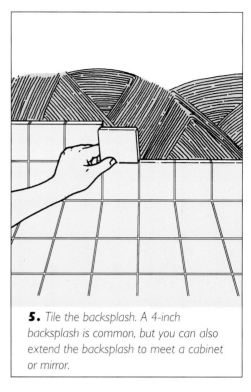

5. *Tile the backsplash. A 4-inch backsplash is common, but you can also extend the backsplash to meet a cabinet or mirror.*

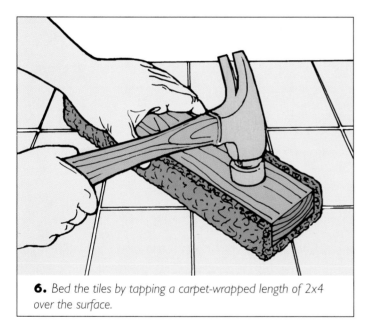

6. *Bed the tiles by tapping a carpet-wrapped length of 2x4 over the surface.*

7. *Press grout into joints with a squeegee.*

use the notched side to create ridges of the correct setting depth. Next "butter" the backs of the tiles and position them so they align with the loose tiles on the top. Then lay any trim tiles around sink openings or corners.

Step 4. *Install the Surface Tiles.* Lift some of the dry-laid tiles and apply adhesive to the countertop with the notched trowel. Take care not to spread adhesive over too great an area, so that you have time to set the tiles before the adhesive begins to harden. Press each tile firmly in place with a slight wiggle to ensure a good bond.

Step 5. *Tile the Backsplash.* Apply tiles to the backsplash the same way as the trim tiles. Make sure you turn off the power to any switch or outlet you tile around.

Step 6. *Bed the Tiles.* Use the piece of carpet-wrapped 2x4 to bed the tiles into the adhesive. Tap the top gently while moving it over the tiles.

Step 7. *Grout the Joints.* First place a strip of wide masking tape along the underside of the front trim tiles to prevent the grout from falling out of the joints. Also mask any surrounding walls or surfaces you want to protect.

Then mix the grout according to the manufacturer's directions (using colorant if desired) and press it into the joints with a squeegee. When the grout is firm, but not dry, clean the surface with a damp sponge. When the grout dries to a hazy residue on the surface of the tiles, clean the haze off with a dry cloth.

Installing a Basin in a Plastic Laminated Countertop

Use the following guidelines for installing a basin into a vanity countertop. See Chapter 11 for help with the fittings and plumbing. If you must cut a hole in the countertop, it's usually easier to make the cutout before securing the countertop to the base cabinet.

Difficulty Level: 🔨 🔨

Tools and Materials

☐ Saber saw
☐ Adjustable wrench
☐ Spud wrench
☐ Utility knife
☐ Masking tape
☐ Length of rope
☐ Brick
☐ Countertop

☐ Drill with bit
☐ Basin wrench
☐ Screwdriver
☐ Caulking Gun
☐ Silicone caulk
☐ 2x4s
☐ Basin

Step 1. *Position the Basin.* First make a line marking where you want the center of the basin to fall on the countertop. If your basin is self-rimming, place it upside down, center it over the line you drew, and trace around the outer edge of the rim. Remove the basin and mark the actual cutting line inside the outer line. Determine the dimensions of the cutout from the basin or the manufacturer's instructions. If your basin is metal rimmed, lay the metal trim over the countertop and use it as a template to mark the cutout. Drill 1/4-inch holes at the corners (or wide and narrow points of an oval basin) to establish the extent of the cutout on the underside of the countertop.

Step 2. *Add Supports.* Install braces below the sides of the basin, unless the countertop consists of two layers of 3/4-inch plywood or solid-surface material.

Step 3. *Cut the Opening.* Use a saber saw to make the cutout.

Step 4. *Install the Basin.* The specific method of installation depends on the type of basin.

◆ Self-Rimming Basins. You can install a self-rimming basin on any countertop, after cutting a hole smaller than the outer rim (see Step 1). Place a bead of silicone caulk over the countertop where the rim will go. Then position the basin in the opening and press it into the sealant. Install the four metal clips that come with the basin on the underside and tighten each clip's screw snugly but not all the way. Gradually tighten the screws enough to hold the basin firmly. Finally, run your finger around the edge to shape the caulk, then remove any excess sealant from the countertop.

◆ Metal-Rimmed Basins. Lay a bead of silicone caulk around the cutout and place the metal rim into the caulk. Have a helper push

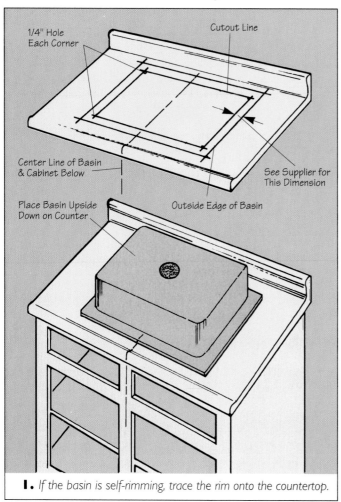

1. *If the basin is self-rimming, trace the rim onto the countertop.*

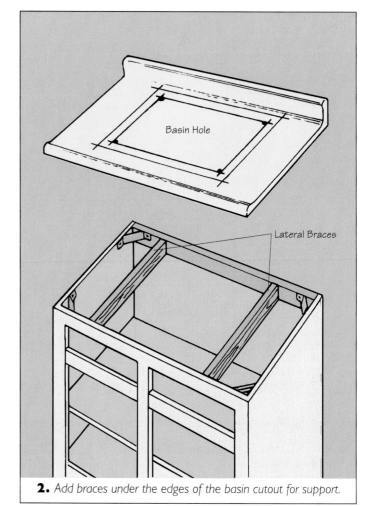

2. *Add braces under the edges of the basin cutout for support.*

the basin up from below to meet the trim and allow you to tighten the clips. If you have to work alone, suspend the basin into position, held in place by a 2x4 across the top and another across the bottom, with a rope connecting the two. Before tightening the rope, place a bead of caulk between the basin edge and metal trim. Then tighten the rope by twisting a screwdriver in the rope, to pull the basin up to meet the metal trim. Finally, tighten the set screws on the clips below and clean off any excess caulk.

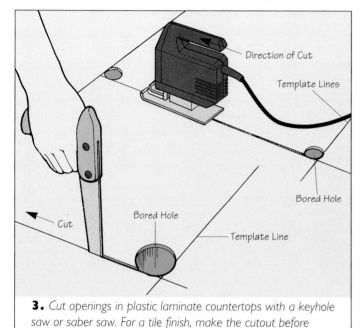

3. *Cut openings in plastic laminate countertops with a keyhole saw or saber saw. For a tile finish, make the cutout before setting the tiles.*

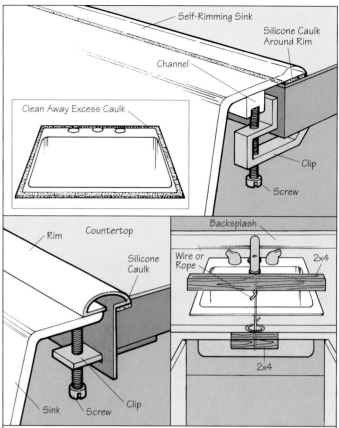

4. *Self-rimming basins are set in caulk and held with clips (top). Set the metal rim into sealant and push the basin up from below (bottom). If you are working alone, use two 2x4s and rope.*

Installing a Basin in Tile

There are three ways to install a basin in a tile countertop:

♦ Drop the basin into the opening after tiling the countertop. To do this, set the basin into a bed of caulk and secure with clips from below.

♦ Rout out a recess for the basin rim in the countertop to allow the rim to set flush with the untiled surface. Then install the basin in the countertop before tiling. Install tile over the edge of the basin.

♦ Install the basin in the cutout first, then tile up to the basin's trim edge.

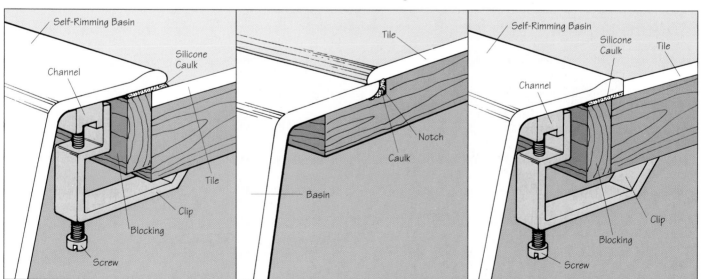

The basin is installed into a bed of silicone caulk laid over the tile (left). If you want the tile to overlap the basin, rout out a notch or recess in the countertop so the basin's edge is flush with the untiled surface (center). Install the basin in the countertop. Then tile up to the basin's edge (right).

Installing a Basin in a Solid-Surface Countertop

If the basin is not an integral part of the countertop, you can mount a self-rimming basin into the cutout. Order the counter-top piece with the cutout already made, if possible. If you have to cut it yourself, mark the cutout, drill a pilot hole along the line, and cut the opening with a saber saw equipped with a carbide-tipped blade. Install the basin into the cutout as described in "Installing a Basin in Tile," page 169.

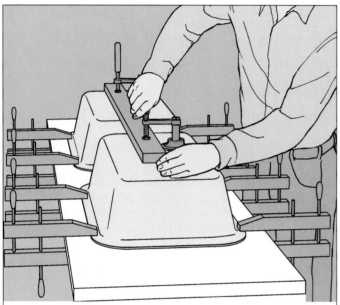

Glue the basin to underside of solid-surface countertop, then apply pressure by clamping through the drain hole and around the edges, using wood blocks to protect basin's edges.

Putting in a Medicine Cabinet

How to Install a Surface-Mounted Medicine Cabinet

Medicine cabinets that stick out from the wall may not be as elegant as cabinets recessed into the wall, but hanging them is far simpler. If the wall contains piping or electrical items, a surface-mounted unit may be the only practical option.

Difficulty Level: 🔨

Tools and Materials

☐ Basic carpentry tools   ☐ Medicine cabinet
☐ Screwdriver bit for drill   ☐ Electric drill
☐ 1½-inch no. 24 pan-head screws   ☐ Masking tape
☐ Magnetic wall stud locator (optional)

Step 1. *Mark the Position on the Wall.* Use a carpenter's level to mark a line on the wall that will represent the top of the cabinet. This line will be 72 inches from the floor for most people, but you can make it a few inches higher or lower to suit the height of the people who will be using it. Next, have a helper hold the cabinet against the wall and up to the line while you mark the outline of the cabinet on the wall. If you can't use a pencil (such as on tile), use masking tape.

Step 2. *Locate the Wall Studs.* Locate the wall studs that fall within the area of the medicine cabinet. Use a magnetic stud finder or drill small-diameter holes across the wall surface until you find a stud. (This is sloppy, but you can fill in any holes not covered by the cabinet.) Measure the positions of the studs from one edge and transpose this to the back of the medicine cabinet. Drill holes through the back panel of the cabinet near the top. Ideally, there will be at least two holes, one near each cabinet edge.

Step 3. *Attach the Cabinet to the Wall.* Have your helper hold the cabinet in place while you mark the position of the pilot

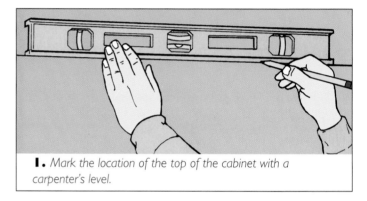

1. *Mark the location of the top of the cabinet with a carpenter's level.*

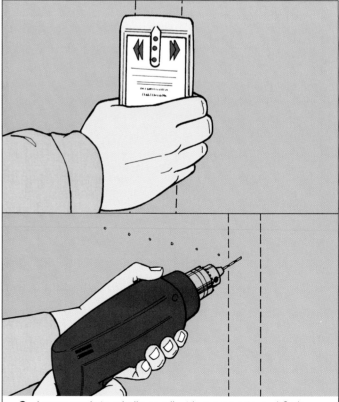

2. *Locate studs in a hollow wall with a magnetic stud finder (top). To locate studs without a stud finder, drill small holes at 1-inch intervals until you hit a stud. Then measure off 16 inches, the usual space between studs, to find a second one (bottom).*

3. *With one or more helpers holding the cabinet in place, mark the pilot holes.*

holes. Take the cabinet down and drill pilot holes in the wall, slightly smaller than the diameter of the screws. If you must drill through tile, use a carbide-tipped bit slightly larger than the screws to drill through the tile, then switch to a smaller bit. While your assistant lifts the cabinet back into position, insert the screws and tighten them. If the cabinet comes with a top- or side-mounted light fixture, attach it and complete the wiring, following the manufacturer's instructions (see Chapter 12 for help).

How to Install a Recessed Cabinet

Recessed medicine cabinets are sized to fit into walls framed with 2x4s. If you are lucky, the studs will be just in the right position to enable you to insert a 14½-inch cabinet (or a double-width cabinet by removing a center stud). Just as likely, the studs will not be in the

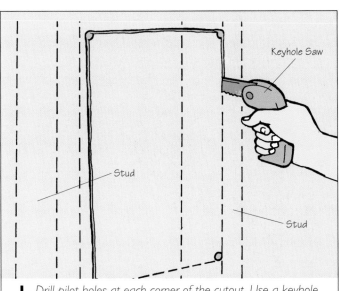

1. *Drill pilot holes at each corner of the cutout. Use a keyhole saw to cut through the wall.*

best place for the cabinet. You'll need to cut out some studs and add some new ones at the sides.

Cutting an opening in a stud wall faced with drywall is relatively simple. Opening up a tile-faced wall is tougher, and surgery into a plaster wall is both difficult and messy. Be prepared for fine dust spreading throughout the room and into adjacent rooms; protect yourself by wearing a respirator. If you have to install a new header for a bearing wall, allow 1½ inches at each side of the opening for the supporting studs.

Difficulty Level: 🔨 🔨

Tools and Materials

☐ Basic carpentry tools | ☐ Electric drill
☐ Keyhole saw | ☐ Chisel
☐ Screwdriver bit for drill | ☐ Backsaw
☐ Wood plane | ☐ Rasp
☐ Drywall finishing knife | ☐ 2x4s
☐ 3½-inch-long L-clip | ☐ 6d common nails
☐ Screws to attach cabinet | ☐ Drywall pieces
☐ Drywall tape | ☐ Drywall compound
☐ Sandpaper | ☐ Paint
☐ Paintbrush | ☐ Medicine cabinet
☐ 10d common nails (for larger cabinet)

Cabinets That Fit between Two Studs

Step 1. *Remove the Wall Finish.* Locate the wall studs as described in Step 2 under "How to Install a Surface-Mounted Medicine Cabinet," on page 170. Unless you are certain that no electrical wires run through the area to be cut out, shut off the circuit breaker that controls the electricity in the area. Drill a pilot hole 3/4-inch or larger diameter at each corner of the cutout. Cut through plaster or drywall with a keyhole saw. If the wall is faced with ceramic tile, remove the tile in the area of the cutout with a hammer and chisel before sawing through the substrate.

2. *Install the head and sill blocking with L-clips attached to the exposed ends of each piece.*

3. *Screw the sides of the cabinet into the studs.*

Cabinet
Side

Step 2. *Install the Head and Sill Pieces.* Measure the exact distance between the studs (normally 14½ inches). Cut two pieces of 2x4 to this dimension; they will serve as blocking (head and sill) at the top and bottom of the opening. Attach a 3½-inch-long L-clip to the end of each 2x4 with 3d nails. Hammer two 6d nails partway into the studs below the sill to provide a temporary support to keep the sill from falling into the wall. Then rest the sill piece on these nails, with the L-clips facing up, and attach the L-clips to the studs with three 3d nails (use screws for plaster-faced walls). Reverse the procedure at the top, except you won't need the supporting nails.

Step 3. *Attach the Cabinet.* Insert the cabinet into the opening and screw it to the studs through the holes provided in the overlapping sides. If there are no holes or they are poorly located, drill new ones.

Cabinets That Span Several Studs

Step 1. *Locate the Studs and Mark the Wall.* Shut off the circuit breaker that controls any power or wiring that may run through the area. Find the studs behind the wall in the location of the new medicine cabinet (see Step 2 under "How to Install a Surface-Mounted Medicine Cabinet," page 170). Use a carpenter's level to mark the top line of the medicine cabinet. This is generally 72 inches above the floor, but adjust this for your own comfort and use. Measure the height of the portion of the cabinet that will go into the wall and add 3 inches to allow for header and sill blocking. Mark a horizontal line at the bottom of the cutout. Mark the outer studs, using a level held vertically as your guide.

Step 2. *Remove the Wall Finish.* Drill a pilot hole at least 3/4 inch in diameter at each corner of the cutout. Next, cut the wall finish, using a keyhole saw. If the wall is faced with ceramic tile, strip it off before cutting through the drywall or plaster substrate.

Step 3. *Remove the Studs.* After the studs have been exposed, determine which ones need to be cut. But before cutting, make sure the wall is not a load-bearing wall. If it is, you'll need to provide a header above the remaining studs (see Chapter 10). Use a backsaw to cut through the studs.

Step 4. *Install Head and Sill Pieces.* Measure the horizontal distance between the edge studs and cut two pieces of 2x4 to this dimension to serve as the header and sill. Drive pairs of 10d nails through the header and sill into the ends of the cut studs. Then toenail the header and sill to the edge studs with 8d nails.

Step 5. *Install the Trimmer Studs.* If necessary, cut 2x4 trimmers to reduce one or both sides of the opening to the size required for the cabinet. Install 2x4 blocking on the head and sill, to support the trimmer, then nail the trimmers into the blocks.

Step 6. *Patch the Wall Finish.* Cut strips of drywall to cover the exposed studs, leaving the recess for the cabinet open. Tape and finish the drywall joints as describe in Chapter 9.

Step 7. *Attach Cabinet.* Insert the cabinet into the opening and screw it to the edge framing through the holes provided in the sides. Complete any electrical wiring if the unit comes with a lighting fixture.

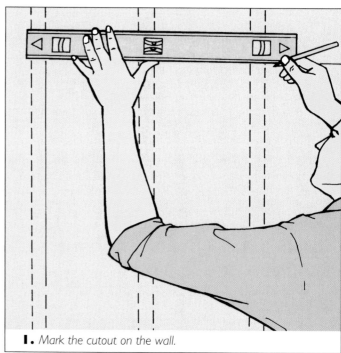

1. *Mark the cutout on the wall.*

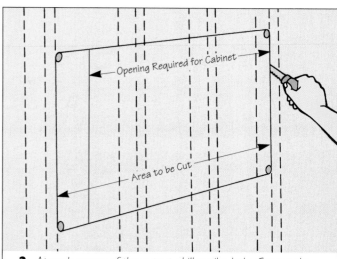

Opening Required for Cabinet

Area to be Cut

2. *At each corner of the cutout, drill a pilot hole. Cut out the wall with a keyhole saw.*

3. *Cut through the studs with a backsaw.*

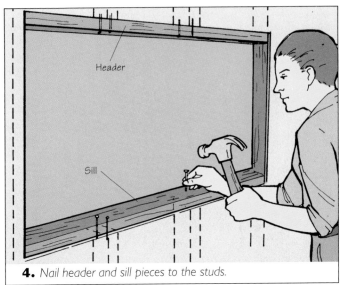

Header

Sill

4. *Nail header and sill pieces to the studs.*

2x4 Blocking

Trimmer

5. *Use one or two trimmer studs to reduce the size of the opening.*

6. *Cover the exposed studs with wallboard.*

7. *Place the cabinet in the opening, and securely fasten.*

14

Finishing Floors, Walls, and Ceilings

The plumbing is installed, the wiring is done. Now it's time to make the new bathroom beautiful by installing your finished floor and by finishing your walls and ceilings. In this chapter you'll learn to apply resilient flooring and ceramic tile, today's most practical and beautiful flooring options. You'll also learn how to repair walls and how to finish them with tape, compound and paint, or with wall tile.

Laying Resilient Floor Tiles

Installing resilient floor tiles is fairly simple and requires only a few tools. To get a successful job, though, you'll need to plan the layout and prepare the substrate properly. Try to complete the installation all at one time when you won't be interrupted. Most resilient floor tiles now come in 12-inch squares. Trim strips in various accent colors are available in 1/4- to 6-inch widths. When ordering, figure the areas in square feet to be covered (length times width) and add 5 to 10 percent for waste.

Start with the Right Base

When you pick out a resilient flooring material, check the manufacturer's instructions for acceptable substrates. This will guide you as to the type of underlayment to put down and the corresponding adhesive. Here are some commonly acceptable substrates for resilient tile and sheet flooring and what to watch out for (see "Selecting the Right Underlayment," page 74).

Old resilient tile, sheet flooring, and linoleum. Clean, free of wax, tightly adhered with no curled edges or bubbles.

Ceramic tile. Clean and free of wax. If surface is porous, make sure it is completely dry. Joints should be grouted full and leveled.

Concrete. Smooth and dry. Fill cracks and dimples with a latex underlayment compound.

Wood flooring. Strip flooring will serve as an underlayment only if it is completely smooth, dry, free of wax, and has all joints filled. Even then, the wood strips can shrink and swell, so a better bet is to put down an underlayment of 1/2-inch underlayment-grade plywood or 1/4-inch lauan plywood.

Plywood. Fir or pine plywood that bears the stamp "Underlayment Grade" (as rated by the American Plywood Association) provides the best underlayment for resilient flooring. Use only material of 1/4-inch or greater thickness. Lauan, a tropical hardwood, is also used, but make sure you get Type 1, with exterior-grade glue. All plywood should be firmly attached, with surface cracks and holes filled and sanded smooth. Nail 1/4-inch-thick plywood at 4-inch intervals around the edges and at 6-inch intervals inside the panel.

Unacceptable Substrates

Particleboard. Never use particleboard for resilient flooring, due to its tendency to swell when moist. If you have particleboard on the floor now, remove it or top it with underlayment-grade plywood or 1/4-inch lauan plywood.

Hardboard. Though often used as a substrate, hardboard is specifically rejected by some manufacturers.

A Solid Color or Pattern?

Unlike sheet flooring, resilient tile flooring gives you the opportunity to mix squares of different colors to create a custom pattern. If this intrigues you, measure the floor and draw it to scale

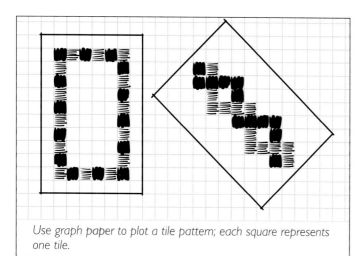

Use graph paper to plot a tile pattern; each square represents one tile.

on a sheet of graph paper. Use colored pencils or markers to explore a few patterns. Your options are greatest if the room is large. Bathrooms tend not to have much unused floor space, though, so too much pattern on the floor can make the room feel cluttered. Muted colors are safest to use—save bright colors for towels, vases, bottles, and other items that can be changed.

Difficulty Level: 🔨 🔨

Tools and Materials

☐ Framing square ☐ Chalkline
☐ Measuring tape ☐ Scribing or utility knife
☐ Rolling pin ☐ Resilient tiles
☐ Adhesive ☐ Solvent
☐ Notched trowel (notch size as specified by adhesive manufacturer)

Preparing the Layout

Step 1. *Mark the Floor.* Measure the room to find the center point of the walls. Have a helper hold one end of a chalkline at the center of one wall, while you hold the line at the other and snap a line on the floor. Then do the same for the two opposite walls. Use a framing square to make sure the intersection of the lines is square. If not, change one chalk line (it will mean cutting the tiles along one wall at a slight angle).

For a diagonal pattern, you'll run diagonal lines through the center of the intersecting lines. In a rectangular room, measure the shorter chalk line from the intersection to the long wall. Mark that measurement twice on each long wall, measuring from the midpoint of the wall and going in both directions along the wall. Run a chalk line diagonally from one of the points you just marked across to the corresponding point on the opposite wall and snap the line. Do the same with the other diagonally opposite points.

Step 2. *Make a Dry Run.* Place a row of tiles along each of the chalk lines to check your layout. If the last tile will have to be cut down to the size of a skinny strip, move the appropriate chalk line up or down on the floor a few inches. Test a diagonal pattern by first laying tiles down, point to point, along the perpendicular lines, then laying two rows along the diagonal line.

1. *Find the center points of the surrounding walls and, with a helper to hold one end of the chalkline, snap lines on the floor between the points to make work lines. For diagonal patterns, measure the shorter dimension (x) of the two intersecting work lines and mark it on the long walls. Then run a chalk line diagonally between the marks on opposite walls to create diagonal work lines on the floor (inset).*

2. *Lay the tiles out on the work lines. If the fit isn't right, adjust the lines. Place a row of tiles along each of the chalk lines to check your layout. If the last tile will have to be cut down too much, move the appropriate work line (top left). Test a diagonal pattern by first laying tiles down, point to point, along the perpendicular lines, then laying two rows along the diagonal line (top right).*

Setting the Tiles

When you are satisfied with your layout, adjust your drawing so you can remember how you placed the tiles, then remove them.

Step 1. *Spread the Adhesive.* Beginning at the intersection of the chalk lines, spread adhesive along one line with the smooth side of a notched trowel. Then distribute the adhesive into even grooves by holding the trowel notched side down at an angle of about 45 degrees. Leave part of the line exposed, for reference. Set a row of tiles into place; drop, rather than slide, the tiles into position. Starting at the center, set an intersecting row of tiles, then fill tiles in the spaces between the two guide rows.

Begin a diagonal pattern at the intersection of the diagonal lines and lay a row along one diagonal. This row will serve as the baseline for the rest of the pattern.

Step 2. *Roll the Tiles.* Use a rolling pin to apply pressure to each row of tiles as you set them.

Step 3. *Trim the Edges.* Place a dry tile exactly above the last set tile from the wall. Then put a third tile over these two tiles, pushed to the wall. Using the edge of the topmost tile as a guide, scribe the middle tile with a utility knife and snap in two to make a trim piece.

A diagonal pattern requires two different shapes of edge tiles: a small triangle (A) and a larger 5-sided piece (B), unless the wall line happens to fall exactly on a tile diagonal. Place a tile over the laid tiles with one point touching the wall. Mark off a line where the left side of the tile intersects the first joint line and cut to make an A piece. Place another tile similarly, but mark where the right side of the tile intersects the joint. Cut this tile to give you a B piece.

Step 4. *Trim the Outside Corners.* Put a tile directly above the last set tile at the left side of a corner. Place a third tile over these two and position it 1/8 inch from the wall. Mark the edge with a pencil, then without turning it, align it on the last set tile to the right of the corner. Mark it in a similar fashion. Cut the marked tile with a knife to remove the corner section. Fit the remaining part around the corner. When all tiles are laid, use the solvent recommended by the adhesive manufacturer to clean any adhesive from the top of the tiles.

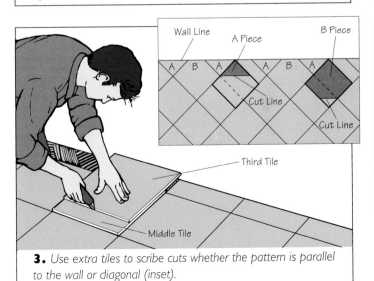

1. *Spread adhesive in a relatively small area, so that you can lay the tiles before it starts to dry.*

2. *Embed the tiles into the adhesive with a rolling pin.*

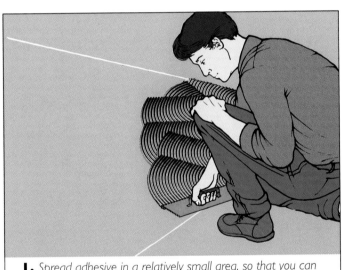

3. *Use extra tiles to scribe cuts whether the pattern is parallel to the wall or diagonal (inset).*

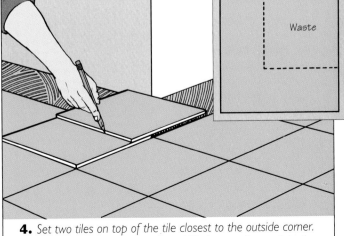

4. *Set two tiles on top of the tile closest to the outside corner. Mark one cutout dimension, then shift the two tiles to the other side of the corner to mark the other dimension.*

Putting Down Sheet Flooring

Unlike setting tiles, putting down sheet flooring will require you to manipulate a roll of material inside a small room—a challenge for anyone. So think twice about doing it yourself.

If you do decide you are up to the challenge, begin with a scale drawing of the room on graph paper, showing the exact outline of the flooring. Bring the roll into the bathroom and let it acclimate to the room's temperature and humidity for at least 24 hours. Some resilient sheet flooring requires no adhesive, some requires adhesive around the outer edge, and some is stuck down with double-sided tape. The tried-and-true method described below is for adhesive-applied flooring. In any case, begin on a good base (see "Start with the Right Base", page 175). Remove any edge trim, such as the base shoe, before you start.

Difficulty Level: ᛏ ᛏ ᛏ

Tools and Materials

☐ Linoleum roller (rent one from your flooring supplier)

☐ 6- or 12-foot-wide roll of resilient flooring

☐ Notched trowel (notch size as specified by adhesive manufacturer)

☐ Framing square   ☐ Chalkline
☐ Measuring tape   ☐ Utility knife
☐ Straightedge   ☐ 24-inch-long 2x4
☐ Handsaw   ☐ Seam roller
☐ Rolling pin   ☐ Adhesive
☐ Solvent

Cutting and Fitting

Step 1. *Make the Rough Cuts.* Unroll the flooring in a room big enough to lay out the whole sheet. With a marker, draw the bathroom's edges on the flooring; add an extra 3 inches on all sides. Cut the flooring to the marks with a straightedge and a utility knife. Roll up the cut piece and take it into the bathroom, then lay the longest edge against the longest wall. Position the piece so that about 3 inches of excess goes up every wall.

Step 2. *Fit the Flooring Around All Objects.* If fixtures are not yet in place, roll the flooring out over the toilet flange and cut the outline with a knife. For fixtures already in place, precut a hole to match the outline of the fixture's base, but smaller by 3 inches on all sides. You can trim it later. Then cut a slit from the cutout to the closest edge of the roll.

Step 3. *Lay the Second Piece (if Necessary).* Sometimes it isn't possible or practical to cover the floor with a single sheet. A deep jog in the wall may require seaming a second piece to the main piece. With the first piece in position, measure and cut the second piece as you did with the first one, leaving a 3-inch overlap at the seam.

Step 4. *Trim the Corners.* At the outside corners, cut a slit straight down through the margin to the floor. Trim the inside corners by cutting the margin away with increasingly lower

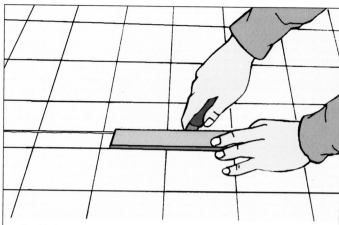

1. *Make the rough cut with a knife and straightedge in an area where you can lay out the entire piece of flooring.*

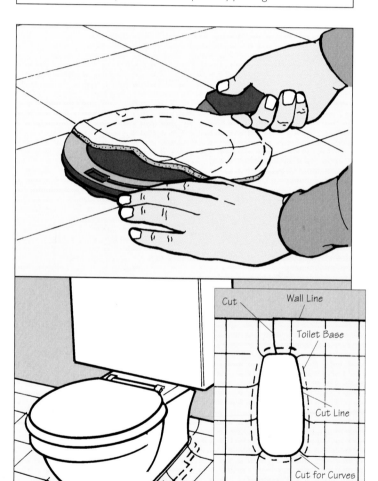

2. *Cut around the toilet flange by pressing the floor covering down so you can feel the edge. Cut as closely as possible to the edge, but don't worry about exactness, because the toilet base will cover the cut (top). Cut around the toilet base, leaving a 3-inch margin all around. Then cut a slit at the back of the toilet to the wall. Slit the 3-inch margin to let the flooring lie on the floor (bottom).*

3. *If you can't make the installation without a seam, roll out a second piece and pull it over the first piece until the patterns match. Cut it to the approximate size.*

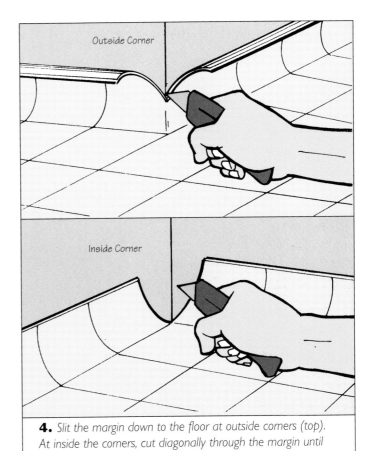

Outside Corner

Inside Corner

4. *Slit the margin down to the floor at outside corners (top). At inside the corners, cut diagonally through the margin until the flooring lies flat (bottom).*

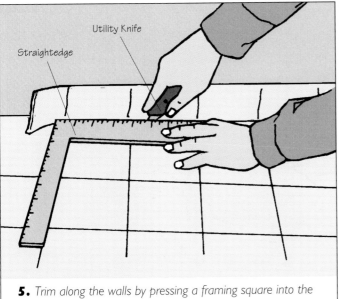

Utility Knife

Straightedge

5. *Trim along the walls by pressing a framing square into the corner and cutting away the excess.*

6. *Cut a recess below the door casings with a handsaw.*

diagonal cuts on each side of the corner. Eventually you will have made a split wide enough to allow the flooring to lie flat.

Step 5. *Trim the Flooring at the Walls.* Crease the flooring into the joint at the wall with a 2-foot-long piece of 2x4. Then place a framing square in the crease and cut along the wall with a utility knife, leaving a gap of 1/8 inch between the wall and the flooring.

Step 6. *Trim the Flooring at the Door Casing.* Use a handsaw to cut a recess in the wood door casing just above the underlayment and wide enough to slide the flooring beneath. Trim the flooring to match the angles and corners of the door casing; allow about 1/2 inch of the flooring to slip under the casing.

1. *Roll the floor covering back to the center of the room, apply adhesive, roll the covering back down. Repeat for the other half of the flooring.*

2. *To make a seam, align the smaller piece with the first piece, matching the pattern. The two pieces should overlap by about 3 inches.*

Second Piece

Pieces to be Removed   First Piece

3. *Use a rented seam roller to force out any ridges and air bubbles in the flooring; roll from the center to the edges.*

Completing the Operation

Step 1. *Apply the Adhesive.* Roll back the flooring to the center and apply adhesive to the floor with the smooth edge of a notched trowel, following the manufacturer's directions. Comb out with the notched edge. Push the flooring immediately into the adhesive. Repeat for the other half of the flooring.

Step 2. *Making a Seam (if Necessary).* If a second or third sheet of flooring must join the first, stop the adhesive short of the edge to be seamed by 2 inches or so. Spread adhesive on the floor to receive the second piece, stopping 2 inches from the first sheet. Position and align the second piece carefully. With a straightedge and utility knife, cut through both sheets along the seam line. Remove the waste. Lift up both edges and apply adhesive. Clean the seam and use the seam sealer recommended for your flooring.

Step 3. *Clean Up and Roll Down.* Clean excess adhesive off the surface with the solvent recommended by the manufacturer. Then roll the flooring firmly into the adhesive with a roller, working from the center outward. Finally, replace the baseboard and shoe molding. When replacing the shoe, nail it into the wall rather than the floor covering to allow the floor covering to expand and contract.

Thin-Setting Tiles on Bathroom Floors

Ceramic and stone tiles can be set into adhesive (thin set) over a plywood or cement board underlayment or over smooth concrete using the guidelines to follow. Tiles inside showers should be set into a bed of mortar over a metal or plastic shower pan (a task that demands a level of skill beyond that possessed by most do-it-yourselfers).

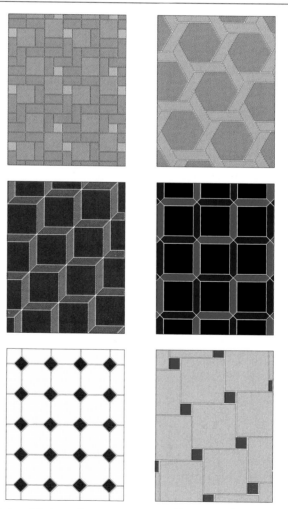

It is possible to make many patterns with ceramic floor tiles, but nonrectangular tiles can be challenging to cut at the edges of the floor.

Tile is an expensive finish that lasts for years, so choose your material carefully and install it with patience and care. Sizes range from 1 to 12 inches square. There are many shapes to choose from, so you can create your own interesting patterns. Keep in mind, though, that trimming out nonrectangular tiles can be challenging.

Difficulty Level: ⚒ ⚒ ⚒

Tools and Materials

- [ ] Hammer
- [ ] Pail
- [ ] Soft cloth
- [ ] Tile spacers
- [ ] Jointing tool or toothbrush
- [ ] Rubber float
- [ ] Sponge
- [ ] Tiles
- [ ] Grout
- [ ] 1x2 or 1x4 battens
- [ ] Notched trowel (notch size as recommended for the tile and adhesive you want to use)
- [ ] Tile cutter (rent from supplier)
- [ ] Tile nippers (rent from supplier)
- [ ] 12-inch piece of 2x4 wrapped with carpet
- [ ] Adhesive (type and quantity as recommended by supplier)
- [ ] Solvent (as recommended for the adhesive)

Step 1. *Mark the Floor and Attach the Guides.* You can lay tiles from one corner or from the center of the floor, using chalk lines as described in Step 1 under "Preparing the Layout," page 176. If the floor is small and the tiles are larger than 4x4 inches, one way to lay out the design is to use the tiles as templates and mark each tile's position on the floor. In any case, it is usually easier to have something other than the chalk line itself to work from.

Some tiles have nubs on the edges that space the tiles apart for grout lines. Plastic spacers are available for tiles without nubs.

To lay out the pattern from one corner of the room, make guide strips by temporarily nailing 1x2 or 1x4 battens to the underlayment (if tiling to concrete, weigh down the ends of the guides with heavy weights, such as a few stacked bricks). Place a strip parallel to each of two adjacent walls, with their leading edges positioned on the first joint line. To make sure the strips are at right angles, measure 3 units (36 inches, if the room is big enough) from the corner along the guide line (or strip) and mark the spot. Measure out 4 units (48 inches) along the long guide line, and mark the spot. Now measure the diagonal between the two points. If the diagonal measures 5 units (60 inches), the two guides are at right angles. Adjust the lines (or strips) as necessary.

Step 2. *Make a Dry Run.* Check the layout with a dry run. Use tile spacers to indicate the width of the grout joint; if using mesh-backed tile sheets, you don't have to worry about joint spacing. Try to lay out the tiles to avoid narrow pieces of tile (less than 1 inch) abutting a wall. If this happens, adjust the layout.

Step 3. *Spread the Adhesive.* Remove the tiles from the floor. Spread adhesive over about a 16-inch square area of the substrate with the smooth side of a notched trowel, following the manufacturer's directions. Comb out with the notched edge.

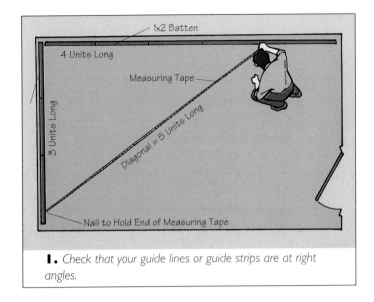

1. *Check that your guide lines or guide strips are at right angles.*

2. *Lay out the tiles dry to check their position. Avoid skinny pieces of tile next to the walls.*

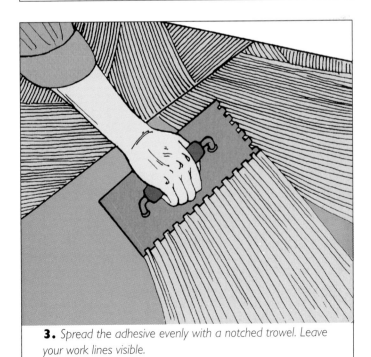

3. *Spread the adhesive evenly with a notched trowel. Leave your work lines visible.*

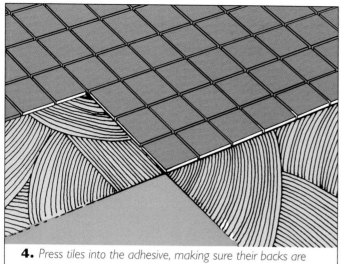

4. *Press tiles into the adhesive, making sure their backs are completely covered.*

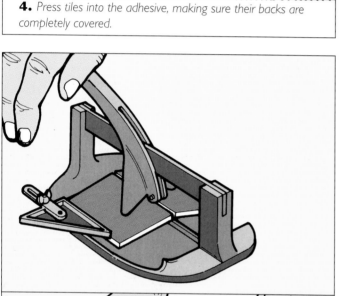

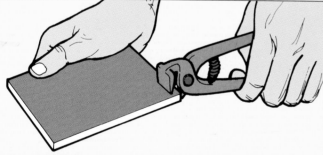

6. *Cut whole tiles with a tile cutter. Moving the lever across the tile scores the cut line. Pressing down then snaps the tile apart (top). Make minor or irregular cuts by biting off small pieces of the tile with a pair of tile nippers. Keep jaws parallel to get an even cut (bottom).*

Note that you may have only a limited time to work before the adhesive sets up. If you are not using wood strips as guides, take care not to cover the chalk lines with adhesive.

Step 4. *Set the Tiles into the Adhesive.* Press each tile or sheet of tiles into the adhesive. Set mosaic tiles by rolling each sheet up loosely, then setting one edge and rolling the rest of the sheet out. Insert a spacer (except with mosaics) and lay up the next tile or sheet. If you notice that the tiles are getting progres-

Bedding Block

5. *Embed the tiles into the adhesive by moving a padded board over the surface and tapping with a hammer.*

sively out of line with each other, wiggle them into position instead of lifting them out of the adhesive. Make frequent checks for alignment—every two sheets with mosaic tiles, every row with individual tiles. Before adhesive dries, wipe off any excess from the surface of the tiles.

Step 5. *Embed the Tiles.* After laying several rows of tile, embed them into the adhesive with a carpet-wrapped 2x4. As you move the board around, tap it firmly with a hammer. Use a framing square to make sure the surface is level, row to row.

Step 6. *Cut the Edge Tiles.* Use a tile cutter to make long straight cuts and a nipper to make irregular cuts.

Laying a Saddle (Threshold)

The transition from the tiled bathroom floor to an adjacent floor of a different material and, possibly, height, is made with a saddle. Choose among trim pieces of tile that come with a molded edge, a solid-surface saddle (cultured marble), or hardwood. Hardwood offers the chance to cut and shape the piece to blend floors of two different heights. Apply adhesive to the floor and bottom of the saddle. Allow space between the saddle and tile for a grout joint.

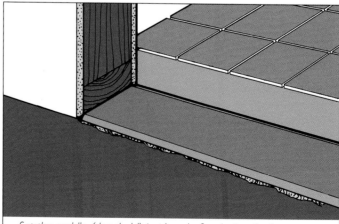

Set the saddle (threshold) in place before laying the last row of tiles.

Grouting the Joints

Allow the adhesive to dry for the length of time recommended by the manufacturer before filling in the joints with grout. Pre-mixed grout is ready to apply. If you buy the grout as powder, mix it as directed. Grout is usually white; if you want colored joints to match or complement the tile color, ask your tile dealer to show you the range of colorants available, and follow the directions on the package for mixing.

Step 1. *Apply the Grout.* Spread the grout over the tiles and press it into the joints with a rubber float held at a slight angle. Work diagonally over the tiles, taking care to fill all joints.

Step 2. *Remove the Excess Grout.* After the surface is well covered, remove any excess grout with the rubber float. To avoid removing too much grout, work across the tiles diagonally.

Step 3. *Wipe Off Any Remaining Grout.* Wipe the surface with a wet sponge, squeezed out frequently in a pail of water. Get as much of the grout off the surface of the tiles as you can without eroding the joints. Then wait 30 minutes or so until the residue dries to a thin haze. Wipe this off with a soft cloth.

Step 4. *Tool the Joints.* For large tiles, you may want the joints to be smoother than they emerge after the grouting and cleaning steps. Tool the joints with a jointing tool you can obtain from your tile supplier or use the end of a toothbrush.

Step 5. *Seal the Surface.* To prevent moisture from penetrating the grouted joints and any unglazed tiles, seal the surface with a sealant recommended by your supplier. Some sealants are applied with a roller; others come in a spray can. Allow two weeks for the grout to dry thoroughly, and then apply one coat of sealant. Apply another coat after the tiles have been down about two years.

1. *Force grout into the joints with a rubber float.*

2. *Remove the excess grout by working the rubber float diagonally across the joints.*

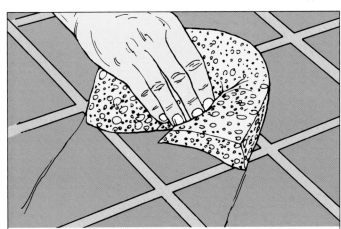

3. *Wipe the remaining grout off the tiles with a dampened sponge.*

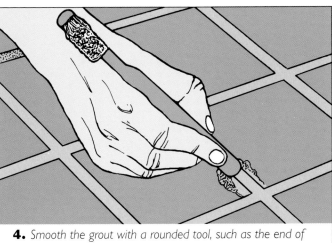

4. *Smooth the grout with a rounded tool, such as the end of a toothbrush, making a slight depression.*

5. *Seal unglazed tile and grout with a sealant made for that purpose.*

Tiling Walls

The first step is selecting wall tiles is to decide how much of the wall surface will get tiled and to plan a pattern. You can tile walls partway up (wainscot) or all the way to the ceiling. You can develop patterns by mixing tiles of different colors and shapes. A trim band is useful to tie several features of the room together visually.

Tiling walls uses the same tools and steps described for tiling floors, but the walls should probably be done before the floor, to avoid messing up your floor job. To install the tiles, begin with Step 3 of "Thin-Setting Tiles on Bathroom Floors" (on page 181) and follow the steps through "Grouting the Joints."

Laying out the tile arrangement is a bit different for walls than floors, because you can't lay the tiles down dry over the surface, as you can on a floor. If your proposed pattern is anything but simple, plan the arrangement by drawing the wall(s) to scale on graph paper, letting each square equal one tile. If the walls are not plumb, plan the edge tiles carefully to allow enough trim width to take up the difference in dimension, top to bottom.

Laying Out the Pattern

Step 1. *Mark a Vertical Work Line.* A vertical line near the middle of the wall makes a convenient work line. Lay a row of tiles out on the floor in front of the wall, adjusting their position until you get the right spacing to minimize the trim cuts. Be sure to allow for the width of the grout joints. Then use a carpenter's level to mark a vertical line up from a tile near the wall's midpoint.

Step 2. *Mark a Horizontal Work Line.* You can determine a horizontal reference line in different ways. If you want to line up a trim row with the top of the sink or vanity, place a carpenter's level on the top and draw a line on the wall against the bottom of the level. To tile only several feet of the wall, use tiles to measure off the desired number of increments (allowing for grout joint widths) to the desired height, then use the level to help you draw a line at this height. Use a similar method if you want to tile the wall to the ceiling, but pick a joint line about halfway up as the baseline (you can also work directly off the floor, if it is level).

Step 3. *Mark for the Accessories.* Locate any accessories that mount into the wall, such as soap dishes, and mark their positions. Some accessories have flanges that overlap the surrounding wall tiles.

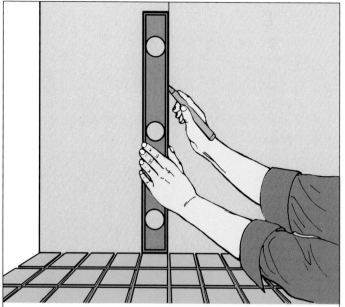

1. *Draw a vertical work line by laying tiles loosely next to the wall, spaced for the width of grout joints. Use a level to help you draw a line up from the edge of a tile near the midpoint of the wall.*

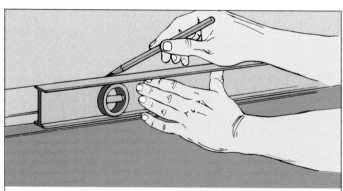

2. *If the floor is not level, establish a horizontal work line on the wall with a level.*

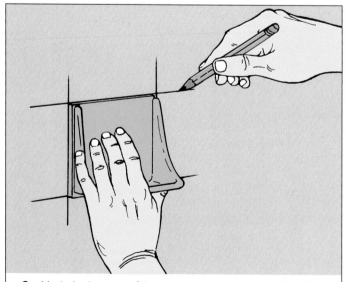

3. *Mark the location of the accessories to be inset before tiling.*

Painting

The easiest and most economical finish for bathroom walls, ceilings, and wood trim, paint is also the easiest to apply. Unlike more demanding finishes, paint is forgiving, allowing you easily to make corrections and change the color. With all these pluses, paint can also provide a durable finish, if you prepare the substrate properly and take measures to deal with the heavy amount of moisture that bathrooms generate.

Even the best paint will grow mildew when subjected to continuously high humidity, so begin by installing an exhaust fan (see "Installing an Exhaust Fan," page 154). Choose paint with a high sheen. Gloss and semigloss paints resist moisture and are easier to clean than more porous flat or eggshell paints. Because oil-based paints are being phased out by antipollution legislation, the steps below apply to water-based latex paints.

You can paint intricate surfaces, such as wood trim or cabinets, and small wall areas with a brush only. If the project extends to larger walls or ceilings, you'll save time and effort by using a roller.

Difficulty Level: 🔨

Tools and Materials

Tools for Preparation
☐ Masking tape
☐ 4-inch-wide drywall knife
☐ Nail punch
☐ Spackling compound
☐ 100-grit sandpaper
☐ Phosphate-free trisodium
☐ Fine- and medium-grit sandpaper
☐ Denatured alcohol (solvent for shellac)
☐ Caulk (match type to task)
☐ Fiberglass joint tape and drywall joint compound (for large plaster cracks)

☐ Putty knife
☐ Hammer
☐ Screwdriver
☐ Crack and hole filler
☐ Caulking gun
☐ White shellac

Tools for Painting by Brush
☐ 1½- or 2-inch sash brush
☐ Pail
☐ Paint shield

☐ 4-inch paintbrush
☐ Dropcloth
☐ Razor blades

Tools for Painting by Brush and Roller
☐ 1½- or 2-inch sash brush
☐ Roller with 1/4-inch nap cover
☐ Razor blade
☐ Roller handle extension (optional)

☐ Roller pan
☐ Paint shield
☐ Dropcloth

Preparing the Surface

The key to a successful paint job is what lies below the paint. Paints with a gloss or semigloss sheen reveal imperfections more than flat-sheen paints, so begin with a good substrate. Seal cracks between wood trim and walls with acrylic latex caulk. To seal cracks between a finished floor and wood baseboard, protect the floor with masking tape, then caulk the joint with urethane butyl caulk (one that will expand).

Wash previously painted surfaces with phosphate-free trisodium and water. If stains or marks remain after washing, brush white shellac over them.

To remove any adhesive that clings after stripping off an old wallcovering, brush on wallpaper remover solvent diluted with water (according to the instructions).

Preparing Drywall

Finish new drywall by taping all joints and sanding the surface completely smooth (see "Finishing Drywall," page 87). Prepare old drywall as described below:

Step 1. *Fix Popped Nails.* Drive new nails or drywall screws 1 or 2 inches above and below any popped nails, then reset the popped nails.

Step 2. *Fill Any Voids.* Fill holes above reset nails with spackling compound. Fill any cracks, dents, or other surface irregularities.

I. *Reset a popped nail, then drive a new nail or screw above and below it.*

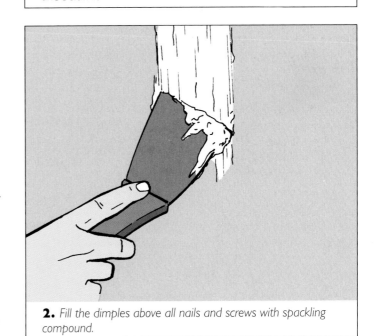

2. *Fill the dimples above all nails and screws with spackling compound.*

3. *Sand spackling compound until smooth.*

4. *Spot prime all filled areas and unpainted surfaces.*

Step 3. *Sand the Spackling Compound Smooth.* After the spackling compound has dried completely, sand all filled areas completely smooth with 100- or 150-grit paper.

Step 4. *Spot Prime the Walls.* Spot prime all filled areas and unpainted surfaces. Use a latex-based primer if the topcoats will be medium to dark colored. To ensure an even color for very light topcoats, use a white shellac primer.

Preparing Old Plaster

Before repainting old plaster, take a hard look at its overall condition. If it has too many defects, such as being loose in spots and crumbling in others, you may be better off applying new drywall over the top or ripping it off and applying a new finish (see "Gutting a Wall or Ceiling," page 81). If the plaster is basically sound, use the following steps to repair the imperfections:

Step 1. *Widen Hairline Cracks.* Use a pointed tool such as a utility knife or can opener to enlarge hairline plaster cracks and provide a toothed base for the filler. Clean the joint with a dampened brush and let dry.

Step 2. *Fill the Cracks and Sand Them Smooth.* Fill widened cracks with spackling compound or joint compound and sand smooth, using 100- or 150-grit paper.

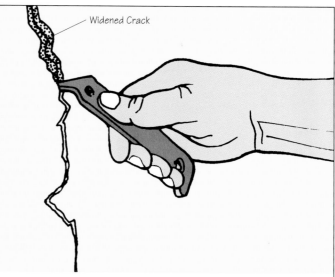

1. *Widen hairline plaster cracks with a sharp tool to make a base that will hold the filler.*

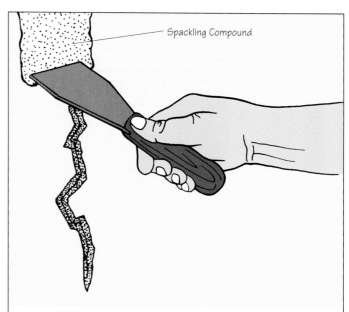

2. *Fill widened cracks with spackling compound or drywall joint compound and sand smooth.*

3. *Fill deep or wide cracks with spackling compound and let dry. Apply fiberglass mesh tape (above). Cover with joint compound, sand smooth and recoat (bottom).*

Step 3. *Repair Large Cracks.* Larger plaster cracks are likely to reopen. To prevent this, gouge out the crack with a pointed tool, fill with spackling compound, and let dry. Then apply fiberglass mesh joint tape over the crack and finish with joint compound. Sand smooth, recoat, and sand again. Spot prime all filled spots as was described under "Preparing Drywall," page 185.

Preparing Woodwork

How you prepare wood, particleboard, or plywood depends on its present condition and what you want to end up with. You can repaint previously painted woodwork after repairing surface defects. To apply a natural finish, you need to start with raw wood or strip off any previous coating with a chemical stripper.

Step 1. *Set the Nails.* Use a hammer and nail punch to set nailheads slightly below the wood surface.

Step 2. *Fill Holes and Sand Smooth.* Fill all holes and cracks with the appropriate filler and sand smooth. If the wood is to be painted (or repainted) use a powder-base or premixed wood filler. For natural finished woodwork, you will want the filled spots

1. *Use a hammer and nail punch to set nails on new woodwork and drive any popped nails back into the surface.*

2. *Fill all holes and cracks with the appropriate filler and sand smooth.*

to match the color of the wood when finished. Doing this is more art than science, and may take a few tries. Select the closest premixed wood filler color to the species of wood and fill a hole in a scrap of the same color. When dry, apply the natural finish and evaluate the resulting color. Try a darker or lighter filler, as necessary to get a close match.

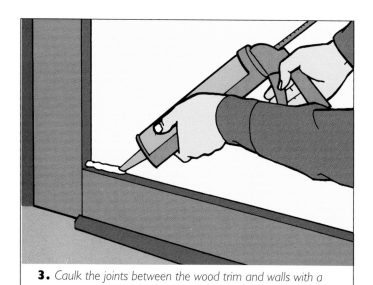

3. *Caulk the joints between the wood trim and walls with a high-grade flexible caulk.*

4. *Prime woodwork with the appropriate first coat for a natural or paint finish.*

Step 3. Caulk the Joints. Caulk joints between wood trim and walls with a high-grade flexible caulk, such as acrylic latex (polyurethane is good but messier to work with).

Step 4. Prime the Surface. Prime the woodwork as required to achieve the desired finish. Some of the options are listed below:

Wood/Finish	Prime Coat(s)
Penetrating finish (oil)	Penetrating oil; one or more coats
Surface finish	Stain (if desired); two coats clear surface finish
Bare wood, paint finish	Two coats latex wood primer or white shellac
Prepainted wood, paint finish	Spot prime filled areas with latex wood primer or white shellac

Painting Walls and Ceilings

To get the best finish on new surfaces, figure on one coat of primer and two coats of semigloss or gloss enamel. Most paint covers about 400 square feet per gallon, so estimate the amount you will need by first determining the square footage of walls and ceilings, multiplying by the number of coats, and allowing for waste. Before beginning, protect fixtures and floor surfaces with dropcloths. The usual sequence is to do the large surfaces first and wood trim later. But if all surfaces are to be painted with the same color and type of paint, it will be simpler to begin with the brushwork—wood trim, adjacent walls, and inside corners—and then do the large surfaces with a roller.

Step 1. *Remove Cover and Trim Plates.* It's tempting to try to paint around switch plates, pipe escutcheons, and fixture trim strips, but removing these items is usually easy and you'll get a much better job for your efforts. When you remove the cover plates, you also risk electrical shock or short circuit if you happen to jab a finger or wet brush into a bared receptacle, so it's a good idea to shut off the power to the circuit before painting.

Step 2. *Cut In the Ceiling.* Use a sash brush to cut in (trim) around the walls and edges around fixture openings. Overlap the joint where the ceiling meets the wall.

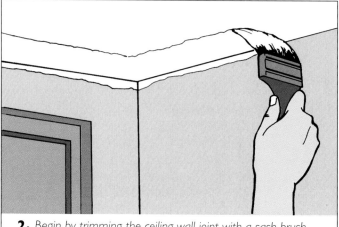

1. *For a neater job, remove all cover plates, trim strips, and escutcheons before painting. Shut off electrical power before painting around electrical boxes.*

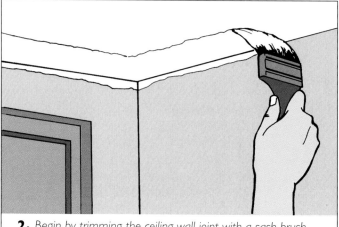

2. *Begin by trimming the ceiling-wall joint with a sash brush. Don't worry about overlapping the wall—it's easier to cut a finish trim line on the wall than the ceiling.*

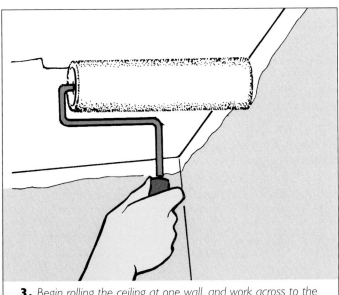

3. *Begin rolling the ceiling at one wall, and work across to the opposite wall.*

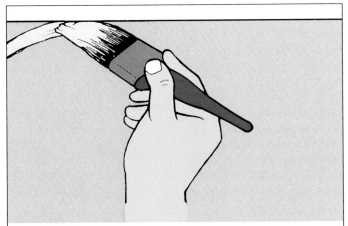

4. *If the ceiling is a different color than the wall, cut the trim line on the wall with a sash brush, working the paint up against the ceiling line as shown.*

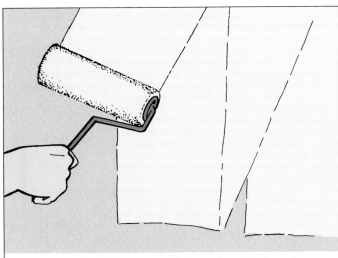

5. *Use a roller for large areas. Paint each section in a zigzag pattern, then finish off with up and down strokes until all spots are covered equally.*

Step 3. *Paint the Ceiling Field.* Use a wide brush or roller to finish off the large surface (field) of the ceiling, beginning at one wall and working across the ceiling to the opposite wall. If the ceiling area is extensive, consider adding an extension handle to the roller. This will allow you to paint the ceiling from a standing position on the floor. After dipping the roller in the pan, roll paint onto the surface in a zigzag pattern about two roller-widths wide and 36 inches long. Finish off by rolling the spots between with smooth, vertical strokes.

Step 4. *Cut In the Walls.* Paint the corners and edges around open wall surfaces with a sash brush. If the wall color differs from the ceiling, let the ceiling dry completely, then cut the wall-ceiling joint carefully.

Step 5. *Paint the Wall Field.* Use a roller to paint the wall field. Start at one corner and work across the wall, applying the paint to rectangular sections as described in Step 3.

Painting Woodwork

Remove any knobs from doors and cabinets before painting, to get a clean job. Unless you need to paint large surfaces, use a small sash brush (1½ to 2 inches wide) to paint all wood in the bathroom. Paint the edges of doors first, ending with the larger surfaces. Use a paint shield to protect the floor while painting baseboards.

When painting window sash, cut the trim as close as practical to the glass, but don't worry about paint that slops over onto the glass. Go back when the paint dries and scrape any spills off the glass with a razor blade. You can't remove paint quite so easily from tile, so if you are not confident of cutting a clean edge on wood trim next to tile, protect the tile with masking tape.

A paint shield may help you protect adjacent surfaces when painting against materials such as tile and wood.

GLOSSARY

Anti-Scald Valve (Pressure-Balancing Valve) Single control fitting that contains a piston that automatically responds to changes in line water pressure to maintain shower temperature; the valve blocks abrupt drops or rises in temperature.

Backsplash The tiled wall area behind a sink, countertop, or stove.

Barrier-Free Fixtures Fixtures specifically designed for people who use wheelchairs or who have limited mobility.

Base Plan Transferring rough measurements of an existing room to a scale drawing; a convenient scale for planning a bathroom is to make 1/2 inch equal 1 foot.

Bearing Wall A wall that supports the floor or roof above it.

Bidet A bowl-shaped bathroom fixture that supplies water for personal hygiene.

Blanket Insulation Flexible insulation, such as fiberglass or mineral wool, that comes packaged in long single rolls.

Blocking Bracing, such as 2x4s, attached to framing.

Cement Backer Board Also called cementitious backer units, or CBUs, cement board is a rigid, portland cement-based panel designed for use as a substrate or underlayment for ceramic tile in wet or dry areas.

Cleat A piece of lumber fastened, e.g., to a joist or post, as a support for other lumber.

Double-Glazed Window A window consisting of two panes of glass separated by a space that contains air or argon gas. The space provides most of the insulation.

Drain Any pipe that carries waste water through a drainage network and into the municipal sewer or private septic system.

Dry Run Before applying grout, the process of placing the tiles to check the layout; usually tile spacers are used to indicate the width of the grout joints.

Escutcheon A decorative plate that covers a hole in the wall in which the stem or cartridge fits.

Fixed Windows Windows that do not open. They come as glass sheets to be installed into a finished opening or as ready-to-install units enclosed in wood, metal, or plastic frames.

Full Bath A bathroom that contains a sink, toilet, and tub/shower.

Furring (Strapping) Wood strips used to level parts of a ceiling, wall, or floor before adding the finish surface; commonly used to secure panels of rigid foam insulation.

Ground Fault Circuit Interrupter (GFCI). A safety circuit breaker that compares the amount of current entering a receptacle with the amount leaving. If there is a discrepancy of .005 volt, the GFCI breaks the circuit in 1/40 of a second. Required by the National Electrical Code in areas that are subject to dampness, such as bathrooms.

Grout A binder and filler applied in the joints between ceramic tile. May come with or without sand added.

Half Bath (Powder Room) Bathrooms that contain a toilet plus a sink.

Hardboard Manufactured pressed-wood panels; hardboard is specifically rejected by some manufacturers as an acceptable substrate for resilient floors.

Luxury Bath A full bath with a bidet and/or second sink.

Middle-of-the-Run Electrical box with its outlets or switch lying between the power source and another box.

Nonbearing Wall A wall that does not support a load from above.

On Center A point of reference for measuring. For example, "16 inches on center" means 16 inches from the center of one framing member to the center of the next.

O-Ring A ring of rubber used as a gasket.

Overflow An outlet positioned in a tub or sink to allow water to escape in case a faucet is left on.

Particleboard Reconstituted wood particles that are bonded with resin under heat and pressure and made into panels. Particleboard has a tendency to swell when exposed to moisture.

Resilient Flooring Thin floor coverings composed of materials such as vinyl, rubber, cork, or linoleum; comes in a wide range of colors and patterns in both tile and sheet form.

Rigid Foam Insulation Boards of insulation that are composed of various types of plastics. Rigid insulation offers the highest R-value per inch of thickness.

Riser Pipe A supply pipe that extends vertically, carrying water, steam, or gas.

Rubber Float A flat, rubber-faced tool used to apply grout.

R-Value A number assigned to thermal insulation to measure the insulation's resistance to heat flow. The higher the number, the better the insulation.

Sister Joist A reinforcing joist added to the side of a cut or damaged joist for additional support.

Spas A bath-like unit, usually with a high, rounded shape that is deeper than a whirlpool. Unlike a whirlpool bath, spas are not usually drained after each use. Because they cannot double as bathtubs, spas are better adapted for outside installation.

Spud Washer On a toilet that has a separate tank, the spud washer is the large rubber ring placed over the drain hole. The tank is placed over the spud washer.

Stops Strips of wood nailed to the head and side jambs to prevent a door from swinging too far when it closes. Stops also keep window sash in line.

Stud Vertical member of a frame wall, placed at both ends and usually every 16 inches on center. Provides structural framing and facilitates covering with drywall or plywood.

Subfloor The floor surface below a finished floor. In newer homes the subfloor is usually made of sheet material such as plywood; in older houses it is likely to consist of diagonally attached boards.

Tacknail To nail one structural member to another temporarily with a minimum of nails.

Thick-Bed Mortar A layer of mortar more than 1/2 inch thick that is used to level an uneven surface for tiling.

Thin-Set Adhesive (Mortar) Any cement-based or organic adhesive applied in a layer less than 1/2 inch thick and used for setting tile.

Three-Quarter Bath A bathroom that contains a toilet, sink and shower.

Toenail Joining two boards together by nailing at an angle through the end, or toe, of one board and into the face of another.

Tongue-and-Groove Flooring Floor boards that are milled with a tongue on one edge and a groove on the other edge. The tongue of one board fits into the groove of the next to make a tight, strong floor.

Top Plate Horizontal framing member, usually consisting of 2x4s, that forms the top of a wall and supports floor joists and rafters.

Trap A section of pipe that is bent to form a seal of water against sewer gasses.

Wax Ring A wax seal used to seal the base of a toilet so it won't leak.